Building the Cold War Consensus

Building the Cold War Consensus

The Political Economy of U.S. National Security Policy, 1949–51

BENJAMIN O. FORDHAM

Ann Arbor

THE UNIVERSITY OF MICHIGAN PRESS

2001   2000   1999   1998   4   3   2   1

A CIP catalog record for this book is available from the British Library.

Library of Congress Cataloging-in-Publication Data

Fordham, Benjamin O.
     Building the Cold War consensus : the political economy of U.S.
     national security policy, 1949–51 / Benjamin O. Fordham.
        p.   cm.
     Includes bibliographical references (p.   ) and index.
     ISBN 0-472-10887-5 (cloth)
        1. United States—Foreign relations—1945–1953.   2. United
     States—Politics and government—1945–1953.   3. National
     security—United States—History—20th century.   4. Internal
     security—United States—History—20th century.   5. Cold War.
     I. Title.
     E813.F55   1998
     327.73'009'045—dc21   97-45391
                                                                          CIP

11703373

Contents

Acknowledgments

Without the help and support of many people, I could never have completed this work. Timothy McKeown patiently read and commented on many drafts, providing crucial suggestions and all the attention one could ask from a dissertation adviser. Also at the University of North Carolina, I benefited from the comments (skeptical as well as supportive) of the other members of my committee, Richard Kohn, Eric Mlyn, Lars Schoultz, and Terry Sullivan. Several others read all or part of the manuscript and provided valuable comments and suggestions. I would like to thank Erik Devereux, Gavan Duffy, Thomas Ferguson, Aaron Friedberg, David Gibbs, Frank Kofsky, Gregory Nowell, David Painter, Paul Papayoanou, Athan Theoharis, and Ellen Schrecker for their help.

Many other people and institutions have provided special help. George Rabinowitz, Michael Munger, and Mira Wilkins provided important suggestions for handling the quantitative data. The staff at the Truman Presidential Library was exceptionally helpful and made research there a pleasure. Charles Myers at the University of Michigan Press has been an understanding and helpful editor. Many other friends and colleagues have responded to the ideas presented here and provided help of all kinds along the way. I have also benefited from the generosity of the University of North Carolina, the Harry S. Truman Library Institute, the Triangle Institute for Security Studies, and the Research Program in International Security at the Princeton University Center of International Studies. The responsibility for any errors in this work is mine.

Abbreviations

ADA	Americans for Democratic Action
AFL	American Federation of Labor
CEA	Council of Economic Advisers
CED	Council for Economic Development
CIO	Congress of Industrial Organizations
CIA	Central Intelligence Agency
CR	*Congressional Record*
DDRS	Declassified Documents Reference System
DNC	Democratic National Committee
ECA	Economic Cooperation Administration
FBI	Federal Bureau of Investigation
FRUS	*Foreign Relations of the United States*
FY	Fiscal Year
GATT	General Agreement on Tariffs and Trade
GE	General Electric
IAC	Industrial Advisory Committee (of the ILRC)
IBM	International Business Machines
ICIS	Interdepartmental Committee on Internal Security
ICPSR	Inter-university Consortium for Political and Social Research
IERB	Industrial Employment Review Board (an interdepartmental committee)
IIC	Interdepartmental Intelligence Conference
ILRC	Industrial Labor Relations Committee (of the Munitions Board)
ILWU	International Longshoremen's and Warehousemen's Union
ITT	International Telephone and Telegraph
IUE	International Union of Electrical Workers
IWW	International Workers of the World
JCS	Joint Chiefs of Staff
MDAP	Mutual Defense Assistance Program
NAM	National Association of Manufacturers
NATO	North Atlantic Treaty Organization

NKVD	Soviet People's Commissariat of Internal Affairs
NLRB	National Labor Relations Board
NSC	National Security Council
NSRB	National Security Resources Board
NUMCS	National Union of Marine Cooks and Stewards
OF	President's Official File
ONI	Office of Naval Intelligence
OSD	Office of the Secretary of Defense
PPF	President's Personal File
PPP: HST	*Public Papers of the Presidents: Harry S. Truman*
PSEA	Physical Security Equipment Agency
PSF	President's Secretary's Files
RG	Record Group
RNC	Republican National Committee
SACB	Subversive Activities Control Board
SANACC	State-Army-Navy-Air Coordinating Committee
SIC	Standard Industrial Classification
UAW	United Automobile Workers
UE	United Electrical Workers
USCC	United States Chamber of Commerce

CHAPTER 1

The Domestic Political Economy and
U.S. National Security Policy

> The significance of events was shrouded in ambiguity. We groped after
> interpretations of them, sometimes reversed lines of action based on ear-
> lier views, and hesitated long before grasping what now seems obvious.
> —Dean Acheson (1969, 3–4)

The period between the summer of 1949 and the winter of 1951 was a crucial one in the history of American domestic and foreign policy. During
this time, the annual military budget roughly tripled, rising from $13.5 bil-
lion to nearly $45 billion, only a fraction of which was earmarked for the
war in Korea. Military budgets have not since returned to the relatively
low levels prevailing between 1946 and 1950. At the same time, domestic
social welfare programs, such as President Truman's plan for a national
health care system, disappeared from the agenda in the United States.
These programs had played a central role in Truman's successful 1948
reelection campaign and remained very important in other developed
democracies. In 1950, the hunt for communist influence in American life,
on the rise since the end of World War II, reached remarkable new heights
with the passage of a law calling for the registration of all communist-
affiliated individuals and organizations and providing for their imprison-
ment in times of national emergency. The Federal Bureau of Investigation
and other government agencies greatly expanded their efforts to identify
radicals and remove them from the American labor force.

How can we explain these important historical developments? The
starting point for this book is the idea that domestic and foreign policy
outcomes are related. The Truman administration's efforts to fund its
ambitious and expensive foreign policy required it to sacrifice much of its
domestic agenda and acquiesce to conservative demands for a campaign
against radicals in the labor movement and elsewhere. The president and
others in his administration regretted the demise of their domestic initiatives and remained skeptical of the crusade against domestic communism,
but they were unwilling to accept the potential damage that blocking these

developments might have done to their foreign policy agenda. Similarly, the administration's opponents, particularly conservative Republicans, were uneasy with the administration's foreign policy, but they were unwilling to endanger their domestic policy gains in order to stop it. The durability of Cold War assumptions makes it easy to see the dominant world role of the United States since World War II, and the linkage between the international confrontation with the Soviet Union and domestic anticommunism, as logical and inevitable. In fact, advocates of Cold War foreign policy tended to oppose the domestic policies that came to be associated with it, and advocates of the Cold War domestic agenda tended to oppose the foreign policy. As the Acheson quote above implies, policies that seem obvious now were not obvious in 1950. Other outcomes were possible. Both the individual policies and the association between them are best understood as the results of a struggle between domestic political factions rooted in the American political economy, rather than as natural or obvious products of some clear set of policy imperatives in the postwar international environment.

This is not the way the development of U.S. national security policy during the early Cold War era is usually understood. Most historical accounts of it do not devote much attention to domestic political conflict, and they rarely link foreign and domestic policy outcomes. In international relations theory, this case is usually considered a strong one for accounts of policy-making that focus on exogenous international threats and treat foreign-policy makers as if they were insulated from the pressures of political coalition building. A better explanation of foreign policy locates its origins in conflicting interests within the domestic political economy and focuses on bargaining among political actors representing different coalitions of these interests. This approach explains features of the policy-making process that are problematic in other accounts and offers insights about a range of questions they do not address.

A Domestic Political Economy Theory of National Security Policy

In recent years, it has become routine to acknowledge the importance of domestic politics. Indeed, even many analysts who had adhered to realist assumptions in their previous work, such as Snyder (1991) and Bueno de Mesquita and Lalman (1992), have added domestic political variables in their most recent work. Since there is widespread agreement that domestic politics "matter," why devote more attention to the subject?

Although discussion of domestic political influences on foreign policy is widespread, many recent treatments of the topic obscure its most important implications. As most analysts frame it, the debate over domestic politics concerns the relative importance of domestic and international considerations in driving state behavior (Snyder 1991; Zakaria 1992; Rosecrance and Stein 1993). An analytically prior question, however, is whether it is meaningful to speak of "international pressures" without knowing the identity of the domestic actor on whom these pressures are exerted. It is obviously true that international conditions have an important effect on foreign policy, since the policy must act on the international environment. However, not all domestic actors share the same interests and perceive the same international threats. To the extent that perceptions differ, it makes no sense to examine threats and interests without knowing the identity of the domestic actor or coalition controlling the policy-making apparatus. The most important issue in the debate over domestic politics is not whether domestic or international factors matter more, but whether the appropriate unit of analysis for understanding international events and conditions is the unitary state or a set of contending domestic political actors.

Departing from the assumption that international events and conditions have some objective or consensual meaning raises important theoretical questions. If their meaning is not obvious, what determines how particular domestic actors interpret international events and conditions, and what policies they prefer as a result? How are these conflicting preferences articulated in the policy-making process? What determines which policy is ultimately enacted? A domestic political economy theory of the policy-making process offers some answers to these questions.

The Sources of Divergent Preferences on National Security Policy

National security policy is often defined as an effort to protect consensual "core values" from international threats (Buzan 1983; Leffler 1991). While this definition gives little reason to expect much domestic conflict on the matter, there is no denying that national security policy is often controversial. The early Cold War period is a case in point. Internationalists sought a greater economic and political role for the United States in the international system. Nationalists, on the other hand, wanted to exclude foreign competition from U.S. markets and avoid the risks of extensive involvement in international economic and political affairs. For both groups, economic and military means and ends were inextricably intertwined. The internationalist effort to establish an international system open to American trade and investment required a strong military force to insure the physical security of critical areas of the world. Furthermore, internationalists believed that the long-term security of the United States itself was best insured by the maintenance of such an open international political and economic system. On the other hand, nationalists believed that the effort to establish and maintain this sort of international system would lead to war and would undermine democracy at home. They warned of a "garrison state" and sought to protect the physical security of the United States while limiting military spending, foreign aid, and international commitments.[1]

Cleavages in the domestic political economy are an important source of conflict over national security policy, including the division between nationalists and internationalists. National security policy protects particular values, including not only the political independence and territorial integrity of the state itself, but also international prerogatives such as access to markets and investments in other parts of the world. Political conflict over national security policy occurs because not everyone attaches equal importance to the values the policy seeks to protect. Indeed, sometimes even states facing a foreign invasion contain groups that would be better off under the political order imposed by the invader. When the immediate physical security of the state is not at stake, there may be even less consensus. During the early Cold War era, internationally oriented commercial and financial interests played an important role in the Democratic party. These interests had an enormous stake in the values protected by the administration's ambitious foreign policy. The chief architects of this policy came from internationally oriented investment banks and law firms on the eastern seaboard.[2] Nationalists had similar ties to domestically oriented sectors of the economy without such a stake in the administration's policy.

Although alternative explanations for the origins of divergent foreign policy preferences are possible, an account based on interests has considerable practical and theoretical advantages over one based on ideas and ideology.[3] From a practical standpoint, an examination of actors' interests more easily generates empirically falsifiable propositions about their political behavior. Data on various political actors' positions in the economy, which can be used to discern their interests, are both less ambiguous and less easily manipulated by the actors themselves than is information about their ideology. Advocates of sharply differing policy positions may justify their arguments with appeals to the same ideas and values. Political actors may also frame their public statements strategically in the terms they believe will best promote their preferred policy outcomes in the public arena. Such statements may present a distorted picture of their genuine motives and beliefs. Even in private communications, where political actors have less incentive to misrepresent their positions, statements about specific issues may reflect either general principles or just tactical convenience. Given these sources of ambiguity in ideological discourse, determining the genuine ideological differences between political actors is difficult without referring to the policies they advocate. Since these policy positions are precisely what we are seeking to explain here, inferring ideology from them would create a tautology.

There is also reason to suspect that ideas and ideologies can only produce effective political action if they are backed by material power. Material interests are much less likely to have a similar problem finding ideas that support positions they favor. For example, in spite of the consensus in the scientific community about the health consequences of smoking, the tobacco industry is able to produce scientists to support its position that tobacco products are not necessarily harmful. Ideologies may also be flexible enough to include a broad range of possible policy positions depending on which aspect of the ideology, and of the policy, one chooses to emphasize. Even some of the recent literature on the importance of ideas concedes the need for effective material political backing.[4] The assertion that interest tends to dominate reason is also fundamental to classical realist thought. Niebuhr (1932, xiv–xv) argues that "reason is always, to some degree, the servant of interest in a social situation."

The argument that interests are more important than ideas or ideology in determining policy does not necessarily imply that decision makers are cynical, or that ideas cannot exist apart from political power. Individual decision makers may believe sincerely in the ideas they use to justify their preferred course of action. However, individuals whose ideas attract material support are much more likely to achieve positions of power where they can put those ideas into practice. If one is willing to search broadly, a very wide range of policy-relevant ideas can be found. However, a much narrower range of these ideas will attract enough material support to become politically practical.

Like most other examinations of economic divisions over foreign policy, this book will examine divisions between industrial sectors rather than between the owners of different factors, such as capital and labor.[5] If political coalitions on trade issues were based on the ownership of common factors, a convincing account of the politics of foreign policy would focus primarily on class conflict, rather than on divisions between factions of capital. Such accounts are plausible and have been pursued elsewhere.[6] However, most research on the politics of trade supports the argument that capital and labor in different sectors have conflicting interests. Relative factor immobility between sectors shapes political action. Magee, Brock, and Young (1989, 101–10) present evidence that, at least in the short run, even the relatively scarce factor—which should benefit from trade—will oppose liberalization if it is located in an import-competing sector. Using data from the lobbying effort over the 1973 Trade Reform Act, they found that trade associations and labor organizations from the same sector tended to agree on the advocacy of either free trade or protection. The limits on geographical factor mobility also support a sectoral approach. Arguments that distinct regions specialize in particular sectors of the economy are a staple of the literature on political geography.[7] In their discussion of the tariff cycle, Cassing, McKeown, and Ochs (1986) also point out that factors are limited in their mobility not only across sectors but also across regions, and that certain sectors tend to dominate particular geographic areas. Geographic factor immobility and regional concentration in a few sectors would tend to reinforce sector-based cleavages because these considerations would further bind both labor and capital in particular geographic areas to each other, rather than to labor and capital in other sectors or other regions.

The Articulation of Divergent Interests in the Policy-Making Process

Determining the origins of conflicting views on the goals and priorities of national security policy is only one aspect of a domestic political account of the policy-making process. The relationship between societal interests and official policymakers is also critical. In some cases, policymakers may be drawn directly from the interested groups, but more often the relationship is less direct. Both elected politicians and appointed bureaucrats need political support in order to retain power and implement policy. Because economic interests can provide politicians and bureaucrats with money, access to media, and other political resources, they may decisively influence the policies major political actors support.

The relationship between societal interests and policymakers is not necessarily a simple exchange of political resources for policies. Although this is a useful metaphor for the influence of interests, and such an exchange certainly occurs in some cases, there are other ways policymakers may come to advocate the positions interest groups support. The structure of the economy influences the socialization of individual politicians. The economic activities prevailing in the policymaker's social milieu are likely to have an important effect on his or her general ideas about "the national interest." An individual rooted in a social setting dominated by people involved in export industries or international investment will probably have a very different view of the national interest than an individual from a setting in which most people earn their living through small business or domestically oriented industry. Even if the individuals to whom the policymaker turns for validation are not always consciously self-interested, few people can bring themselves to support policy positions that seriously undermine their own basic interests. Many of the most influential foreign-policy makers in the Truman administration came from a social and economic environment where the importance of international trade and investment were taken for granted. They may not have conceived of their policy positions in terms of their own self-interest, but their arguments nevertheless reflected their background.[8]

The exchange metaphor also obscures the fact that interests do not simply lobby politicians once they are in office. They have a crucial influence over whether they are elected in the first place. Recent research points to the usefulness of understanding political parties as sets of interests united around candidates that support policies they favor. Ferguson's (1983; 1995) investment theory of parties is perhaps the most completely articulated version of this theoretical argument, but he is not alone in using this approach. Other treatments of the United States and other industrialized countries also link political parties and various interested business elites.[9] The centrality of business interests comes not from any "magical powers" of business leaders, but from their control of important political resources—such as money and access to media—and their ability to monitor policy outcomes closely (cf. Weir and Skocpol 1985, 114–15). As Olson (1965) has pointed out, unorganized groups of voters face collective-action problems that make it difficult for them to engage in political action. These problems are much less serious for large business interests, since their greater resources allow a much smaller group of them to affect outcomes.[10]

Treating parties as coalitions of interests has a number of theoretical advantages. Above all, it provides a link between broad economic divisions in the society and the individuals who actually make policy. The argument that sets of interests shape the positions politicians take on major issues greatly simplifies the task of determining why members of each party take the positions they do. Furthermore, this argument can be tested against both statistical and qualitative historical evidence.

Societal interests influence not only elected politicians, but also appointed bureaucrats. In order to protect their budgets and prerogatives, bureaucratic leaders develop political constituencies and alliances with sympathetic elected politicians. The resulting constellations of societal interests, elected politicians, and bureaucrats with complementary organizational interests resemble what Joseph (1987) calls "policy currents."[11] Although the nature of the problem examined here suggests some modifications to Joseph's conception, the concept of elite policy currents is quite useful in examining how interests rooted in the structure of the economy are actually articulated in the policy-making process.

Joseph defines a policy current as a common conception of how power should be exercised, found among both state policymakers and interested members of the capitalist class outside the state (51–52). Policy currents are composed of common policy positions, although they can also be understood more concretely as the individuals and groups advocating these common positions. Because the adherents of a particular policy current may favor the common position for different reasons, the current itself is not reducible to the interests of any single group within it. Each element of the policy current has a different set of political resources with which to promote the common policy interest. No single actor controls the others, but they may assist one another at particular junctures in the policy-making process. The value of this concept is that it points to the convergence of societal and governmental actors around particular sets of policies based on common interests rather than any formal association. The success of a policy is determined by the ability of its supporters in the executive branch, in Congress, and outside the government to assist one another effectively.

This concept clarifies the relationships between governmental actors and their societal supporters in this case. For example, it is a good description of the linkages between the actors in the executive branch, the Congress, and the broader society that supported an antilabor internal security program. The specific actors included in this policy current, such as J. Edgar Hoover's FBI, congressional Republicans such as Styles Bridges, and representatives of particular firms and business associations concerned about the growing power of the labor movement, helped one another in promoting their shared policy objective, even when they were not all aware of the activities in which the others were engaged. The position of the FBI in the executive branch, as well as the activities of other elements of this policy current, made it very difficult for the White House to control the campaign against domestic radicals and influenced the nature of the trade-off between domestic and foreign policy. A similar story can be told about the influence of internationalists in the State Department.

Although Joseph does not locate the origins of policy currents in "different segments of capital" because bureaucratic participants do not necessarily share these interests, there are some advantages to treating these societal interests as more fundamental under certain conditions. In particular, when a new set of policies is emerging, societal interests are less malleable than the policy positions of official policymakers and the structure of bureaucracies. Although state intervention may alter the structure of the economy in the long run, it is difficult to imagine such an intervention succeeding quickly enough to provide immediate support for a newly developed set of policies.[12] The balance of policy interests within the state can be altered relatively quickly, by the reorganization or abolition of existing bureaucracies, the creation of new ones, or the replacement of key personnel within them. When a new set of policies is being developed, the relevant set of policy currents is more likely to reflect the distribution of societal interests than existing bureaucratic interests. The fact that development of Cold War national security policy was marked by the creation of significant new bureaucracies, such as the Central Intelligence Agency and the Air Force, and the reorganization of existing ones, such as the Department of Defense, supports the argument that the societal interests were more fundamental.

Political Bargaining and Policy Outcomes

Some account of bargaining between the president and his opponents in Congress is required to explain the development of early Cold War foreign and domestic policy. Although the Democratic party controlled both Congress and the presidency during the 1949–51 period, it could not simply impose its policy preferences on the Republican minority. The administration's goals in the spring of 1950 entailed sustaining a large increase in defense spending over a long period of time. While the president could depend on the support of the liberal wing of his party, the conservatives were much less reliable. Furthermore, nationalist Republicans who strongly opposed the administration's national security program dominated their party in the Senate. Before the Korean War, most contemporary observers believed that the military and foreign aid budgets would be cut even below the reduced levels set by the administration in late 1949. Furthermore, some important administration officials worried that even though the Korean War had forced Congress to support increased military budgets in the short run, these budgets might be cut immediately after the war ended.

   The policies that emerged from the 1949–51 period reflected the efforts of the leaders of both parties to maintain their political constituency. Their priorities reflected the relative importance of different segments of their societal constituency. The outcome of the bargaining process, in turn, reflected their priorities. The administration valued its national security program more highly than it valued its social welfare agenda, in part because placating the interests supporting this agenda, particularly organized labor, was less important for maintaining the Democratic coalition than was satisfying the interests backing the administration's foreign policy. On the other hand, the administration's Republican opponents valued their domestic policy goals more highly than they did their foreign policy agenda. Conservatives had opposed the labor and social welfare programs of the New Deal since their inception. With the enormous wave of strikes that followed the end of World War II, and the administration's continuing proposals to expand the welfare state, the concerns of labor-sensitive industries associated with the Republican party were especially acute. The two parties' different priorities implied a trade-off in which each would get the policy item it valued most highly. Figure 1 summarizes the bargaining situation.

The bargaining process had to be carried on by the party leadership, not representatives of the interests themselves. The coalitions involved encompassed many diverse groups united by compatible interests and support for a common set of candidates rather than by an organizational structure. Diffuse sets of interests do not have the centralized decision-making capacity necessary to commit themselves to act strategically. Even if they did, members of the coalition have no incentive to remain loyal if their interests are not served, and no reason to agree to a compromise that sacrifices those interests. Among such decentralized political formations, a lasting explicit bargain sacrificing the interests of some major investors is highly unlikely.

Although diffuse and incompletely organized sets of interests cannot bargain with one another, party leaders can. Political bargaining of this sort can only occur among politicians with coalitions of supporting interests broad enough to be able to sacrifice some of them in order to secure others. The broader the range of interests with which a politician is associated, the easier it will be for that politician to sacrifice a few of them in the course of a bargaining process. Since national political figures such as presidents and congressional leaders are likely to be associated with a broad range of policy currents across many different issues, they are more easily able to make these trade-offs than are lesser political figures with narrower constituencies.[13] High-level political leaders with broad constituencies are driven by the need to maintain the integrity of their coalition rather than the need to satisfy a particular set of interests within it.

This high-level bargaining process is likely to be a tacit one resembling that described by Downs and Rocke (1990) in the context of international bargaining over arms control. In a tacit bargaining process, each side takes actions to signal its intentions and its commitment to a particular position rather than relying on words alone. This type of bargaining, usually discussed in an international context, is likely to occur domestically in this case for several reasons. An explicit acknowledgment that certain interests are being traded away can only complicate the task of man-

	More military spending	Less military spending
	Administration's preferred outcome	**Demilitarized welfare state**
More social welfare spending; maintain power of labor movement	Losers: Labor-sensitive sectors Domestically oriented sectors	Losers: Labor-sensitive sectors Internationally oriented sectors
	Winners: Internationally oriented sectors Labor movement	Winners: Domestically oriented sectors Labor movement
	Actual outcome	**Nationalist Republicans' preferred outcome**
Less social welfare spending; reduce power of labor movement	Losers: Domestically oriented sectors Labor movement	Winners: Domestically oriented sectors Labor-sensitive sectors
	Winners: Internationally oriented sectors Labor-sensitive sectors	Losers: Internationally oriented sectors Labor movement

Fig. 1. Bargaining over national security and social welfare policy

aging a political coalition, so political leaders are unlikely to admit when they do so. Actions taken in a tacit bargaining process can be explained in a variety of ways to different audiences and thus do not pose this problem as sharply as explicit bargaining does. Furthermore, the leaders of opposing political parties may not trust one another to carry out the terms of informal or secret agreements. In a tacit bargaining process, actors may commit themselves to a course of action in ways that are less easily revoked than verbal promises. They may, for example, accept an institutional arrangement limiting their own future choices in order to assure the other side of their intention to cooperate.

While the societal constituencies of the major actors determined their priorities and shaped the outcome, the institutional context of the early Cold War era influenced bargaining tactics. Both sides used their institutional positions to attach additional rewards or penalties to particular options open to the opposing political leadership. The decision to intervene in Korea made it much more difficult for Republicans to oppose increased levels of military spending. The administration's use of the crisis in Korea to promote its national security program frustrated Republican leaders but did not change their minds about the value of the program itself. Rather than pay the costs of opposing it, they sought to use the crisis for their own purposes. They attached elements of their own domestic program to it, cutting social welfare spending and moving ahead with their attack on radicals in the labor movement.

National Interests, International Threats, and National Security Policy

The domestic political economy theory differs from most theoretical accounts of the national security policy-making process as well as from most historical accounts of the reasons for the 1950 military buildup. Most discussions of national security policy in both international relations theory and the historiography of the Cold War focus on decision makers' responses to international threats. The essentials of these accounts are simple and straightforward. They begin by confronting state officials with a set of problems they must solve, and threats they must face, in the international environment. The nature of these problems and threats does not depend on who the officials are but is instead an exogenous, objective feature of the international environment. If another domestic faction were to seize control of the state, it would face the same set of international threats as the faction it replaced. High-level policymakers may not always make wise choices about the achievement of these goals. Indeed, in extreme cases, they may even disregard them because of organizational interests, domestic political distractions, or their own psychological limitations. However, unless policymakers are constrained by other factors, it makes sense to assume that they will act in terms of exogenous goals imposed on them by international events and conditions.

This treatment of international threats carries some important theoretical baggage. Above all, it implies that the state can be treated as a unitary actor on foreign policy issues. Without a unitary actor assumption, it makes no sense to discuss the exogenous influence of international threats. Threats cannot exist apart from some set of interests or values. If there are exogenous threats that do not depend on the identity of the observer in a particular state, there must also be an exogenous set of threatened "national interests."

The notion of the national interest and related discussions of international threats have a long history in international relations theory. Hans Morgenthau (1956, 7), for example, in the introduction to his well-known textbook on international relations, argued that while national leaders do not always act in terms of the national interest defined as power, the national interest is nevertheless the best basis for a theory of foreign policy. The idea of the national interest is also commonly used in everyday discourse about international relations. Advocates and opponents of different foreign policies in the public arena commonly appeal to the national interest as a justification for the courses of action they recommend.

Despite its broad currency among policymakers and its historical role in international relations theory, few recent scholarly works explicitly use the concept of the national interest, even though their arguments imply that one exists.[14] The most important issue confronting theories or historical accounts that use or imply a unitary national interest is the problem of multiple interpretations. As Beard and Smith (1934), Rosenau (1968), and Nowell (1994, 11–14), among others, have pointed out, the nature of the interests and threats a state confronts in the international system is unclear and can be interpreted differently by observers with different interests and values. International events rarely affect an entire society in the same way or evoke a single, universal response. Nation-states, divided as they are by class, region, economic sector, and many other factors, cannot be realistically depicted as responding to events in the international system like a unified leviathan. The assertion that the national interest forms the basis for policy begs the question of how it was identified from among the welter of conflicting interests in society. Individuals and groups in the state and society may believe that their understanding of the national interest is genuinely "national," but, however sincere this belief, it is unlikely to have much basis in the perceptions of differently situated individuals and groups. As Rosenau (1969, 37) put it, "a description of the national interest can never be anything more than a set of conclusions derived from the analytic and evaluative framework of the describer."

Accounts of the policy-making process that use the unitary actor assumption, or arguments about international threats that imply one, must explain how a particular set of international threats and pressures is transmitted to decision makers. Resolving the multiple interpretation problem requires more than an appeal to the median voter or some other process of political negotiation and compromise. Conflicting interests and values cannot be aggregated into a single set of rational preferences resembling a national interest through political bargaining among interest groups or bureaucratic factions within the state. The work of social choice theorists since Arrow (1963) indicates that there are very few conditions under which different societal preferences can be aggregated into a single set of rationally ordered preferences.[15] Policy choices may result from the domestic decision-making process, but a unitary set of rational preferences will not.

Most theoretical accounts of the policy-making process that invoke or imply some conception of the national interest address the multiple interpretation problem using two related arguments. Realists contend that the need to survive in the anarchic international system imposes demands on state decision makers that are readily apparent under most conditions in practice. As McKeown (1986, 43–44) aptly puts it, this explanatory strategy is essentially a bet that "analysts will be able to identify a set of antecedent environmental conditions with sufficient precision that one and only one response will follow from each environmental condition." While realists stress the pressures generated by the international system, statists posit the historical development of a consensual set of values that shapes policymakers' interpretations of international conditions. These theoretical arguments are not mutually exclusive, and both are deployed in historical accounts of the decision-making process that use some notion of the national interest, or a related account of international threats.

Realists argue that the competitive pressures generated by the anarchic international system will force states to adopt certain basic sets of policies in order to survive. Waltz (1979, 172–73) argues that the requirements for survival in the anarchic international system force states to behave in particular ways. He uses the Cold War behavior of the United States and the Soviet Union to illustrate his argument.

> In a world in which two states united in their mutual antagonism far overshadow any other, the incentives to a calculated response stand out most clearly, and the sanctions against irresponsible behavior achieve their greatest force. Thus two states, isolationist by tradition, untutored in the ways of international politics, and famed for impulsive behavior, soon showed themselves—not always and everywhere, but always in crucial cases—to be wary, alert, cautious, flexible, and forbearing.

Part of the "calculated response" required by the position of the United States in the international system in the immediate postwar period was a military buildup, since the great powers in a bipolar system cannot rely on alliances for security. For Waltz, the structure of the international system determined the national security policy of the United States, in spite of its domestic politics. The national interest triumphed over ideology and historical tradition.[16]

Waltz avoids the need to present a theoretical account of the policy-making process by excluding foreign policy from the domain of his theory. Others have been less reluctant to apply realist arguments to the foreign policy-making process, however. These realists treat the policy implications of international conditions as if they were readily discernible in practice unless obscured by other considerations. Posen (1984, 221) argues that it is unfair to impute a unitary rational actor assumption to more recent formulations of realist theory. "These are more concerned with the *con-*

straints and *incentives* inherent in an anarchical international system than they are with the accuracy of a unitary rational actor assumption." Most of these accounts hold that various features of the policy-making process, such as organizational imperatives (Posen 1984) or domestic politics (Snyder 1991; Stein 1993), may prevent policymakers from effectively meeting the exogenous policy demands of the international system under certain circumstances. The unitary interests of the state and the corresponding international threats nevertheless play an important role in these accounts, both as a normative standard against which to judge defective policy choices and as an empirical baseline for measuring the influence of other complicating factors. Indeed, both Snyder and Posen treat deviations from the policy implied by the state's position in the international system as the result of exceptional circumstances, such as the "hijacking" of the state by cartelized interests, or organizational pressures under conditions of very low international threat.

The approach to solving the problem of multiple interpretations used in most of the recent historiography of the early Cold War era resembles a statist approach in most respects. In these accounts, decision makers interpret international conditions in terms of a consensual set of policy interests. Presenting his statist account of the national interest, Krasner (1978, 13–14) argues that the basic policy goals associated with it "must be related to general societal goals, persist over time, and have a consistent ranking in order of importance." The notion of "general societal goals" strongly resembles Leffler's (1991, 202) argument that security policy is intended to protect "domestic core values from external threats." Leffler argues that culture, ideology, and economic interests all contribute to the development of these core values.[17] Although their account of the origins of basic policy goals differs from that offered by realists, Krasner and Leffler resemble the realists in treating these goals as exogenous to the policy-making process and in using them to explain the policy that ultimately develops. In Krasner's account, state officials' conception of the national interest is the main explanation for policy outcomes. If one assumes the core values are indeed consensual, the proper analytical focus is on official understandings of the international threats to them. This is precisely what Leffler emphasizes. While he argues (1984, 346) that many societal influences shaped the "American conception of national security," he devotes little attention to them in his lengthy 1992 narrative, focusing instead on the specifics of the international threats to these values, much as realists do.[18]

Leffler's approach departs from the strict stress on security concerns found in the work of other "postrevisionists" like Gaddis (1982; 1983) and earlier "orthodox" historians such as Halle (1967).[19] While Leffler includes economic goals among his core values, Gaddis (1983, 175) contends that "economic instruments were used to serve political ends, not the other way around as the Leninist model of imperialism would seem to imply." Gaddis's position echoes the realist argument that the survival interests of the state as a unitary actor in the international system will override other interests.[20] Gaddis (1982, 353) summarizes the policy problems facing U.S. decision makers during the Cold War as a process of overcoming various political and cognitive barriers to understanding what is required to meet exogenous threats. A strategy that avoids overextension is difficult because "one must distinguish rationally, even cold-bloodedly, between vital and peripheral interests, tolerable and intolerable threats, and feasible and unfeasible responses. There is little protection against psychological insecurities, always a problem in a democracy." While Leffler's statist version of the policy-making process is not quite the same as Gaddis's realist account, both assert that there were clear security imperatives in the international system and that these concerns drove policy.

In realist and statist accounts, domestic politics plays a marginal role. It does not shape basic policy goals, which are exogenously given, although it sometimes interferes with the optimal pursuit of these goals. Even accounts like Snyder (1991) and Stein (1993), which explicitly examine the effects of domestic politics on foreign policy, treat political conflict as a constraint on policymakers' responses to objective international constraints and incentives. In Snyder's account, cartelized interests may produce an "overexpansionist" foreign policy that deviates from the one implied by the position of the state in the international system, but only if they "hijack the state" (14). Such a condition is exceptional. Snyder's argument implies that, under normal circumstances, such narrow interests do not dominate the policy-making process, and it is therefore much more responsive to the dictates of the international system. Stein's argument about U.S. foreign policy during the 1938–50 period also treats domestic politics as a set of constraints on an appropriate U.S. response to its position as a great power. When these constraints were removed by international crises, policymakers were able to act in accordance with realist expectations. Although domestic politics plays a central role in both of these accounts, it acts within a realist framework. Only deviations from realist expectations are caused by the action of domestic interests. Policies that respond to what the authors take to be the imperatives of the international system are not explained in this way.

Many recent historical accounts of early Cold War U.S. foreign policy also minimize the importance of political conflict over the policy's basic outlines. While no one argues that there was no opposition to the Truman administration's foreign policy, Eden (1993, 196–98) notes that its importance in the process is often minimized. Leffler (1992, 15, 140, 371) repeatedly insists that the Truman administration's opponents offered no alternative, and he pays very little attention to the process through which the administration secured their acquiescence. He accords little practical importance to the administration's domestic opponents, noting that "[m]ost people were willing to follow the administration in the direction that it wanted to lead. So long as the administration practiced containment and deterrence, so long as it rejected a policy of reassurance and accommodation, it could do pretty much as it liked" (140). Leffler notes that increasing Republican opposition in the spring of 1950 forced administration policymakers "to move cautiously, plan carefully, and design a compelling case for anything they wanted to do," but he does not argue that it had any effect on their choices (344). Indeed, if he did, his central theoretical device for interpreting the policy-making process—the defense of core values—would be harder to sustain. Domestic political processes shaped core values in Leffler's account, but his account of the policy-making process begins with these core values already well established.

Gaddis, Leffler, and other historians who use exogenous international threats or consensual core values to explain the development of Cold War national security policy might prefer to avoid this linkage with realist or statist international relations theory.[21] Nevertheless, the theoretical implications of their historical accounts are unavoidable. The explicit or implicit frameworks they use act as analytical tools for understanding historical evidence. These frameworks shape expectations about policy development and so determine what historians see as problematic, what they set aside as uninteresting or irrelevant, and how they fill in the gaps in the documentary record. As I will discuss in greater detail later, these theoretical positions also lead them to positions concerning the impact of international events that are not supported by evidence but are logically necessary to sustain their general argument.

Theories of "Policy-Making" and Theories of "Decision Making"

The problems faced by realist and statist accounts of the policy-making process in this case do not mean these approaches are never appropriate. However, they are likely to produce the best results when applied to cases where their central assumptions are more realistic. In some cases, it may make sense to depict policy goals as if they were consensual, foreign policy as if it were separated from other issues, and decision makers as if they were insulated from societal pressures. These cases are associated with what I will call a "decision-making" context to distinguish them from the broader range of circumstances I wish to imply by the term "policy-making."

In the sense in which I will use it here, "policy-making" refers to the selection of policy goals and the allocation of material, organizational, and other resources with which to achieve them. By extension, "national security policy" is the identification of national security goals and threats, and the development and allocation of resources to achieve those goals and protect against those threats. Understood in this way, policy may be directed at concerns that are neither present nor immediately anticipated. Policy-making can be distinguished from "decision making," by which I mean a discrete choice by an actor in response to a specific contingency. Policy is made for the long term, to deal with general issues, while decisions are made in response to immediate events. The Kennedy administration's handling of the Cuban missile crisis is a case of decision making, while the rearmament program envisioned in NSC 68, which took several months to produce and even longer to put into effect, is an example of policy-making. Although decisions made in specific crises may be bounded by prior decisions about policy, and general policies may be reinforced or undermined by decisions made in response to discrete crises, the two concepts are not identical.

As routes to state action, "policies" and "decisions" are related. The relationship is not necessarily a simple one, however. Decisions do not necessarily result in policy, since even responses to some intrinsically important events may not influence the identification of policy problems or the allocation of resources in the long term. On the other hand, while prior policy does not determine what decisions will be made in a particular case, it is likely to have significant influence in the issue area with which it is concerned. Prior national security policy may not dictate the choice made by a decision maker, but it will almost certainly determine the range of diplomatic and military options available. For example, if the United States had not maintained sufficient transport aircraft in 1948, Truman would not have had the option of responding to the Soviet blockade of Berlin with an airlift. The distinction between policy and decision, like that made between the levels of analysis in international relations, looms larger when its theoretical implications are examined more closely.

Policies may be explained by a different set of factors than are decisions, even when they are related. Political actors are likely to have much greater autonomy in making discrete decisions than they do in making policy. Indeed, policies, like budgets, may be best understood as the outcome of a political process reconciling the competing aspirations of many actors.[22] The final result may be one that none of the participants in the policy-making process would have chosen individually. Since readily identifiable groups of people make decisions, their personal psychology and the group dynamics taking place among them are likely to be critically important. Policy, on the other hand, may not be the result of specific sets of decisions by readily identifiable actors. A policy may emerge from many contradictory decisions made by many different people over a long period of time. This process diminishes the importance of the individual actors' personal idiosyncrasies and increases the importance of the political context determining which decisions will have long-term influence, and of the specific political arrangements providing the support necessary to keep a policy in place over time.

Since policies and decisions cannot always be explained by the same factors, an approach focusing exclusively on decision making is likely to miss some important factors shaping policy. As Snyder, Bruck, and Sapin (1954) pointed out, a decision-making approach focuses on factors affecting the conscious calculations of decision makers. This approach is not appropriate for all questions. Two important sets of problems arise from applying decision-making models to questions of national security policy more appropriately analyzed in a policy-making context. The first set of problems arises from the implicit separation between national security policy and other issues. The second set stems from treating decision makers as if they were insulated from the rest of society.

Policy-making processes in different issue areas are unavoidably linked by budgetary trade-offs between competing priorities. As statements about the allocation of resources, budgets are central to the policy-making process. Without adequate resources, no program, however well planned, will be effective. Political actors during the 1949–51 period understood the importance of budgets for policy-making. Wilfred McNeil, then comptroller of the Department of Defense, expressed this point succinctly when asked about the relationship between the policy of containment and his efforts in planning the defense budget: "If you are talking about containment, I can tell you whether you can do it or not by whether you can get the dough."[23] Without the billions of dollars required to put its recommendations into effect, the program outlined in NSC 68 could never have been implemented. Once these billions were allocated to military use, they were no longer available for other policy priorities. Because they have implications for resource allocation, statements about national security policy are also implicit statements about what will be done in other areas of policy as well.

Another problem with separating national security policy from other policy matters is that all of these issues are handled by the same individuals and coalitions. At its highest level, the state is not divided into discrete segments that deal separately with domestic and foreign policy issues. The president introduces policies concerning both domestic and international issues and confronts many of the same members of Congress in both issue areas. Political parties and coalitions usually remain intact across both foreign and domestic policy issues. They are not created anew in each issue area. There is no reason to assume that the development of policy will proceed separately on different issues. Indeed, given the political and budgetary connections among them, policy choices in different areas are arguably just individual elements of a single complicated political problem. Political actors must find a solution that both optimizes the resources available to them and draws the support of a coalition sufficient to defeat alternative sets of policies.[24]

In addition to the problems of separating national security policy from other issues, decision-making theories also treat policymakers as if they were insulated from the rest of society, examining only the factors the decision makers themselves consider. However, social forces that the decision makers themselves never consider may also influence policy. The reaction of other political actors, such as members of Congress, may move policy in an unanticipated direction, perhaps even one never imagined by those who initially selected it. Also, factors that lead to the selection of policymakers from a particular segment of society may have more influence on the selection of policy than the conscious considerations of these individuals once they are in office. The forces that determine which policies are politically feasible may also be decisive even if decision makers do not fully comprehend them. If the range of politically viable choices is sufficiently narrow, the decision-making process may be insignificant. Individual policymakers may arrive at a decision for many different reasons. Whatever the individual motives involved, though, not every decision will meet with a level of support in the state and society necessary to sustain it in the short term, let alone establish it as a long-term policy. Without considering the socioeconomic context of policy-making, a theory about the process can only be partial and incomplete. It may offer an excellent account of decision making but fail to explain why many plausible alternatives were excluded before the decision-making process even began.

Although they have not framed their arguments in these terms, a distinction between policy and decision contexts is implied in some other discussions of foreign policy. These analyses indicate that accounts focusing exclusively on decision making are likely to underestimate the role of actors and sociopolitical pressures outside of the state. Charles Hermann (1972), in his discussion of crisis decision making, contends that the short time allowed to make decisions in crises tends to restrict the scope of the group making the decision. By contrast, the longer a policy-making process continues, the greater the opportunity for participation by a wide range of actors, including those outside the state. Since policy-making, as I have defined it here, is a long-term process, it follows that it is more likely to be influenced by actors outside the state than is crisis decision making.

Similarly, Thomas McCormick (1982, 320) comments that diplomatic history has "a fixation with crisis-events" that leads its practitioners to avoid the consideration of the larger social and political context of decision making. McCormick argues that the excessive focus on crises exaggerates the importance of the state, since "[t]he state, after all, does play peculiarly important functions in a crisis. If one's focus is crisis-event, one's focus is also the State." By restricting the range of relevant actors to state decision makers, realist and statist accounts treat policy-making as if it resembled crisis decision making. In fact, long-term decisions about national security policy are made and implemented over a long period of time, with ample opportunity to be blocked or changed by a wide range of political actors. The NSC 68 rearmament program, for example, had to be approved by Congress and implemented over a period of several years.

Unfortunately, McCormick's critique is quite applicable to many historical accounts of U.S. national security policy during the early Cold War era. Even a work as large and impressive as that of Melvyn Leffler (1992) offers little discussion of the effects of domestic political conflict on foreign policy, or the impact of foreign policy on domestic politics. Leffler offers virtually no account of the sources of support for or opposition to Truman's national security policy outside the executive branch. Indeed, his discussion of congressional approval of the rearmament program is confined to a single sentence: "After some wrangling, Congress gave the president the authority he requested" (371). Leffler's subsequent work (1994) pays more attention to the political context of these policies in the United States, but he does not change his assessment of its significance for policy outcomes.

This sort of history can provide, as Leffler's does, a careful and detailed account of decision making, but it gives an incomplete version of the development of policy. In this area, it leaves untouched some of the most important issues, including the question of how American society was mobilized to support this unprecedented and costly effort to secure new goals it had consistently rejected throughout its prior existence as a nation. Even where Leffler makes the decision makers' thinking clear, he does not explain how these decisions became an enduring policy. Leffler's book is not the only one to ignore the socioeconomic context of policy-making, but the fact that this problem exists in a work that is so outstanding in other respects indicates the prevalence of the assumptions of the decision-making approach in the historiography of American foreign policy. The problems in his account are not caused by insufficient research, but by an implicit prior theory about how policy is made.

Conclusion: Evaluating Conflicting Theories of the Policy-Making Process

The two theoretical approaches to the policy-making process outlined here lead to very different versions of the early Cold War era. Although historical accounts of policy-making are not always framed in terms of an explicit theory, they are necessarily theoretical. Researchers require a framework of expectations about the context in which documents and other evidence about the process were produced—not all of which can be ascertained from the documents themselves—in order to evaluate their importance. At a minimum, this theoretical framework provides a set of expectations about what actors are relevant to the outcome, and the considerations that govern their choices. These theoretical expectations guide research decisions about what evidence to examine. They shape researchers' judgments on whether particular pieces of information about the process are problematic or obvious to the explanation, important or irrelevant to the outcome, routine or unusual for the actors involved. These expectations also determine where researchers perceive gaps in the available evidence and provide the theory-laden arguments through which those gaps are filled. Good narrative writing may create the illusion of a seamless chain of events, re-created as it actually happened. In practice, though, historical processes have to be re-created from isolated bits of evidence such as documents or the memories of the participants. These pieces of information must be related to a larger pattern by the researcher.

The remainder of this book will evaluate the usefulness of the domestic political economy theory of the policy-making process by comparing it to the realist-statist approach. In order to avoid constructing a "straw man" to represent the realist-statist approach, I will rely on particularly good historical accounts of this case that share realist-statist assumptions and use related concepts. Since Melvyn Leffler's 1992 work is both recent and highly acclaimed, I will focus primarily on it. My criticisms apply to Leffler's theoretical framework rather than his prodigious and admirable research effort. They apply with even greater force to weaker accounts. While the realist-statist approach is useful for some purposes, it does not produce a satisfactory explanation of this important historical case. The domestic political economy theory produces more consistently correct expectations about the policy-making process than does the realist-statist approach. It also explains important features of this process that are exogenous to realist and statist theories, such as the origins of conflicting policy preferences and the linkages between national security policy and other issues. Because this case is generally considered a strong one for theoretical arguments treating external events as if they were interpreted in a unitary actor, my findings suggest that the applicability of the realist-statist approach has been overstated.

CHAPTER 2

The Politics of Rearmament in the Executive Branch I: The Fiscal 1951 Budget

It is not within the province or competence of the economist to pass judgment on the necessary level of expenditures in these fields [defense and foreign aid]. It is within his province, however, to point out the dangers to the domestic economy arising out of continuing deficits and with a growing national debt in times of relatively high business activity. These are dangers to the security of the Nation no less real than the dangers of military aggression or international economic retardation.

—Edwin Nourse

I asked one of the services, the other day, what they needed for the defense of America. That service had a program, on charts and all, that would cost 30 to 50 billion dollars a year. After 30 or 40 minutes of it I said, "Now forget this presentation. This is what I want: a sufficient defense within the economy of the United States. I want something that is practical. Quit that dreaming."

—Louis Johnson

I was sent over by the State Department to follow the joint effort at military planning [by Britain, France, and the Low Countries]. . . . They estimated that the cost of the military equipment necessary for a force strong enough to hold the Soviets at the Rhine was $45 billion in 1949 dollars. That was triple the cost of the entire Marshall Plan. Could the United States institute a military aid program to help?

—Paul Nitze

Accounts of the defense buildup that began in 1950 nearly always center around a National Security Council report best known by its file number, NSC 68. The report, which was submitted to the president by a joint State-Defense working group on April 7, 1950, argued that the Soviet Union was engaged in an all-out effort to extend its influence and control over all regions of the world. It asserted that the means available to the Kremlin were considerable and growing constantly. Noting that "[t]hese risks crowd in on us, in a shrinking world of polarized power, so as to give us no choice, ultimately, between meeting them effectively and being overcome by them," the report concluded that "it is clear that a substantial and rapid military building up of strength in the free world is necessary to support a firm policy necessary to check and roll back the Kremlin's drive for world domination."[1]

The rhetoric of NSC 68 echoes realist arguments about the pressures of the international system on a unitary state. Furthermore, NSC 68 was developed in secret at the highest levels of government and involved basic national security policy questions. Both its subject matter and its institutional setting suggest that the development and acceptance of this policy statement within the executive branch should be a very strong case for realist or statist explanations stressing unitary state action to meet the imperatives of the international system and protect core values from external threats. However, close examination of historical evidence about this process reveals that even the best of these accounts are quite problematic. The domestic political economy theory offers a better way to reconstruct the policy-making process in this case.

The account of policy development in the executive branch presented in the next two chapters has two goals. The first is to demonstrate that the development and acceptance of NSC 68 is better explained in terms of domestic coalition building and maintenance than as a response to external threats to core values. Major developments in the process corresponded to changes in the demands of coalition building and maintenance rather than to particular external events. Decision makers disagreed about the meaning of the events usually thought to have motivated rearmament. Neither the writing of NSC 68 nor the decision to accept its call for rearmament can be convincingly linked to the external shocks usually offered to explain them. These events were important, but they did not drive the development of policy. The second goal is to show that high-ranking executive branch decision makers reflect the broader economic and political divisions in society. These societal linkages are important in determining the positions they take on foreign policy issues. The idea that these decision makers act on a set of core values or a "national" interest is deeply problematic, even on national security issues.

Realist and statist historical accounts logically require linkages between the policy-making process and external events because they rule out serious conflict over basic policy goals and priorities. The notion of "core values" and arguments about the imperatives of the international system imply unity within the state on national security issues. External shocks drive the process by clarifying the demands of the international system or the requirements of defending core values. Unfortunately, this account of the process is not sustained by a close examination of the evidence. In fact, the administration's decision to proceed with rearmament was not driven by particular external events, but by the resolution of a domestic political conflict between opposing sets of policy priorities. External events may make a great impression on individual policymakers, but domestic actors with different interests may disagree about their significance. The influence of an event depends on the interests comprising the dominant domestic coalition. The requirements of building and maintaining such a coalition may lead central decision makers to discount potentially significant external events and may produce policy changes even when there is no precipitating international event.

Any account of executive branch decision making is, in some sense, a story of bureaucratic politics. Since the publication of Graham Allison's well-known article and book on the subject (1969; 1971), accounts of this sort have become commonplace. Allison and others present bureaucratic politics as an alternative to unitary actor models. However, while historical accounts of bureaucratic struggles over policy challenge realist-statist arguments about consensus on core values, they often share other important realist-statist assumptions. Although they do not conceptualize the state as a unitary rational actor, theories of bureaucratic politics often focus just as rigidly on central government decision makers as do realist and statist approaches. They often discuss conflict within the government without examining its deeper roots in society. Indeed, some discussions of the internal politics of the executive branch, such as Huntington (1963), argue explicitly that conflict over national security policy is confined to the executive branch.

Another way of treating bureaucratic politics is to recognize that it reflects broader societal conflicts. In this conception of the policy-making process, bureaucrats can influence policy to the extent that they can draw political support from interested groups in society. Rather than simply taking the existence and interests of bureaucratic actors as given, it makes sense to examine the role they play in the larger society and the ties they maintain to interests within it. A large body of work exists treating bureaucratic politics in this way.[2] Archival evidence suggests that in this case, too, bureaucratic politics is best understood as part of a wider struggle taking place both inside and outside the government. The way policy divisions within the executive branch are nested in broader social cleavages will affect the behavior of executive branch actors, the political options open to them, and the final outcome of policy debates. The term *bureaucratic politics* is probably too narrow to capture these dynamics. Joseph's 1987 notion of conflict between "policy currents" linking actors in the state and society is preferable.

Both the policy positions and the influence of particular executive branch officials during the 1949–51 period are difficult to understand without examining their links to the broader society. For example, Louis Johnson, the secretary of defense from April 1949 until September 1950, advocated lower military budgets during most of his tenure in office. Given the organizational interests of the Department of Defense, Johnson's position is difficult to understand. His attitude makes more sense in light of his ongoing efforts to build a political constituency to run for president in 1952. Similarly, the director of the FBI, J. Edgar Hoover, had far more power over the administration's internal security policy than one would expect given his institutional position as a subordinate of the attorney general and his tense relationship with the president. His influence makes more sense when one considers his ability to call on sympathetic societal interests and members of Congress to support his position.

The next two chapters present a process-tracing analysis of the development of NSC 68 within the Truman administration. This chapter covers the process leading to the late 1949 decision to reduce the fiscal 1951 military and foreign aid budget below the levels envisioned in early 1949. The next chapter addresses the reversal of this decision in the spring of 1950 associated with NSC 68. The details of the decision-making process presented here are important for theory-testing as well as for developing a rich historical account. The ability of each theoretical approach to fit these details into a broader conceptual account of the policy-making process determines its usefulness as an explanatory tool.[3]

"No less a risk than our military and diplomatic risks"

Between the summer of 1949 and the spring of 1950, the administration completely reversed its position on the level of spending required to protect U.S. national security. The most common explanation for this change shares some critical premises with realist and statist theory. It stresses the role of external events, especially the Soviet acquisition of the atomic bomb and the Chinese revolution. These events are treated as if they had but one plausible interpretation. Samuel Wells (1979, 117) characterizes them as "hammer blows" that forced U.S. policymakers to reconsider their views about the requirements of American security. According to Wells, the new conception of these requirements embodied in NSC 68 finally gained acceptance within the administration because of the North Korean attack on South Korea. Melvyn Leffler's account (1992, 355–60) resembles the one offered by Wells in most respects, adding that NSC 68 was not itself very important because it did not deviate from previous policy in most respects. The Korean War forced a reluctant administration to accept rearmament.[4] Both Wells and Leffler depict an administration reacting to events in the international system, if not as an entirely unitary actor, then certainly as one united in its understanding of policy priorities and necessities. Neither takes contemporary alternative views of American priorities very seriously. This account of the rearmament decision is plausible, but a closer examination of the available evidence about the process does not support the reactions it posits to particular external events.

Examining the competing policy preferences in the executive branch and considering the president's need to select a politically sustainable policy lead to a better account of the NSC 68 process. Long-standing policy currents that linked decision makers with interests in society—and that were not dependent on particular, discrete events—account for the positions taken by the major actors. U.S. policymakers viewed the major international events that preceded NSC 68 with much less alarm than Wells implies. There was no generalized sense of crisis before the Korean War compelling policymakers to proceed with the massive buildup that ultimately resulted from NSC 68. Indeed, those who favored the buildup worried that the lack of public and elite concern would prevent them from enacting the program. Furthermore, the best available evidence indicates that Truman had decided to proceed with a defense buildup in response to NSC 68 before the beginning of the Korean War. While the events used to explain NSC 68 are certainly consequential in their own right, they do not explain the resolution of the policy debate over rearmament. The failure of particular external shocks to explain the development of NSC 68 raises serious questions about the viability of realist and statist accounts of the policy-making process.

The acceptance of NSC 68 in the executive branch resulted from the political victory of a policy current concerned about the long-range problems caused by the approaching end of the Marshall Plan. Although they undoubtedly interpreted events to support their position, the supporters of rearmament were not convinced by any particular external shock.[5] The struggle between this group and its opponents in the executive branch foreshadowed the conflict that subsequently took place between the administration and Congress. The societal ties of those in the executive branch who favored a small defense budget were similar to the societal ties of those in Congress who favored the same policy.

The Bureau of the Budget was the center of executive branch opposition to large military budgets. Under James Webb and his successor, Frank Pace, the bureau had developed significant authority over the administration's budgetary and legislative strategy. It not only reviewed all executive budget requests, but also made final recommendations to the president on whether he should sign or veto legislation passed by Congress. The economic effects of federal deficits deeply concerned Webb and Pace. Both men sought to limit spending, especially by the military services, which had the largest single share of the total budget. The political forces favoring a smaller military budget were not confined to the Bureau of the Budget, however. In the planning stages of the fiscal 1951 budget, Pace sought allies both within and outside the administration. In 1949, the proponents of a small budget were a formidable political force. Their sudden eclipse deserves more attention than it has received.

The small-budget faction enjoyed early success shaping the fiscal 1951 defense budget. Truman had committed himself to an eventual balanced budget when he submitted the fiscal 1950 budget to Congress in January 1949. In April, Pace informed the president that the federal budget would have to be cut in order to achieve this goal on schedule, because he expected the slowing economy of early 1949 to cause a drop in revenues. Planners at the National Military Establishment had been developing war plans and programs under the assumption that they would receive at least $15 billion. Based on reduced government revenue projections, the Bureau of the Budget reduced the fiscal 1951 budget ceiling for the National Military Establishment to $13.5 billion dollars.[6] The president approved Pace's request and announced his decision at a meeting of officials from the affected departments on July 1.

Frank Pace was not a major political figure in his own right. However, his public relations efforts as director of the Bureau of the Budget indicate that he may have hoped to build a political career for himself—or at least a base of political support for his policy views—by cultivating those favoring a balanced budget and reduced federal expenditures. He published a condensed and simplified version of the administration's plans to balance the budget and sought to distribute it as widely as possible. In staff meetings, he referred to this publicity effort as a matter of "extreme importance."[7] "Budget in Brief" brought Pace some favorable press, including a glowing profile in *U.S. News and World Report* describing the 37-year-old director as a "boy wonder." Pace drew this article to the attention of Louis Johnson and the president.[8] His zeal on behalf of a balanced budget was not always appreciated by the White House, however. David Bell, a speechwriter on the White House staff, objected to a statement Pace wrote for the *New York Daily Compass.* When Pace sought White House clearance for its publication, Bell wrote that he was disturbed by Pace's failure to consider policy priorities other than balancing the budget, especially in the area of foreign policy. Bell contended that these other priorities might prevent the administration from balancing the budget and that statements like the one Pace proposed might later become a source of embarrassment. The White House subsequently refused to grant Pace permission to publish the article.[9]

Pace sought to build support for himself and his programs in other ways. He contacted Charles Dawes, a member of the board of the City National Bank and Trust in Chicago and the director of the Bureau of the Budget under Herbert Hoover. Dawes wrote back lamenting the increased size of the government and offering Pace his help and support. Much of Pace's correspondence with Dawes appears to be missing from his papers, so it is difficult to determine what sort of support or assistance, if any, Dawes gave Pace.[10] Pace also maintained contact with a number of local and state Democratic party officials from the South, especially his home state of Arkansas. He spoke publicly on the importance of a balanced budget to Democratic party groups and financial organizations such as the Association of Stock Exchange Firms. In short, Pace was extremely active in promoting a balanced budget, and he developed a high-profile public commitment to this goal.

Pace's concerns about a possible federal deficit were shared by Edwin G. Nourse, the chairman of the Council of Economic Advisers (CEA). Like Pace, Nourse saw inflation as the greatest potential threat to the health of the U.S. economy. When Truman reduced the fiscal 1951 budget ceilings, he requested that the CEA prepare a report comparing the economic effects of these cuts with those of continuing budget deficits due to a large diversion of resources to the military and foreign aid.[11] Pace had requested that Truman ask for such a report, no doubt anticipating that Nourse would support his position. Pace also asked Truman to invite Nourse to the meetings of the National Security Council at which budgetary issues were discussed. Although Nourse supported Pace's views on the budget, he lacked the political connections and the personal style necessary to be an effective ally in the ensuing policy struggle.

If Nourse lacked the will to fight the political battle over the budget, Louis Johnson had more than his share. History has not been kind to Johnson, who chaired Truman's 1948 campaign finance committee and became secretary of defense at the beginning of Truman's second term. Johnson has often been blamed for the fiscal 1951 budget cuts and for the alleged lack of preparedness during the early stages of the war in Korea. This charge is unfair. Although Johnson eventually became the most visible proponent of reducing the military budget, Frank Pace initiated the fiscal 1951 cuts. Johnson was first informed of the planned reductions in the fiscal 1951 budget ceiling at a May 12, 1949, meeting with Pace. Initially, Johnson appears to have resisted the cuts, ordering the Joint Chiefs of Staff to proceed with planning under the previous estimate of $16.5 billion. Eventually, however, he came to believe not only that the president was fully committed to a smaller budget, as Pace had indicated, but also that the Congress might trim the budget to as little as $10 billion (Rearden 1984, 369–71).

Whatever his previous feelings about small military budgets, Johnson quickly adopted the effort to trim the defense budget as a personal crusade. He used the budget cuts to gain political allies for his anticipated run for the presidency in 1952. Johnson struck up a friendship with Frank Pace in the summer of 1949, after the budget ceiling had been imposed. The two men became involved in the Citizen's Committee for the Hoover Report, a presidential-commission study calling for government reorganization and a balanced budget. Johnson had served with Pace's father during World War I and passed along glowing reviews of the younger Pace's work to his father.[12] Pace was already a friend of Stephen T. Early, the former press secretary to Franklin Roosevelt whom Johnson had appointed assistant secretary of defense.[13] Since Early's principal function in the Department of Defense was "to groom Louis Johnson to be President," according to one Defense Department official, the relationship may also have had some political significance.[14]

Johnson cultivated small businesses and domestically oriented industries opposed to large defense budgets. Francis Matthews, the widely ridiculed secretary of the navy, had assisted Johnson in raising funds for Truman. Matthews's understanding of naval issues may have been limited, but he had first-rate connections to the most conservative elements of American business. As an officer in the United States Chamber of Commerce, he had directed their campaign against domestic communism through 1947.[15] Johnson spoke before the Chamber of Commerce in May 1949, stressing his efforts to get small businesses a larger share of Defense Department contracts.[16] He delivered similar messages before a variety of local business and civic organizations around the country. Johnson's highly visible budget-cutting efforts drew praise from conservatives and scorn from the internationalist news media. *Time* argued that Johnson had "ruthlessly sliced away muscle" with his economy program.[17] Joseph and Stewart Alsop blasted his opposition to greater military spending in their *Washington Post* column throughout the winter and spring of 1950.

Johnson's efforts to mobilize political support were not limited to small business. During his tenure as secretary of defense, he met with an impressive list of corporate officials, ostensibly to discuss international business conditions. These meetings were arranged by Frank Page, an ITT executive, and included representatives of U.S. Steel Export Company, Chase National Bank, IBM, General Electric, Kennecott Copper,

National City Bank, and others.[18] Cultivating a positive media image was also a priority for Johnson, although he had only limited success. He hosted a series of luncheons with representatives of major media organizations, especially large contingents from the Washington press corps.[19] His concern with the media led him to confront John Osborne and Henry Luce about criticism of his programs in *Time*. Osborne later wrote to reassure Johnson that "nobody is 'gunning' for you in this organization."[20] Nevertheless, the magazine's criticism of Johnson continued.

The small-budget faction was strengthened by its ties to Nationalist Republicans in Congress also interested in keeping defense spending down. Johnson was on good terms with Senate Minority Leader Kenneth Wherry, a strident administration critic. Both men had ties to the American Legion, of which Johnson had been national commander.[21] The bipartisan effort to promote the Hoover Commission report, which called for a balanced budget, provided a rallying point for conservatives in both parties. In addition to Johnson and Pace, many conservative Republicans such as Wherry, Styles Bridges, and Robert Taft endorsed the Hoover Commission's call for cuts in defense spending as a way to balance the federal budget.[22] Even after the beginning of the Korean War, when Johnson's efforts to hold down military spending might have made an inviting target, Republicans concentrated their attacks on Secretary of State Dean Acheson and left Johnson alone.[23]

Although no one protested the budget cuts during the July 1 meeting with President Truman, discontent about them soon developed. Opponents of the cuts fought a losing battle during the second half of 1949, but they succeeded in changing administration policy the next year. In 1949, opposition to the cuts came from the State Department, where reductions in foreign aid were a source of concern, and from the Joint Chiefs of Staff, who were alarmed by the implications of the cuts for their war plans. In addition to the CEA's report on the economic impact of the budget cuts, Truman asked that the NSC review their effects on national security programs. This review process became the focus of those who opposed the budget cuts.

Although the Joint Chiefs of Staff did not try to persuade Johnson or Truman to raise the new budget ceiling, they remained concerned about its effects. Dwight Eisenhower, then serving as NATO Supreme Commander, argued that the reduced funding made a greater reliance on air power unavoidable and urged that more of the total be allocated to the Air Force. Johnson, who had been a director of Consolidated Vultee Aircraft, shared these views on air power (Burch 1980, 87). The Navy requested additional funding to increase the size of its force beyond what Johnson had proposed (Rearden 1984, 372–76). In general, while all of the services expressed concern about the cuts, their protests were relatively mild compared to their efforts to alter the fiscal 1949 and 1950 budgets. They pointed out inadequacies in the state of readiness allowed by the new budget, but they did not attempt to undermine the budget in Congress, as the Air Force had done in 1948 and the Navy earlier in 1949.[24]

Leffler (1992, 308) attributes the quiescence of the Joint Chiefs of Staff and the military services to their perception that war was unlikely. This argument does not explain why their attitude persisted well into 1950, however—a time when, Leffler and others have argued, perceptions of the Soviet threat were becoming more dire and concern about the possibility of war was growing. Much of the credit (or blame) for their relative political inactivity should probably be given to Louis Johnson and his much-maligned style of management in the Pentagon. Armed with the 1949 amendments to the National Security Act strengthening his authority over the service secretaries, Johnson resolutely imposed his will on the military services. Where his predecessor, James Forrestal, had been willing to take military requests for additional funding to the president, Johnson simply refused to consider them.[25] He also restricted contact between the Pentagon and other branches of the government, insisting that all such contacts be cleared by him or by James Burns, his designated representative.[26] While Johnson made life difficult for many in the Department of Defense and won few friends there, he also prevented the military services from undermining his authority on budgetary matters, as they had done to Forrestal.

State Department officials fought the budget cuts more vigorously than did the military services. Military aid was increasingly important in the State Department. Paul Nitze has dated his concern about the issue to the spring of 1949, when European officials estimated the cost of building an effective defense at the Rhine at $45 billion at a time when the Congress would appropriate only $1 billion for military aid (Nitze 1980, 171). Furthermore, when the Bureau of the Budget proposed holding all foreign aid under $200 million in fiscal 1951, the Mutual Defense Assistance Program (MDAP) and its initial appropriation of $1.45 billion had not yet even been passed by Congress.

Not surprisingly, State Department planners were not eager to abort a program they had not yet even begun to administer. James Webb and Paul Nitze, the State Department officials assigned to the interagency group reviewing the new budget ceilings for the NSC, insisted on a recommendation for a separate $1–1.5 billion allotment for MDAP, as well as additional sums for aid to Korea, relief of Arab refugees, the Point IV technical assistance program, and other new foreign aid initiatives. When the interagency group's report was distributed to the members of the National Security Council as NSC 52/2, it stated that any smaller aid program "would necessarily be of insufficient size to achieve the desired results and might have an adverse psychological effect."[27] Without sufficient military aid, State Department officials worried that NATO would be a hollow military alliance and would not reassure the Europeans of the U.S. commitment to their defense.

The State Department found allies in the CEA, where the president's requested report on the effects of the budget cuts had sharply divided the council and isolated Nourse. For some time, Nourse had been at odds with the other two members of the council, John D. Clark and Leon Keyserling, over a variety of official and personal issues. Conflict was especially sharp between Nourse and Keyserling, who strongly disagreed about the usefulness of government spending as a means of stimulating the economy. While Nourse believed a continuing budget deficit would cause inflation, Keyserling was more sympathetic to Keynesian ideas. The two men also had an enormous personality conflict that was played out on both major policy issues and less important matters, such as Keyserling's right to review personally the loyalty files of his employees. Keyserling used his friendship with White House Special Counsel Clark Clifford to bypass Nourse. Nourse, in turn, tried to have Keyserling fired.[28] Unable to reconcile their views on the fiscal 1951 budget, the CEA members sent two separate and conflicting reports on the new budget ceilings to the president on August 26. Nourse's report called for even greater reductions in government spending, while Clark and Keyserling argued that more spending was possible without damage to the economy.

Nourse's report to the president stated that the economic assumptions that had justified the budget cuts were excessively optimistic. He argued that the new budget was still too large and would produce an increasing deficit over the next few years. He contended that prices were likely to fall because of an imminent agricultural surplus, reducing revenues below the expected levels. Popular pressure for tax cuts and the possibility of increasing unemployment might exacerbate the revenue shortfall. In response to the president's question, Nourse also stated that long-term deficits would probably reduce business confidence in the economy and cause inflation. Given the likelihood of a downturn in the economy, he argued that such deficits were quite likely unless spending were further reduced. Nourse concluded his letter by arguing that military and foreign aid programs were especially undesirable and should be reduced as much as possible. While spending on domestic programs might serve other desirable ends and have positive secondary effects on economic well-being,

Nourse argued that military and foreign aid expenditures held no such advantages. In any event, he concluded, "[o]ur ability to make good on our military position and aid the revival and progress of world industry and trade over a long period ahead will depend also on the maintenance [of] soundness and confidence at home."[29]

Clark and Keyserling directly contradicted Nourse on most issues in their report. They endorsed the Bureau of the Budget's economic assumptions that Nourse had criticized. They expressed approval of the administration's budget and even stated that "moderate variations upward or downward as you might find necessary to carry out essential national policies" would also be acceptable under current economic conditions. Contrary to Nourse, they contended that a moderate budget deficit during fiscal 1951 would stimulate business activity sufficient both to cover the debt and to produce a budget surplus by fiscal 1953. Keyserling and Clark remarked that "it is always a good policy to reduce the cost of government through efficiency of operations and weeding out of non-essentials, but there is no basis now for reducing costs at the sacrifice of essential programs."[30]

Above all, Clark and Keyserling disagreed with Nourse on the effects of military and foreign aid programs. Although they agreed that the military budget should be kept as low as was consistent with national security, they argued this was only because military programs

> are not wealth-creating in the sense of other programs, and therefore represent an economic loss necessitated by unfortunate world conditions. . . . Nevertheless, we have several times pointed out that our economy can sustain—in fact, must be subjected to policies which *make it able to sustain*—such military outlays as are vital to [national safety and the promotion of optimum opportunity for world peace].

Clark and Keyserling acknowledged that keeping military spending as low as possible was a good idea, but remarked that "our security comes first; and, on that, we are not experts." Concerning foreign aid programs, Clark and Keyserling went even further, arguing that these programs were "wealth-creating in an economic sense" and should not be seen as a drag on the economy in the same way that military programs were. Just as they hoped domestic spending might stimulate the U.S. economy, Keyserling and Clark hoped that foreign aid might spur the economies of other nations and eventually create larger markets for American products.[31]

At Pace's request, Nourse—and not Keyserling or Clark—was invited to participate in the critical September 30, 1949, National Security Council meeting on NSC 52/2, the interagency working group's report on the impact of the fiscal 1951 budget ceilings.[32] Nourse's comments, which became Annex B of NSC 52/3, attacked the interagency report for suggesting that the overall budget ceiling be increased to allow additional expenditures for military aid.

> On the basis of my studies, I believe that incurring a budget deficit of the size contemplated for 1951 would have adverse effects on the functioning of the domestic economy so as to threaten total national security in ways which must be weighed seriously against whatever gains for national security in the strategic and diplomatic sense would result from those levels of expenditure.

Nourse also attributed the threat of "Communistic elements in the unions" in part to the drag on the economy caused by excessive military spending, which, he emphasized, contributed little to domestic well-being. Furthermore, he argued that the large remaining debt from World War II would make financing another war, if one should occur, very difficult.[33]

Ultimately, the president sent a budget to Congress in January that included the proposed cuts in military spending. Some of the foreign aid cuts were restored after further State Department pleading, but the small-budget forces had carried the day. The budget for national security programs was heading down in early 1950.

The results of the September 30 meeting are difficult to reconcile with the explanations offered in the realist-statist historiography. Samuel Wells (1979, 117) has argued that a series of external events, especially the fall of China and the discovery that the Soviets possessed an atomic bomb, were the main forces driving the development of NSC 68.[34] Although both of these events preceded the discussion of NSC 52/2, neither was mentioned in the meeting summary or the documents discussed there. In fact, there are no references to any increase in the seriousness of the Soviet threat, even from those fighting the budget cuts. If the fall of China and the advent of the Soviet atomic bomb struck some people as "hammer blows," those present at the September 30 NSC meeting—as well as the president who subsequently accepted their recommendations—do not appear to have been among them.

Even if one were to contend that there was a lag in the influence of the Soviet atomic bomb test and the fall of China, an ad hoc argument neither Wells nor Leffler makes, evidence about how policymakers perceived these events does not support the argument that they created a sense of alarm. The fall of the Nationalist regime in China had been anticipated for more than a year before the proclamation of the People's Republic in October 1949. Virtually every intelligence report and policy discussion of China after the Marshall mission in 1947 either predicted or assumed the collapse of the Nationalist regime. For example, a CIA Special Evaluation dated July 21, 1948, commented that "[t]he Chinese National Government is now so unstable that its collapse or overthrow could occur at any time."[35] Acheson repeated the same argument at an NSC meeting in February 1949. "[Acheson] said there was general agreement that, from a strategic point of view, China was an area of lower priority, especially since the house appeared to be falling down and there was not much to be done until it had come down."[36] The State Department's China White Paper, released in July, publicly acknowledged what was being said privately: the civil war in China was effectively over, and the United States had to "face the situation as it exists in fact."[37] If the fall of China is to be seen as a "hammer blow," the fact that the State Department—the organization most closely associated with promoting the subsequent defense buildup—was so unconcerned about it is very difficult to explain. Although some die-hard supporters of the Nationalist regime protested State Department indifference to its fate, they were unable to mobilize much support for the actions they proposed before the Korean War (Tucker 1983, 167).

Similarly, the Soviet atomic test occurred before the September 30 NSC meeting, and it was also substantially discounted at the time. Although the president had announced the detection of this test to the public only a week before, on September 23, this event did not prevent the NSC from approving plans to cut the defense budget on September 30. While it may have made the advocates of greater defense spending more vehement in their position, there is no evidence that it converted any of the opponents of such a program. George Kennan, for example, wrote Acheson in February 1950, while planning for NSC 68 was under way, that "[t]he demonstration of an 'atomic capability' on the part of the U.S.S.R. likewise adds no new fundamental element to the picture. . . . The fact that this situation became a reality a year or two before it was expected is of no fundamental significance."[38] Leffler (1992, 326) notes that public reaction to the event also quickly subsided and was not a major consideration in subsequent decisions about American weapons development.[39] Indeed, rather than raising alarm about the administration's national security policy, Republicans accused the administration of timing its announcement to ease the passage of the Mutual Defense Assistance Act.[40] Although the Soviets had acquired the weapons earlier than had been anticipated, there was no immediate expectation that possession of the new technology would change Soviet foreign policy. An October 1949 edition of the State Department's secret "Weekly Review" of world events stated that there was no evidence the new weapon would change Soviet foreign policy and commented that the United States still retained the upper hand. In Truman's copy of this document, the passage making this point is underlined in red.[41]

Leffler's treatment (1992, 309–10) of the 1949 decisions concerning the fiscal 1951 budget suffers from a similar failure to account for the chronology of events. He contends that the issue of the budget cuts remained unresolved because Truman neither accepted nor rejected NSC 52/2, despite the fact that the cuts were included in the January 1950 budget. He then explains the eventual decision to accept NSC 68 in terms of the same events cited by Wells, albeit in much greater detail and with an additional focus on the dollar gap. Like Wells, Leffler ignores the timing of these events. His use of the fall of China and the Soviet atomic bomb suffer from the same difficulties these events posed for Wells. Neither explains why there was such a lag between the events that allegedly triggered rearmament and the advent of the program. Indeed, this explanatory task is complicated by the fact that the immediate response to these events was to approve the decision to proceed with a small military and foreign aid budget. While the president never officially approved NSC 52/2, he proposed a budget that matched it on January 9.

While Wells relies on generalization, Leffler refers to specific documents to indicate the growing Soviet threat. To justify the eventual increase beyond the Bureau of the Budget's ceiling for MDAP, Leffler (1992, 309) cites a CIA report warning that if the Soviets conquered Europe, it "might in ten years result in the creation of an industrial power equivalent to that of the United States today." However, this report dates from July 1949—nearly six months before the issue was resolved, and certainly in time to have been considered before the September 30 deliberations.

The existence of alarming intelligence reports issued before the September 30 NSC meeting simply does not support arguments that external events explain policy. The fact that Truman went ahead with his plans to cut the military budget, albeit with some additional foreign aid funding, indicates that the prevailing view in the administration in January 1950 was that these international trends and events did not require much additional action. Other intelligence reports more likely to have been under immediate consideration by decision makers at the time of the September 30 meeting also came to the unsurprising conclusion that cuts in international programs would have negative effects on the international position of the United States. A CIA report developed to estimate the effects of the reductions in international programs contemplated under the July 1 budget ceilings concluded that the reduction would significantly reduce the capacity of the United States to meet the goals set out in NSC 20/4 and would produce a variety of other negative effects.[42] The existence of these intelligence reports implies that the question at hand was not simply the effect of budget cuts on international programs, which everyone knew would be negative, but whether the domestic and fiscal policy sacrifices required to have a larger budget were worth making.

The decision to reduce military spending at the end of 1949 cannot be explained in terms of pressure from the international system. The events of late 1949 were certainly important, but they did not resolve the policy debate in Washington. Different individuals drew different implications from conditions in the international system. While Acheson, Nitze, and others in the State Department were beginning to advocate great increases in the resources dedicated to the national security program, Johnson, Pace, and Nourse successfully secured cuts in military spending. The proponents of a small military budget did not argue that it would have no effect on the international position of the United States, but that other priorities, especially domestic ones, should take precedence. Few individuals appear to have changed their minds on this issue. The principal figures involved in the writing of NSC 68, such as Paul Nitze, did not require a conversion after the summer of 1949; they already believed a larger defense budget was desirable. Furthermore, as I will explain in more detail in the next chapter, those in the executive branch who had favored the low budget ceilings that summer were simply removed from the decision-making process, rather than converted by events.

CHAPTER 3

The Politics of Rearmament in
the Executive Branch II: NSC 68
and Rearmament

The purpose of NSC-68 was to so bludgeon the mind of "top govern-ment" that not only could the President make a decision but that the decision could be carried out.

—Dean Acheson

This was in the late spring of 1950, we, in this operation—this is the only time I suppose that I ever went regularly to the meetings of the NSC staff, but we were trying to find out through this machinery, using all the President's advisers and the departments, what was the best thing to do about our defense posture. We came, I think, to a firm judgment that our course ought to be sharply changed from what it had been.

—Charles Murphy, White House Special Counsel, 1949–53

If the decision to reduce the fiscal 1951 military budget is difficult to explain in realist or statist terms, the abrupt reversal of that decision in the spring of 1950 is even more problematic. President Truman's decision to accept NSC 68's call for more military spending is better explained by the requirements of maintaining the political coalition supporting his admin-istration than as a response to particular external shocks. This chapter will present evidence that this decision was made before the North Korean attack on South Korea. Since the events of 1949 were not sufficient to con-vince the administration to devote more resources to the national security program, it is extremely difficult to explain how such a decision could have been reached on this basis in the spring of 1950. The Korean War clearly affected the amount of money spent. However, it does not explain why President Truman accepted the need for a larger military budget before June 25, a choice that may have influenced the administration response to the North Korean attack on that day. Changes in the dominant group within the administration provide a better explanation for the acceptance of NSC 68 than changes in the international environment.

"To so bludgeon the mind of 'top government'"

Although the advocates of a small military budget were successful in 1949, their victory was short-lived. Nourse's disgust with the inability of the Council of Economic Advisers to agree on the fiscal 1951 budget led directly to his resignation. According to Nourse (1953, 283), when the council met with the president on August 26 to present its conflicting reports on the budget, Keyserling tried to play down the differences between the two sets of recommendations. Nourse wrote at the time that Keyserling's attitude "seems to me to completely negate any proper function of objective professional advice for a Council of Economic Advisers." He declined to explain his differences with Keyserling and Clark to the president at the August 26 meeting but hoped instead that his memo would speak for itself. He trusted Pace and apparently preferred to rely on him to get the proper recommendations enacted as policy. "He seems quite sympathetic to the points of view which I have expressed."[1] Despite his success in cutting the budget, the process disgusted and exhausted Nourse, who publicly accused the military advocates of greater spending of "trying to preserve a vested interest or gain new superiority with little evidence of concern as to the repercussions for military efficiency or economy, or the drain imposed on the industrial system."[2] Nourse resigned on November 1, 1949, disregarding both the president's request that he stay on and the lack of any designated successor. Leon Keyserling then became the acting chairman, bringing his very different policy views into the position with him.

After Nourse's departure, things began to go wrong for the advocates of a small defense budget. At a December 1 conference to plan the foreign affairs sections of the president's January 1950 budget message, State Department representatives insisted on at least $1 billion in new appropriations for MDAP in fiscal 1951. The Bureau of the Budget had planned to carve the fiscal 1951 MDAP budget from unexpended funds appropriated for the previous fiscal year. Both sides prepared to appeal their case to President Truman.[3] Acheson spoke out publicly on behalf of the program and may have raised the subject privately with Truman. In any case, the president proposed $1.1 billion in new appropriations for MDAP in his budget message on January 9, 1950.

By the time Truman agreed to the additional MDAP appropriations, however, there were hints that the State Department would soon seek something much more ambitious. There is little evidence of individual conversions brought on by outside events. Instead, the change proceeded through the replacement of key officials with others who envisioned a more central role for military spending in U.S. national security policy. Paul Nitze replaced George Kennan as director of the Policy Planning Staff in January. Kennan and Nitze had disagreed over the amount of military spending required to contain the Soviet Union. Nitze had long favored a much larger program of aid and military spending. Kennan had argued that two or three Marine divisions would be enough to carry out the military aspects of containment, which he envisioned primarily as a political and diplomatic strategy rather than a military one.[4]

While the emergence of the People's Republic of China and the Soviet acquisition of the atomic bomb produced little immediate reaction in the State Department, the persistent balance-of-payments surplus with Europe proved instrumental in mobilizing new supporters for increased military aid. The State Department was becoming increasingly alarmed about the "dollar gap" in late 1949 and early 1950. Block (1977, 92–96, 102–8) points out that these considerations played a critical role in building a consensus behind NSC 68 there. The United States had experienced periods of international tension since the end of World War II without a massive increase in military spending. In 1947 and 1948, however, there had been other means of coping with the persistent balance-of-payments problem. In 1950, these alternatives appeared to have been exhausted. The 1949 recession and the consequent drop in U.S. imports from Europe added to the already large balance-of-payments surplus the United States was running with Europe. On September 18, after months of financial crisis, the British devalued the pound by 30 percent. Because the end of the Marshall Plan was approaching in 1952 and funds provided by this program were vital to covering the dollar gap, another crisis appeared to be just over the horizon unless a new way to finance European imports was found.

Although the British devaluation eased immediate problems, the prevailing view in the State Department was that the dollar gap would persist and that the British might decide to develop a closed trading bloc within the British Empire once the end of the Marshall Plan deprived them of a major source of dollars. Nitze (1980, 171) recalls that, as the writing of NSC 68 began, "our prime concern had remained with the economic situation in Europe." At Truman's request, Acheson prepared a memorandum for the White House on the matter in February. In it, Acheson argued that the end of the Marshall Plan would produce a crisis that would threaten the political stability of Europe and have "serious repercussions on our domestic economy." The memo stated that such a crisis had to be avoided "even if this involves adjustments and sacrifices by particular economic groups in the United States in the interest of the nation as a whole—

even if it requires some modification of current domestic policies—and even if it requires more time than was originally contemplated by the Foreign Assistance Act of 1948."

Acheson concluded that the president should launch a coordinated effort to find programs to close the dollar gap and to get those programs approved by the Congress. He also called for a special staff assistant to the president to coordinate the response to the problem and suggested that a "committee of leading public citizens" be organized to help enlist public support.[5] Acheson secured the approval of the Treasury Department for this memo, a fact that helps explain how the fiscally conservative treasury secretary John Snyder was persuaded to accept rearmament. Snyder had been concerned about the balance-of-payments problem for some time and had traveled to London in 1949 to deal directly with the British on the matter. While in Europe, he received considerable advice and assistance from Dean Acheson and Special Ambassador Averell Harriman.[6]

Acheson sent his memorandum on the dollar gap to the Bureau of the Budget for review, and Frank Pace wrote a comment on it for the president. Pace's memo treated Acheson's argument with some deference but did not endorse its rather extreme account of the urgency of the problem. Pace did not evaluate the State Department position on the dollar gap but only agreed with its recommendation that the issue be studied by a special assistant and the cabinet. He argued, however, that the special assistant should be personally prestigious and not drawn from the current presidential staff. He also suggested that the committee of public citizens should be brought into the planning stages of the program so that they could contribute to it, "rather than ratify a fixed and frozen proposal." Pace also sought to preserve a role for the Bureau of the Budget's fiscal priorities in the course of planning the program. "[B]ecause of the major implications of this operation on the budget position of the U.S. Government over a period of years, I would like to keep in touch personally with developments in this program to advise you of its fiscal implications."[7] Pace did not object to a study of the problem, but he sought to keep the Bureau of the Budget in a position to minimize the impact on the federal budget of any program designed to cover the dollar gap.

The State Department's perspective on the importance of increased foreign aid and military spending was supported by its allies in American society. The connection between the State Department and predominantly eastern, internationally oriented elites has been well documented.[8] Eastern commercial and financial interests had the most to lose if the balance-of-payments problem prompted the Europeans to restrict trade with the United States, perhaps establishing trading blocs with their colonial empires or, worse yet, seeking closer economic relations with Eastern

Europe and the Soviet Union. During the consideration of NSC 68 and the fiscal 1951 budget, representatives of this group expressed their support for State Department efforts to increase the budget for national security programs. Nitze (1980, 173–74; 1989, 98–99), himself a former investment banker, recalls a visit from Alexander Sachs of Lehman Brothers in the spring of 1950, in which Sachs predicted a Soviet-inspired attack on South Korea and urged that the United States do more to counter the Soviet threat. Of the six consultants asked to review early drafts of NSC 68, five—J. Robert Oppenheimer, James Conant, Robert Lovett, Chester Barnard, and Henry Smyth—were drawn from eastern financial and academic institutions. (The sixth, Ernest O. Lawrence, was director of the Radiation Laboratory at the University of California.) Individuals who might have been expected to oppose the program, especially the administration's opponents in Congress, were not consulted. Later, members of this elite supported the administration's efforts to increase the size of the military budget through organizations such as the Committee on the Present Danger.[9]

Those in the State Department who had opposed the 1949 budget cuts were still ready to endorse more spending in early 1950. Concerns about the dollar gap provided another source of support for their position. At the same time, their opponents had grown weaker through the resignation of Nourse and the departure of Kennan from the Policy Planning Staff. After deciding to proceed with the development of the hydrogen bomb, Truman ordered a reassessment of the overall national security policy in light of Soviet atomic capabilities. While the State Department members of the interagency group assigned to write the report interpreted the president's mandate broadly, it is not clear that everyone involved believed the final product would be a complete reconsideration of U.S. national security policy. The president's letter authorizing the study can be read more narrowly as requesting a study on the effects of Soviet atomic capabilities on U.S. strategy. Louis Johnson's objection that the authors of the report had exceeded their mandate may indicate that this was how he interpreted the president's instructions.[10]

Whatever the president's intentions when he authorized the study, it presented policymakers in the State Department, especially Acheson and Nitze, with an opportunity to move policy in a new direction that would solve several problems in a single stroke. First, it gave Nitze the chance to press for a commitment to build a military force sufficient to stop an actual Soviet attack on Europe at the Rhine. As was noted earlier, he had believed since the spring of 1949 that this would require at least $45 billion. Within the group writing the report, spending figures varied widely, ranging from a conservative Defense Department estimate of $17 or $18 billion annually for defense to speculation about the economic feasibility of spending up to 20 percent of GNP on national security programs. At Acheson's request, no spending figures were included in the final report, because the final figure would depend on actual program estimates in any event, and the inclusion of a large number would only have given the opponents of rearmament fodder for criticizing the report.[11] Agreement on the new policy direction was more important to Acheson than the actual dollar figures.

Second, by tying aid to Europe to the military program, rearmament provided a way of getting sufficient aid to Europe to cover the dollar gap without renewing the Marshall Plan, which was considered virtually impossible in Congress. As Block (1980, 36–41) has pointed out, the report discusses the general problem of building a "healthy international environment" as well as the immediate issue of the Soviet military threat to Western Europe. These economic and political-military objectives were linked in the minds of those who wrote NSC 68. Acheson followed the development of NSC 68 closely and took steps to ease its passage through the bureaucracy. Nitze (1989, 94) notes that he kept Acheson fully informed of the progress being made on NSC 68, visiting Acheson's office, which was adjacent to his own, every day. Louis Johnson, on the other hand, remained ignorant of what was being decided until it was too late to reverse the process.

The process of drafting NSC 68 was a tactical opportunity for its State Department supporters because they were able to conduct it without the knowledge of the principal opponents of increasing the budget. The Bureau of the Budget was not included in the interagency group and, given the bureau's lack of involvement in the debates surrounding the H-bomb, Frank Pace may not even have been aware that any such plans were being made. As May (1993, 10–11) notes, the extreme secrecy under which the report was written also kept potential opponents like Pace ignorant. Pace continued speaking publicly on the benefits of a balanced budget through March. During this period, he apparently came into frequent conflict with Leon Keyserling over the acceptable size of the budget, although there is no record of written correspondence between them in either man's papers.[12] After his struggle with the State Department over the military aid budget, and having read Acheson's memo on the dollar gap, Pace knew that foreign policy might undermine his effort to maintain a small federal budget. He confided to a relative that "[t]he cold war is definitely a greater problem both in terms of the fiscal drain on the national resources and in terms of danger to national security than the great majority of Americans realize." He noted that "overt actions" by the Soviets might result in a vastly increased military budget.[13]

Louis Johnson also knew little about the report being prepared by the interagency group. State Department officials, especially Nitze and his Policy Planning Staff, dominated the drafting of NSC 68. Defense Department representatives reportedly entered the process without any clear authority or ideas about what they wanted. Hammond (1962, 300) notes that Truman Landon and Najeeb Halaby, who represented the Joint Chiefs of Staff in the working group, did not expect Johnson to permit more spending in any event, so their failure to spend time developing their position on the matter is understandable. The Joint Chiefs of Staff shared this expectation and did not delegate Landon and Halaby any formal authority to speak for them. The belief that Johnson would interfere with the project if he knew too much about it may also account for James Burns's failure to keep the secretary of defense abreast of progress on the report, in spite of the fact that he was Johnson's principal representative in the working group. Johnson's attitude toward the new plans was not difficult to predict, and keeping him informed would certainly have made the task facing the Defense Department members of the interagency group more difficult. Furthermore, Nitze (1989, 93–94) notes that Burns was in poor health and could only work half days. For whatever reason, Nitze (1989, 94) wrote that Johnson "knew virtually nothing of our deliberations."

Johnson had no particular reason to expect that the report would call for an across-the-board military buildup. After all, the fiscal 1951 budget, which had only recently been sent to Congress, represented a reduction from the previous year's spending. He anticipated a similar ceiling for the fiscal 1952 budget and began the planning process for that budget on February 21 under this assumption (Rearden 1984, 524). Furthermore, since the study had been prompted by the decision to develop the hydrogen bomb, Johnson may have believed that it would support a greater role for air power with which to deliver the new weapon. Johnson favored such a step. Finally, there is no evidence that Johnson had a broad vision of U.S. national security policy comparable to the one held by Acheson and Nitze. His economy program was motivated more by his presidential ambitions than by strategic considerations.

Because Acheson and Nitze were among the few who understood what was happening, they were able to preempt and eliminate opposition to rearmament in the executive branch. Key officials were apprised of the progress of NSC 68 under circumstances crafted to influence their responses to it. First, important individuals outside the administration who might have influenced the president's opinion on the document were brought in individually or in pairs to examine it with the drafters.[14] Although all of these consultants had suggestions and comments concerning the report, few changes were made in the final version sent to the president and the National Security Council. The purpose of the consultation process was the cultivation of sympathetic individuals who were in a position to influence public and elite opinion, not to rewrite the report. Several of the consultants recognized this purpose and called for further efforts to convince the public of the need for rearmament. Chester Barnard, president of the Rockefeller Foundation, suggested several people who could be included in a group to promote the program. Noting the need for "a much vaster propaganda machine to tell our story at home and abroad," Robert Lovett suggested a public relations campaign to enlist the aid of "schools, colleges, churches, and other groups." He also mentioned a list of "elder statesmen" similar to the one suggested by Barnard.[15]

Having begun to cultivate support for NSC 68 outside the government, Acheson and Nitze began to "bludgeon the mind of top government," as Acheson would later put it. Louis Johnson was the first target. A meeting with Acheson, Johnson, and the State-Defense working group was scheduled for March 22 at the State Department. Participants interviewed by Paul Hammond (1962, 321–22) indicated that there was some apprehension before the meeting about Johnson's expected objections to the report's recommendations. Given Johnson's ongoing public advocacy of "economy" in military spending, there was no reason to expect his reaction to be favorable.[16] Furthermore, Johnson had not been kept officially informed of the progress made on the report. The participants Hammond (1962, 322–23) interviewed said that Burns and Halaby prepared a one-page summary of the report for Johnson to read before the meeting and that the group had previously prepared a two-page summary for him. No one was sure that he had actually read either of these papers. When Johnson arrived at the meeting, he said he had not been given a chance to read the group's report and that it had been called to his attention only five hours before.

Johnson was clearly surprised by the report's conclusions, and he reacted angrily. Acheson's colorful account of the meeting (1969, 373) states that "[Johnson] lunged forward with a crash of chair legs on the floor and fist on the table, scaring me out of my shoes." He objected to being asked to submit to such a policy without having adequate time to study it. Arguing that Defense was not being treated as a co-equal department, he refused to endorse the conclusions of the report and stormed out of the meeting after berating Acheson privately in the secretary of state's office. The entire event lasted less than 15 minutes.[17] According to Acheson (1969, 373), the incident was immediately reported to Truman, who was vacationing in Key West, by Sidney Souers and James Lay. (Lay was the executive secretary of the NSC, and Souers, who had held the job before him, was then serving as part-time consultant.) "Within the hour the President telephoned me, expressing his outrage and telling me to carry on exactly as we had been doing." Fortuitously, as Acheson had known before the ill-fated meeting was scheduled, Johnson was about to leave for a NATO defense ministers' conference in The Hague. In his absence, the report was distributed in the Department of Defense.[18] Within a few days of Johnson's return, the report was on his desk with the approval of the Joint Chiefs of Staff and all three service secretaries. Faced with a *fait accompli* and having already embarrassed himself over the issue, Johnson signed the report, and it was formally sent to the White House on April 7, 1950.

Although Johnson told his staff in late April that he and Truman had agreed that his economy program was "dead," he did not give up hope (Hammond 1962, 337). As everyone did, he knew that those favoring a small military budget were quite strong in Congress. Between his return from Europe in early April and the beginning of the Korean War, Johnson kept his options open, positioning himself for any outcome a political battle over the military budget might produce. His April 26 statement before the appropriations subcommittees of both houses of Congress is a model of studied ambiguity. He presented the economy program both as an effort to save money and as a way of improving the efficiency of the military services so that a larger budget could be used efficiently.

> Indeed, the economy program—which has been misconstrued in some quarters—is one of the principal tools used by the Department of Defense in channeling funds into the combatant forces where such funds can be used to give us added strength, and away from such wasteful expenditures as unnecessary overhead, costly duplication, and unnecessary overlaps.[19]

When Johnson went before the Senate Appropriations Committee three months later in connection with the first supplemental appropriations bill, he brought a transcript of his April 26 testimony with him and read from it at length to demonstrate that his economy program had prepared the Department of Defense for eventualities like the Korean War. He repeated his earlier remarks that the economy program prepared the military to use additional funds efficiently "should circumstances so require." After reading this quote from himself, Johnson added dramatically: "Gentlemen, circumstances do so require."[20]

Even before the report was officially submitted to the president, steps had already been taken to secure support for it in the White House. Before a discussion of the State Department's efforts to influence the president's staff on behalf of NSC 68, a few details on the organization of the White

House in 1950 are necessary. Unlike more recent presidents, Truman had no designated chief of staff. Charles Murphy, who replaced Clark Clifford as special counsel in January 1949, acted as the most senior staff adviser on most legislative matters, while John Steelman, "the" assistant to the president, handled mostly administrative issues within the executive branch. Most members of the White House staff were designated simply "assistants to the president" and appear to have been roughly equal in status. Although they were not strictly specialized, some members of the staff did handle particular issues more frequently than others. George Elsey, a Clifford protégé, commonly dealt with foreign policy matters. Stephen Spingarn, a former Treasury Department official with a military counter-intelligence background, handled internal security issues. Others, such as David Lloyd, David Bell, and Richard Neustadt, worked in different policy areas or performed more general tasks, including the drafting of speeches.

The White House staff was diffuse in its politics as well as its organization. The best-known Truman staff members were the assistants to the president who worked closely with Clifford and Murphy. Better-educated and drawn from a more elite social background, they also left behind the most extensive collections of personal papers. However, Truman maintained an additional group of top staff advisers, such as Matthew Connelly and military aide Harry Vaughan, from social backgrounds more like his own who tended to be politically conservative. Unlike the group associated with Clifford and Murphy, they maintained ties to conservative political elites and bureaucracies like the FBI. Although most of these individuals left behind no personal papers, there is good reason to believe that they were just as important to Truman as the group led by Clifford and Murphy.

Matthew Connelly, perhaps the most important figure in this group, was Truman's appointments secretary, serving as his gatekeeper and political adviser throughout his term as president. No one saw the president without Connelly's permission. Connelly was also Truman's chief contact with the Democratic National Committee and the only person permitted to attend the president's weekly meetings with the "Big Four" leaders of the Democratic party in the House and Senate. George Elsey recalled that "Matt was pretty closemouthed and it's understandable and proper that he should have been."[21] Indeed, Connelly left no personal papers behind, despite his central role in the White House. His oral history interview, however, provides a glimpse of the dominant political outlook in this segment of the Truman White House. In it, Connelly expresses his contempt for Clifford, Elsey, some other members of the White House staff, and especially for the State Department.[22] Maintaining two such conflicting sets of advisers probably helped Truman maintain his ties to different wings of the Democratic party.

Although the NSC and the Bureau of the Budget were located in the Executive Office of the President, they were less closely associated with the president himself. Many NSC staff members, for example, including Executive Secretary James Lay, continued to serve in the same positions under Eisenhower. Because there was no national security adviser, the NSC staff was also much less influential than it has since become. The Bureau of the Budget played an important advisory role not only in the determination of the federal budget, but also in shaping the entire legislative program of the administration. Legislation passed by the Congress was cleared by the Bureau of the Budget, which consulted federal agencies affected by the legislation and recommended a course of action to the president. Charles Murphy, Richard Neustadt, and David Bell, three of Truman's best-known staffers, served in the Bureau of the Budget before joining the White House staff. James Webb, who directed the bureau for most of Truman's first term, replaced Robert Lovett as under secretary of state—the second-ranking position in the department—when Dean Acheson became secretary of state in January 1949.

Truman and most of his staff had gone to Key West for an extended vacation beginning on March 12, 1950, so they were not in Washington when Johnson was confronted with NSC 68. On March 26, three days after Johnson met with the State-Defense group, Under Secretary of State James Webb went to Florida, returning to Washington the same day with White House Special Counsel Charles Murphy.[23] Webb was an ideal choice to present the report to the president, because he had worked closely with him as director of the Bureau of the Budget and had advocated balanced budgets until the fight over the military aid program in the fall of 1949. In an oral history interview, Webb recalled that the purpose of his trip to Florida was to present Truman with a copy of NSC 68 and to persuade him to bring John Foster Dulles into the administration so that the rearmament program could be presented to Congress as a bipartisan effort. Webb also said that he and Acheson had decided to ask Truman not to fire Louis Johnson, "but to call him to Key West and give him careful instructions before he took off the next day for Europe." (Johnson did meet with the president the next day, then flew to Europe on March 28.) From the perspective of the State Department, Johnson, as a former advocate of a small defense budget, might have made a more credible spokesperson for a buildup than would a new secretary of defense called in for this purpose.[24]

Finally, Webb said he asked the president to shift Frank Pace from the Bureau of the Budget to the Defense Department as the secretary of the army and move Gordon Gray, the secretary of the army, to the White House, in order to smooth relations between Dean Acheson and Louis Johnson. Webb recalled that "he agreed to Pace and he went over as Secretary of the Army."[25] While it is difficult to see how this move would have done anything to improve State Department relations with Johnson, removing Pace from the Bureau of the Budget certainly solved other problems for those in favor of a military buildup. According to interviews conducted by Hammond (1962, 328–29), Pace had been shown NSC 68, and "[r]eportedly, he quoted to Nitze Bureau of the Budget figures on how much the economy could stand in the way of Federal expenditures, and how necessary expenditures on other things besides foreign and military affairs were."[26]

Pace was removed from his position as director of the Bureau of the Budget and made secretary of the army within two weeks of Webb's trip to Key West. While Pace claims he presented the president with his resignation because of his continuing disagreements with Leon Keyserling, there are good reasons to doubt his version of events. First, because the president was in Key West when Pace resigned and became secretary of the army, Pace's recollection about a meeting with the president during this period is contradicted by other evidence. Pace's detailed calendars indicate that he met last with the president on March 10, shortly before Truman's departure for Key West. There is no record of Pace traveling to Florida in March or April, as there is for other presidential visitors. He was sworn in as secretary of the army on April 12. Second, until just before his resignation, Pace continued to develop long-term arrangements for the Bureau of the Budget and for additional efforts to publicize himself and his activities there. He spoke to the Detroit Economic Club concerning the federal budget deficit on March 13. On March 20, Pace made arrangements to meet with James Lay, the executive secretary of the NSC, every Friday morning. He requested that other officials from the Bureau of the Budget accompany him to these meetings whenever possible. Pace attended only one such meeting, held on Friday, March 31, the same day his move to the Department of the Army was announced in the press. He also met with a reporter concerning a "profile" on that same day. It is unlikely that someone about to resign would do either of these things.[27]

Based on available evidence, Pace was probably informed of the decision to remove him as director of the Bureau of the Budget and make him secretary of the army by Charles Murphy after the special counsel returned from Key West on March 27, although it is also possible the president informed him by phone. Murphy spoke with Pace on the phone once on the twenty-seventh and twice on the twenty-eighth. He met with Pace in person on March 29. Murphy met again with Pace and Roger Jones of the

Bureau of the Budget's Legislative Reference Service, on Thursday, March 30.[28] The following Monday, April 3, Pace began meeting with Gordon Gray, the outgoing secretary of the army, every day until he was sworn in to take his place. In his oral history interview, Pace linked his resignation to his conflict over the budget with Leon Keyserling. There is probably some truth to this recollection, since his replacement appears to have represented a move by Truman to gain greater flexibility on the issue of the budget deficit.

The abrupt removal of Frank Pace as director of the Bureau of the Budget was a major blow to those seeking to maintain a small military budget. There is of course no way to know if Truman's acceptance of Webb's suggestion to make this change constituted knowing approval of such a bureaucratic reorientation, but its effects are clear enough in retrospect. Pace was replaced by Frederick Lawton, who appears to have seen his role as a purely administrative one. He did not involve himself in major policy debates on behalf of fiscal restraint as Webb and Pace had done before him, apparently confining his attention to the administrative and technical aspects of carrying out the policies set forth by the president and the rest of the administration. Lawton also had a different attitude toward publicity than did his predecessors, declining to speak out on behalf of the Hoover Commission report as Pace had done.[29] Lawton did not participate actively in the subsequent consideration of NSC 68, as Pace had in the earlier decisions about the size of the fiscal 1951 defense budget. Instead, he assigned William Schaub, deputy chief of the Division of Estimates, to represent the Bureau of the Budget in the ad hoc committee assigned to develop programs based on the report. Although Schaub objected vigorously to the enormous expenses implied in the document, his comments apparently had no effect on the committee, composed mostly of individuals with more standing in the policy-making arena.[30]

With Johnson and Pace effectively neutralized, convincing the White House staff of the virtues of NSC 68 proved relatively easy. Charles Murphy was probably the first member of the staff to see the report. In his oral history interview, Murphy recalls being given a copy of NSC 68 by the president and being so impressed by it that he stayed home the next day just to study it. The archival record supports Murphy's recollection of his conversion experience. His calendar for March 31, 1950, contains a handwritten note stating: "4:30 James Lay—has paper he wants to bring over this afternoon—in at 6:00 p.m." As Murphy comments in his oral history interview, he does not appear to have received or read the document immediately, but the events that followed his reading of it fit the other elements of his story. On Monday, April 3, a note reads: "James Lay—Mr. Farley brot [*sic*] papers. CSM wants to read papers, GME [George Elsey]

to read also. Nitze Lay at meeting." A note written the next day corrobo-
rates Murphy's claim that he stayed home to consider NSC 68: "9:15—
CSM called—will stay home today."[31]

George Elsey also saw NSC 68 at this point. Elsey had handled foreign policy matters for the White House before, working closely with
Clark Clifford when Clifford was special counsel.[32] In particular, Elsey
had spent time handling the dollar gap issue for the White House. Perhaps
because of his greater familiarity with the subject matter, he was less easily
convinced than Murphy had been. Handwritten comments on Elsey's
copy of NSC 68 reveal some skepticism. Next to the section discussing the
four possible policy responses to the Soviet buildup, Elsey has written: "a
loaded premise if I ever saw one!" Near the portion of the text stating that
potential U.S. military capability is improving but declining relative to
that of the Soviets, a note reads: "not proven in this doc." Elsey's concerns
may have been addressed at his meeting with the State-Defense group that
wrote the report, however, since he does not appear to have carried them
to the president.[33]

On April 5, Murphy and Elsey met with the State-Defense group that
had written NSC 68. The meeting lasted nearly two hours and presumably
allowed the group to go over the report in some detail. Murphy requested
a meeting with the president immediately after Truman returned from Key
West on April 10. He recalled telling the president that the paper should be
referred to the National Security Council and that Leon Keyserling should
be brought in to participate in the discussion as acting chairman of the
Council of Economic Advisers.[34] This is the course of action Truman
chose, and the report was formally discussed by the NSC on April 20. Truman did not attend the meeting, which was anticlimactic in any event. The
NSC simply agreed to refer the report to a special ad hoc committee so
that cost estimates and other program details could be determined.[35]

"A firm judgment that our course ought to be sharply changed"

Most accounts of the early Cold War era hold that the official status of the
report was unclear before the beginning of the Korean War.[36] However,
those who focus specifically on NSC 68 most often argue that the president
was skeptical of the need to increase the military budget and did not accept
the need for rearmament until some time after June 25, 1950. Evidence for
this position is far from conclusive, though. On closer examination, it is
more likely that Truman had accepted the rearmament program and was
preparing for the difficult task of getting the program through Congress.

The timing of presidential approval for the rearmament program is not a minor point. Indeed, it is critical to realist-statist accounts of the policy-making process. Wells and Leffler use the fact that the president did not officially sign the report until September 29 to demonstrate that it was less important than external events—especially the Korean War—in getting Truman to accept rearmament. Wells (1979, 138–39) argues that Truman was unsure about NSC 68 and that the programs envisioned in the report would not have been enacted without the impetus provided by the Korean War. Similarly, Leffler (1992, 358) contends that NSC 68 failed to convince the president to increase the military budget before the Korean War. "He hoped to achieve preponderance on the cheap."

Three categories of evidence are generally presented to support the argument that Truman remained skeptical of the rearmament program before the Korean War. These include the president's failure to approve formally the conclusions of NSC 68 until September 30, the existence of opposition to the report within the administration, and Truman's public comments on the future of the defense budget. An examination of the evidence offered in each of these categories reveals the weakness of the argument that the president did not endorse greater military spending until after the beginning of the Korean War.

It is not difficult to show that the formal approval date of NSC 68 reveals little about the status of the rearmament program. Rearden (1984, 536) argues that Truman's delay in approving the conclusions of NSC 68 was probably intended to give the Bureau of the Budget time to reduce the program estimates it contained to a size acceptable to the president. By September 30, however, the Congress had already voted to approve an administration request that nearly doubled the size of the defense budget, and plans were under way for additional increases. As Nitze (1989, 98) notes, the report was operative policy "well before" Truman formally approved it. An alternative explanation for the delay is that Truman wanted to allow the budget figures—which remained gigantic—and other program details to be completed before the entire program was formally approved. This development process was precisely what State Department officials had expected would follow presidential approval of the report.[37] These budget figures were not completed until September 12. The president signed the report at the next NSC meeting.

Opposition to NSC 68 within the administration is overstated. Wells (1979, 139) makes much of the "very impressive" forces arrayed against NSC 68 in the administration, arguing that they gave the president ample support for his alleged reluctance to accept rearmament. The specific evidence he cites does not support this assertion, though. Wells states that Louis Johnson told his staff that Truman would not agree to increase the defense budget beyond $13 billion. Rearden (1984, 534) also refers to these comments, which Johnson made at a June 7 meeting in the Defense Department. Johnson's public campaign for his economy program had resumed by the late spring. In May, he told an audience that the Soviets planned to defeat the United States "by making us overspend ourselves on national defense until our economy is wrecked."[38] However, Johnson's remarks must be considered in light of other evidence about his expectations, as well as his strong incentive for wishful thinking about the president's position. As was already noted, Hammond (1962, 337) reports that Johnson had informed his staff in April that the economy program in the Department of Defense was "dead." His April 26 testimony to Congress on the fiscal 1951 budget was extremely ambiguous on future plans for the defense budget, even implying that a buildup was possible. Johnson's reputation and future political fortunes were tied to a small defense budget, so he must certainly have hoped Truman would eventually reject NSC 68. His position in the administration was tenuous after his outburst against NSC 68 at the March 22 meeting with the State-Defense working group that had written the report. When he fired Johnson in September, Truman told an aide that he had known "ever since May" that he would eventually do so.[39] Johnson's opinion offers little insight into Truman's thinking.

To provide additional support for his assertion about the strength of those opposed to NSC 68, Wells refers to criticism of the report by the Treasury Department, the Bureau of the Budget, and the CEA in the ad hoc committee assigned to review it. As I have already noted, opposition from the Bureau of the Budget was muted by the removal of Frank Pace as director, an event neither Wells nor Leffler mentions. Pace's successor, Frederick Lawton, kept his distance from the debate over NSC 68. Also, another participant in the ad hoc committee noted at the time that Treasury's opposition to the program was not very significant.[40] Treasury Secretary Snyder's concern about the dollar gap may well have moderated his objections to the fiscal consequences of NSC 68. He had already expressed support for Acheson's February memorandum to the president calling for drastic action to deal with the balance-of-payments problem.

Wells's assertion that the CEA opposed NSC 68 is simply incorrect. In fact, Leon Keyserling could be depended on to argue that the U.S. economy had the capacity to sustain larger expenditures on defense. Charles Murphy recalls that "[h]e always said, 'You can afford to spend more on defense if you need to.'"[41] Edwin Nourse would certainly have opposed NSC 68, but he had left the administration nearly six months before the report was examined by the CEA.[42] The reservations expressed by the council concerned the political viability of the programs associated with the report, not the basic goals of NSC 68 or the principle of spending more on defense: "Unless carefully and imaginatively prepared, their adoption could create concerns on the part of the Congress and the public which could ultimately threaten their success."[43] The strongest advocates of NSC 68 were well aware of these problems and would certainly have agreed with this statement.

Wells (1979, 138) also uses a June 6, 1950, memorandum on a meeting of the Under Secretary of State's Advisory Committee as evidence that James Webb and others in the State Department opposed large defense budgets.[44] Although Webb and the others expressed concern about the program estimates offered by the National Security Resources Board (NSRB) in the Ad Hoc Committee on NSC 68, they did so because they wanted to avoid the public impression that war was imminent, and to prevent other government agencies from linking their budget requests to NSC 68. The Advisory Committee was not hostile to rearmament. Indeed, Paul Nitze himself summarized the paper discussed at the June 6 meeting and was among the strongest critics of the NSRB's proposal. Overall, there is little evidence of serious opposition to NSC 68 in the administration. This is hardly surprising, since the principal advocates of a small military budget had been cut out of the process.

Leffler (1992, 355–60) makes a different claim, arguing that NSC 68 did not represent a new policy departure at all. He notes that NSC 68 reaffirmed the conclusions of the national security policy statement that had preceded it, NSC 20/4. "Hence NSC 68 provoked no great debate. It neither stirred great emotions nor precipitated unusual controversy (except of a personal sort between Johnson and Acheson). It could not do so because it introduced no new goals and no new programs" (359). Like Wells's argument that there was strong opposition to NSC 68, this claim is not well supported by the available archival evidence.

The rhetoric of NSC 68 may have been nothing new, but its call for a greater resource commitment was a break with previous policy. While Acheson and Nitze intentionally included no precise dollar figures in the document, those who wrote NSC 68 had dollar figures in mind, and those reading the report knew it meant a major increase in military spending. Hammond's interview accounts (1962, 321) suggest that there was division over the exact amounts of money in question and the period of time over which they would be appropriated but indicate that everyone agreed it would amount to a "radical departure." In fact, any increase in spending on the national security program would have been a major change from the trend toward smaller budgets established in 1949. Louis Johnson's response when confronted with the document, as well as the apprehension in the State-Defense group prior to its meeting with him, indicates that the meaning of the report for Johnson's economy program was clear. Johnson knew that the State Department was not satisfied with spending on national security programs. NSC 68 probably confirmed his darkest suspicions about what the State Department had in mind for the future of the Pentagon budget. There is no need to interpret his reaction to the report simply as a reflection of his personal distaste for Dean Acheson. NSC 68 was a major blow to both his policy preferences and his political aspirations.

The meaning of NSC 68 was equally clear to others who read the report. Although he disagreed with the interpretation of Soviet intentions contained in the report, Charles Bohlen, one of the State Department's principal experts on the Soviet Union, accepted what he took to be the report's central conclusion: "The issue, of course, is whether our present defense establishment and programs for future development are, in fact, adequate to meet the present world situation and its probable future development. The answer is correctly given that they are not, but I do not believe enough evidence is given to support this contention."[45] Similarly, Charles Murphy summed up his reaction to the report by saying that "it seemed to me to establish an altogether convincing case that we *had* to spend more on defense, that we had to strengthen our defense posture very markedly."[46]

The readers of NSC 68 were probably influenced by the fact that they knew its authors wanted a larger budget for national security programs, and thus they expected an argument for more spending. During the winter and spring of 1950, the secretary of state made it clear in public that he believed military spending was inadequate. Acheson (1969, 375–78) has since stated that he used NSC 68 as the basis for many of his speeches, noting that it played a role as early as his February 8 remarks that the United States should seek to develop "situations of strength." The State Department view that greater military and foreign aid spending were necessary was widely reported in the press, as was Louis Johnson's resistance to it.[47] Leffler is correct in noting that NSC 68 discussed national security in the same terms used in NSC 20/4. However, the meaning the report held for its original audience depended as much on their expectations as on the language of the report itself. What the report says to a more circumspect reader years later is less important for understanding the development of policy than what contemporary readers believed it represented. To policymakers at the time, NSC 68 represented a major departure because higher levels of military spending broke with what had already been planned.

The final category of evidence for the argument that Truman had not accepted NSC 68 before the Korean War includes the president's public comments on the matter. Leffler (1992, 358) argues that, during the spring of 1950, Truman "passed up opportunity after opportunity to make a case for large increments in military expenditures." Although Truman said nothing about rearmament before Korea, a speech on NSC 68 was planned for early June. The public statement was to coincide with the presentation of the new program to Congress.[48] No program could be presented to Congress until cost estimates for it were complete, however. Truman had requested that these estimates be prepared as quickly as possible, but they were not produced until well after the Korean War had begun.[49] In the meantime, as Rearden (1984, 535) points out, the direct comments Truman made about the defense budget—all off-the-cuff remarks at press conferences—were contradictory. On May 4, Truman said the fiscal 1952 budget would be smaller than that proposed for fiscal 1951. At a press conference on May 25, however, he backed away from his earlier statement and declined to reveal what the new budget ceiling for military spending would be on the grounds that final plans had not been made.[50] In general, the president's public remarks on military spending reveal little about his actual thinking on the subject.

While evidence of Truman's doubts about the program is relatively weak, there are a number of strong indications that the president had decided to proceed with a rearmament program, although he was probably uncertain about how large a program Congress would approve. The argument that the president informally approved NSC 68 before the Korean War corresponds to Acheson's recollection (1969, 374) that the report "became national policy" in April. The evidence for this position can be divided into three general categories: Truman's private remarks on the program, his actions regarding it, and the impressions of his views held by those involved in the matter.

Truman gave a few direct indications that he had decided to proceed with the buildup that NSC 68 implied before intervening in Korea. Rearden (1984, 535) cites the president's May 23 comments to Frederick Lawton, his new budget director. Truman encouraged staff members of the Bureau of the Budget to continue to raise any questions they had about the budget for NSC 68 programs and remarked that "it was definitely not as large as some of the people seemed to think." As Rearden notes, these comments indicate both his doubts about the size of the program and a decision to proceed with a buildup of some sort. As I noted earlier, Hammond (1962, 337) reported that Johnson had informed his staff in April that he and Truman had agreed the economy program in the Department of Defense was dead. Both these comments indicate that the president had decided to proceed with some sort of buildup. Truman's uncertainty about the size of the new budget was understandable, since he had no estimates from the Department of Defense and also had to consider what he could induce the Congress to accept. Furthermore, Truman used the Bureau of the Budget to play devil's advocate with appropriations requests, so he could hardly have told its staff to be uncritical. After his abrupt removal of Frank Pace, some encouragement was probably in order.

Truman's actions during the spring of 1950 also support the idea that he had informally accepted NSC 68. In addition to replacing Frank Pace as director of the Bureau of the Budget, Truman finally appointed Leon Keyserling to head the CEA in May, a position he had held on an acting basis for six months. Keyserling's views on the military budget were well known. Indeed, Truman's uneasiness with Keyserling's Keynesian convictions may explain why he waited so long to make the appointment. Knowing that a formal appointment would only strengthen those favoring a military buildup, the president nevertheless gave Keyserling the job. If the president had not intended to proceed with rearmament, a more fiscally conservative choice would have made more sense.

Truman also made several other personnel changes as part of an effort to promote the rearmament program by reviving bipartisanship on foreign policy matters. Of these changes, the one that most clearly reveals the president's intentions regarding NSC 68 is the appointment of Averell Harriman as a special assistant to the president. Prompted by Dean Acheson and James Webb, Sidney Souers suggested to the president on June 8 that he appoint Harriman to oversee matters relating to NATO and the dollar gap problem, "and to interest himself in coordinating the implementation of various phases of NSC 68." According to Souers, Truman approved the idea and "indicated great interest in the program and thought it would be a fine solution."[51] Harriman assumed his new post on June 16.[52] If Truman had not yet accepted NSC 68, he almost certainly would have considered plans for its "implementation" premature.

NSC 68 was not new to Harriman when he arrived at the White House to help sell the program. He had read the report in April and had endorsed its conclusions at the April 20 NSC meeting.[53] He had also been especially concerned about the European balance-of-payments deficit with the United States for months, and he saw NSC 68 as a way to deal with several problems at one time. In March, Harriman and Colonel Charles Bonesteel, the director of the Mutual Defense Assistance Program in London, discussed the overlapping problems of economic recovery and European rearmament. Bonesteel drafted a letter to John Ohly, deputy director of MDAP, arguing that up to $30 billion might be required in order to assemble a military force capable of confronting a possible Soviet attack. The letter, which Harriman edited and approved, suggested that military aid items might be procured in Europe with American aid funds, thereby stimulating European production, alleviating the dollar gap, and contributing to the defense of Europe.[54] The Bonesteel letter's argument for offshore military procurement matched an important line of thinking among the backers of NSC 68 in the State Department and may have prompted Acheson and others to include Harriman, a formidable political figure, in the effort to get the program enacted.[55]

During the second half of May, Richard Bissell, then a Marshall Plan official, kept Harriman informed of the progress being made by the Ad Hoc Committee on NSC 68. On May 12, Bissell reported that the pace of the committee's work had quickened. He noted a general acceptance of the conclusions of the report, despite some opposition from the Bureau of the Budget and, to a lesser extent, the Department of the Treasury. Bissell indicated that he expected an overall increase of about $4–5 billion per year in the current budget as a result of NSC 68, including $1 billion in additional foreign aid and $3–4 billion in additional military spending. While far short of what was actually spent, these figures nevertheless amounted to a 66 percent increase in military aid and a 25–30 percent increase in military spending. He added that these figures were probably lower than what would actually have to be spent once all the necessary programs were estimated in detail. According to Bissell, Charles Murphy had argued in the committee that "the President should soon make a report to the people on our world position and begin the major task of educating American public opinion." The committee was trying to assemble a preliminary estimate of the necessary programs and their cost so that the president could make such a public statement on the matter in early June.[56]

Bissell's letter is not the only evidence that a presidential announcement based on NSC 68 was in the works before the Korean War. James Lay's account of the first meeting of the Ad Hoc Committee on NSC 68 also mentions discussion of a presidential address, although he does not say who suggested this possibility. The State Department's Public Affairs staff anticipated integrating this address into a larger propaganda effort. Assistant Secretary of State for Public Affairs Edward Barrett sent a proposed set of presidential remarks to the White House. Stressing the dire threat of Soviet aggression, the State Department draft states that "[t]he necessary further application of this policy to the persistent problems of the time will require continued hard work and sacrifice on the part of the people of the United States and the free world for an indefinite period."[57] Without the Korean War such an approach might not have worked, but the administration was clearly preparing to try it.

Despite the intentions of the Ad Hoc Committee, the production of cost estimates delayed its work. Bissell informed Harriman on May 26 that, although planning for NSC 68 was indeed "moving at an accelerated pace," a revised version containing cost estimates would not be ready before June 15. The Department of Defense, which had the largest and most complicated planning task, had stated that it could not produce estimates before that date. Bissell was justifiably skeptical even of the June 15 deadline.[58] Indeed, the military representatives on the committee had previously protested that they could not even produce these estimates by the president's original deadline of August 1.[59] The president apparently decided to proceed with a request for additional MDAP funds immediately, without waiting for the completion of program estimates from the Department of Defense. On June 1, the president requested an additional $1 billion appropriation for military aid, as Bissell had told Harriman he would.[60]

Truman's statements and actions on the matter left those involved with the impression that he had effectively approved NSC 68 soon after receiving it and needed only the final program and budget information before formally signing the report. Acheson thought it was "national policy" in April. Charles Murphy, who was apparently convinced of the need for greater defense spending upon reading the report, would not have made plans for a presidential speech on the program if he had not been sure the president supported it. Sidney Souers, who was then serving as a consultant to the NSC, was confident enough of the president's position to approach him about a plan for "implementation" of the program. If Truman did not support the rearmament program, it is hard to understand why he would allow his closest advisers to believe he did and encourage them to make plans for its implementation.

Why NSC 68?

If NSC 68 was adopted as policy in the executive branch before the beginning of the Korean War, and Wells's "hammer blows" appear to have had so little impact, what prompted the president to accept the change in policy? The domestic political economy theory points to the president's need to select a politically viable policy. Because there is little direct evidence of the president's thoughts on NSC 68, any analysis of Harry Truman's consideration of it must necessarily focus on the logic of the situation he faced. Despite his preference for a balanced budget, Truman confronted political circumstances in the spring of 1950 in which the approval of NSC 68 had some clear advantages over his prior policy of fiscal restraint for maintaining his political coalition. Little had changed internationally since the end of 1949, but much had changed within his administration.

One of the biases inherent in archival research is what might be called the "Mount Everest problem." The higher one ascends in the hierarchy, the thinner the documentary record becomes. When it comes to discerning the motives and intentions of the president, documentary evidence is as sparse as oxygen at the summit of a very high mountain. Daniel Ellsberg (1972, 79–80) offers a good explanation.

> The president—having no formal need to persuade a superior, to coordinate a proposal, or to justify a decision internally—puts much less down on paper than others. Because of his *overlapping* roles, he conceals or dissembles his own views even more than other participants, except selectively to his closest associates. They in turn guard them closely, for reasons of loyalty, their own access, and politics, even when they later come to write "history."

Truman appears to have shown different faces to different segments of his staff and administration, making his real sentiments difficult to determine. Furthermore, as the manager of a coalition of potentially conflicting interests, the president may have a motive to obscure the reasons for his decisions. Because the president's opinions and actions are critically important to the policy-making process, some theoretically informed speculation cannot be avoided. In the absence of firm documentary evidence, the best one can do is to examine the situation the president faced and weigh the costs and benefits of the options he had.

Rejecting NSC 68 would have created serious problems within the executive branch. The NSC 68 process can best be understood as a variant of what Wilfrid Kohl (1975, 3) has called the "royal-court model" of decision making, because it was carried on in secret, relatively few actors were involved, and their goal was to gain the eventual approval of the president for their preferred policy. The advocates of rearmament were quite skilled at royal-court politics. Those who might have opposed the program were either excluded from the policy-making process until it was too late for them to affect the outcome or brought into it under circumstances that tended to minimize their influence. By the time Louis Johnson signed the report and formally sent it to the White House, his position in the administration was extremely weak, and his potential allies in the Bureau of the Budget and the CEA were gone. Furthermore, conservative White House staff members such as Matthew Connelly and Harry Vaughan, who might have sided with Johnson, remained in Key West throughout the crucial weeks when the advocates of rearmament built a consensus around the new policy in the State and Defense Departments. Charles Murphy was convinced to support presidential approval of the report before the president returned. Because of the political acumen of Acheson and Nitze, Truman heard few dissenting voices on NSC 68. If Truman had not proceeded with rearmament, it would have constituted a rejection of the advice of most of his economic and foreign policy advisers, as well as important members of his own staff. Such a rejection could not be given lightly because, in many cases, these advisers were linked to important sources of support for his presidency.

Even if those opposed to NSC 68 had been able to mobilize effectively, there were also solid political reasons for the president to prefer the more internationalist position. At the time, Truman had not yet decided whether he would seek another term as president in 1952. Even if he was not planning to run, though, the future of the Democratic party would still have been of some concern to him. Major internationalists, including Averell Harriman, Robert Lovett, and others brought in as consultants during the development of NSC 68, already knew about the report and supported it. While most of these individuals and the interests they represented had supported the president in 1948, Truman must have known that they could still switch their support to a Republican internationalist challenger in 1952. Unlike the labor movement, for example, international commercial and financial interests had ties to both parties. A refusal to proceed with the rearmament program might have alienated this important Democratic constituency and threatened the elite coalition that had sustained the Democratic party for the preceding 15 years.

While Truman might have reoriented the Democratic party toward the interests of the less internationalist segments of the political economy, this option was fraught with political risks. If Truman was considering a third term in 1952, this policy choice would have strengthened Louis Johnson as a potential rival. Whatever Truman's plans and Johnson's role in them, these conservative interests were not a particularly reliable constituency for a Democratic presidential contender in 1952. If the Republicans were to nominate Robert Taft as many in 1950 expected, most conservatives would probably have supported him regardless of Truman's policy choices. Alternatively, as was noted above, if Truman rejected NSC 68 and the Republicans were to nominate an internationalist, an important Democratic constituency might defect. Even if Truman was personally more comfortable with a different political arrangement, moving away from the highly successful New Deal formula linking liberal domestic policies with an internationalist foreign policy would have been a very risky course of action. Getting the rearmament program through Congress was a daunting task, but not trying to do so was even more risky. In the end, probably hoping that Leon Keyserling's reassuring views on fiscal policy would prove correct, Truman sided with the authors of NSC 68.

Viewed from a distance, it may be tempting to attribute presidential approval of NSC 68 to broad concerns about the Soviet threat. This explanation does not account for the actual course of the policy-making process, however. The confrontation with the Soviet Union—a constant consideration throughout Truman's tenure in the White House—did not prevent him from cutting the defense budget in the fall of 1949, even with the additional urgency allegedly created by the events mentioned by Wells and Leffler. The exigencies of the Korean War would provide the best explanation for Truman's acceptance of rearmament, but the best available evidence indicates that the president had decided to proceed with a buildup of some sort before June 25. The international environment had not greatly changed between the fall of 1949 and the spring of 1950. However, the balance of power within the administration had shifted against the advocates of a small military budget. A realist-statist model of national security policy-making is so deeply ingrained in most historical understandings of the early Cold War period that its validity is usually taken for granted despite its conceptual weaknesses and empirical shortcomings. The international imperative and threats to core values may be clear to historians in retrospect, but the use of these concepts obscures other priorities and alternative courses of action open to decision makers at the time. The closer one looks at the historical evidence, the more one realizes that a realist-statist historiographical lens distorts more than it clarifies.

"Something concrete to which your appeal could be tied"

The Korean War is often treated as an example of how international events may lead to policies that would not have been possible without them (Jervis 1980). This line of thinking ignores the fact that it was not only the international event itself—in this case the North Korean attack on South Korea on June 25, 1950—but also the U.S. decision about how to respond to it that gave the event its significance. If the United States had responded to the fall of South Korea in the same way it responded to the collapse of the Nationalist regime in China, the North Korean attack might not have been such a critical moment. Wells, Leffler, and other accounts informed by neorealist theory treat the U.S. response to this event as obvious and unproblematic. They do not take alternative courses of action seriously. In fact, the decision to commit American troops to the defense of South Korea is surprising in view of previous administration policy toward the country. There is at least as much reason to believe that NSC 68 led to the Korean War as there is to believe the usual argument that involvement in Korea led to rearmament.

The decision to go to war in Korea must be considered in the context of serious domestic political problems facing the administration's national security program. Conservatives in Congress maintained that even the reduced fiscal 1951 military budget was too large and planned to cut it further. While Truman awaited the details of the program, he and others began exploring ways to get it through Congress. In the meantime, he ordered that the development of the program be kept strictly secret. If congressional opponents of larger defense budgets had known what the administration was planning, they might have undermined administration efforts to build a political foundation for the program before it was introduced. Several such efforts were under way between early April and late June of 1950.

When James Webb visited Truman in Key West on March 27, he asked the president to bring John Foster Dulles into the administration in an effort to secure greater Republican cooperation. Since illness had removed Arthur Vandenberg from the Senate in October 1949, the arrangements promoting bipartisanship on foreign policy had virtually collapsed. Dulles had worked closely with Vandenberg in the Senate in 1949. Since losing his seat there, he had written to Acheson expressing his support for administration policy and hinting that he could be useful in the State Department. Truman initially refused to accept a Dulles appointment, so Webb instead suggested John Sherman Cooper, a former Republican senator from Kentucky.[61] A few days later, however, Vandenberg informed Acheson that only Dulles had the prestige to secure Republican cooperation with the administration on foreign policy issues and that Dulles had promised not to run for the Senate again in the fall of 1950 if asked to join the administration. Truman relented, and Acheson offered Dulles a position as a consultant to the State Department the following day. Dulles joined the administration on April 26.[62]

In addition to using Dulles as a bridge to congressional Republicans on foreign policy issues, the State Department tried other approaches to mend the tattered fabric of bipartisanship. Soon after Truman returned from Key West, a serious effort was made to set up a formal consultation arrangement with the Senate Republican leadership. On April 18, Truman and Acheson announced an agreement with Styles Bridges, the ranking Republican on the Armed Services and Appropriations Committees, to consult with a committee of five Republican senators. This group included Bridges, Robert Taft (chair of the Republican Policy Committee), Eugene Millikin (chair of the Republican Party Conference), Kenneth Wherry (Senate minority leader), and Alexander Wiley (the ranking Republican on the Foreign Relations Committee).[63] The State Department also initiated a series of informal "smokers" with influential members of Congress, especially Republicans, in April. Robert Taft, for one, received an invitation to one such gathering scheduled for May 10.[64]

Bipartisan cooperation could not be achieved through mere meeting and consultation, however. Nationalist Republicans like Robert Taft greeted news of the Dulles appointment with skepticism. Taft prepared a statement for the smoker to which he had been invited noting that "[n]o policy can become bi-partisan by the appointment of Republicans to executive office, although we hope that recent appointments are intended as a move toward the establishment of closer relations with the elected Republicans in Congress."[65] Letters to Taft from his supporters generally condemned the Dulles appointment as an effort to force Republicans to accept the administration's foreign policy. While he shared their skepticism, Taft had a more acute appreciation of the difficult position the Republican party in the Senate faced on foreign policy. "I cannot understand why Mr. Dulles accepted this position after his past experience. . . . The differences in the Republican party here, however, are so great on this subject that it is hard to take a combative position."[66]

The consultation arrangement set up by Bridges on behalf of the Senate Republican leadership also produced few tangible results. Tom Connally, the Democratic chair of the Senate Foreign Relations Committee, objected to any consultation arrangement that bypassed the members of his committee. Acheson apparently wanted to avoid offending Connally, informing the president that an arrangement had to be developed to make the Republican members of the Foreign Relations Committee "truly represent" the views of their party. No presidential meetings with the Bridges group are recorded.[67] To make matters worse for the State Department, many Nationalist Republicans simply refused to attend the smokers. In the midst of their effort to show that the State Department was riddled with communist sympathizers, they were reluctant to be seen socially with State Department officials.[68]

The White House looked for other ways to build support for the rearmament program. As was noted earlier, Truman asked Averell Harriman to return to Washington from his position coordinating the Marshall Plan so that he could oversee various foreign policy matters as well as "the implementation of various phases of NSC 68."[69] Arriving at the White House shortly before the Korean War, Harriman was initially occupied with the details of NSC 68. Within a few months, however, he began making use of his political connections to promote the administration's military and foreign aid programs. His media contacts included executives and news officials at both NBC and CBS, newspaper columnists, and academics such as Arthur Schlesinger, Jr. Harriman had his staff plan a series of parties and meetings at his Georgetown home for both media figures and potentially sympathetic members of Congress. The purpose of these gatherings, according to the staff member who planned most of them, was to "establish personal relations on the Hill as quickly as possible."[70] The record of these meetings in Harriman's papers makes it clear why Truman and Acheson thought Harriman a potentially useful figure in gaining acceptance for NSC 68.[71]

In addition to his efforts to improve relations with congressional Republicans, the president was prepared to pay a political price for rearmament. The administration's failure to renew its legislative push for most of its major domestic programs, in spite of the president's continuing rhetorical support for them, surprised some political observers.[72] Probably recognizing that they were unlikely to obtain both rearmament and the implementation of the Fair Deal, Truman and his staff had removed some major Fair Deal programs from their legislative agenda by the end of May. A comparison of Stephen Spingarn's list of "top musts" from the president's legislative program made at a White House staff meeting in November 1949 with his list of "urgent legislation" made in May 1950 reveals the deletion of several such proposals. In particular, the repeal of the Taft-Hartley Act, the National Health Insurance Program, and the administration's farm subsidy proposals were no longer on the list of legislative priorities in May, despite the lack of positive action on them.[73] The accidental omission of these popular programs, which were central to the Fair Deal and had been a staple of Truman's 1948 reelection campaign, is very unlikely. Indeed, both White House meetings worked from the same printed list of legislative programs. Changed priorities in light of NSC 68 offer a better explanation. The report had concluded that rearmament would require spending cuts in other areas.[74] The fact that the additional funding requested for military aid on June 1 had been moved to the top of the priority list also supports this interpretation of the changes in Truman's priorities. The president probably did not need NSC 68 to tell him that rearmament would have an important effect on some of his other spending proposals.

Even before these efforts began, Dean Acheson appears to have envisioned the use of an international crisis to solve this problem. Along with Nitze, Assistant Secretary of State for Far Eastern Affairs Dean Rusk, and Assistant Secretary of State for Congressional Relations Jack McFall, Acheson met with Representative Christian Herter (R-MA) on March 21, 1950, the day before they confronted Louis Johnson with NSC 68. According to a memorandum of conversation from the meeting, Herter expressed concern about pending cuts in the national security program, including a reduction in the military budget to as little as $9 billion. He argued that there was "a false sense of security" in the country and that more, rather than less, should be done in the area of national security. Acheson agreed and gave Herter what amounted to a capsule summary of the discussion of the Soviet threat contained in NSC 68. The memorandum's account of their conversation about how a military buildup might be accomplished is worth quoting at some length:

> At this point Mr. Herter said that he wondered whether it would be possible to bring about among the American people a realization of the seriousness of the situation without some domestic crisis, something concrete to which your appeal could be tied, such as a break in diplomatic relations. I [Acheson] replied that I do not believe it will be necessary to create such a situation, the chances are too good that the Russians will do so themselves. I referred to the proposed demonstration on the 28th of May, which might result in 300 odd thousand German youths attacking the population of West Berlin. That would certainly be a messy situation and a crisis. I referred to the next scheduled meeting of the Deputies on the Austrian Peace Treaty when the Soviets may indicate conclusively that there will be no treaty and that they want us to get out of Eastern Austria thus ringing down the iron curtain in that area. Finally, I referred to the possibility of an overall attack on Formosa from the mainland of China where we understand airstrips are being built, Soviet planes are being furnished, and Soviet crews are training Chinese crews. [75]

Acheson did not mention Korea, but it would have fit neatly into his general listing of possible crises. In discussing NSC 68, other State Department officials also anticipated Soviet actions that "will result in solidifying the American people behind the programs the Government may propose."[76]

Acheson's conversation with Christian Herter and the ongoing concern about the fate of rearmament in Congress support Bruce Cumings's argument (1990, 429–35) about Acheson's use of events leading up to the Korean War. In essence, Cumings argues that Acheson and other American decision makers were awaiting some act by the Soviet Union that would help secure congressional approval for an expensive rearmament program. As Cumings points out, Acheson's attitude toward Soviet behavior brings to mind McGeorge Bundy's well-known remark in another context: "Pleikus are streetcars. You could expect one to come along presently and you were ready to board as soon as it did" (432). Acheson's mention of a Chinese invasion of Formosa in his conversation strongly supports the idea that his search for such an incident was a broad one, not confined to those that posed a serious challenge to what he believed to be vital U.S. interests. Less than three months earlier, during the National Security Council's discussion of NSC 48/1 on policy toward

Asia, Acheson had insisted that even a small effort to defend the Nationalist government on Formosa would be counterproductive. "Secretary Acheson said we must consider the effect on the rest of Asia, where we wish to be on the side of the nationalist movements and avoid supporting reactionary governments."[77] Acheson's apparently contradictory positions on Formosa make sense in light of the domestic political context and his general policy goals. Formosa may not have been a vital U.S. interest, but it had the virtue of being under the threat of imminent attack.

As was the case with China and Formosa, avoiding military involvement in Korea was supposed to be a high priority. The U.S. response to the North Korean invasion of the South is hard to reconcile with the official policy set out in the NSC 8 series in 1948 and 1949. Each policy statement in the series holds that, while some limited economic and military aid should be given to South Korea, "the U.S. should not become so irrevocably involved in the Korean situation that any action taken by any faction in Korea or by any other power in Korea could be considered a *casus belli* for the U.S." As Robert Cutler, Eisenhower's national security adviser, explained to the new president in 1953, policymakers had no illusions about what this decision might mean for the pro-U.S. regime in South Korea. "In this paper it was recognized that Soviet policy aimed at eventual domination of the entire peninsula; that Soviet domination of South Korea would be a severe blow to both U.N. and U.S. interests; and that the only certain means of ensuring South Korean independence would be by direct American responsibility to the extent of risking involvement in a major war."[78] In spite of these considerations, the report recommended the withdrawal of U.S. troops. Official policy was to avoid direct military involvement in Korea. When consulted on the matter, Douglas MacArthur concurred in the judgment and held out little hope for South Korea, adding that "[t]he Korean people are by nature susceptible to dictatorial leadership; long-range political stability cannot be expected."[79]

Although Cumings, McGlothlen (1993), Bernstein (1989), and others offer convincing evidence that State Department officials, especially Dean Acheson, viewed Korea as very important and never planned to abandon it, official U.S. policy did not change prior to the North Korean attack. NSC 8/2 reaffirmed the premises and goals of NSC 8, adding that "[a] more immediate objective is the withdrawal of remaining U.S. occupation forces from Korea as early as practicable consistent with the foregoing objectives." The new policy statement was approved in March 1949 and moved the withdrawal date for U.S. troops back to June 30, 1949. Like NSC 8, NSC 8/2 stated that the United States should neither abandon South Korea nor commit itself to maintaining the integrity of the regime there by force of arms. The report did not cast the decision to avoid military commitment to South Korea exclusively in terms of a global war but referred instead to a range of military scenarios following U.S. troop withdrawal, including "a major effort on the part of the Soviet-dominated north Korean regime to overthrow the Republic of Korea through direct military aggression or inspired insurrection." However, it maintained that further delays in withdrawing U.S. troops only created the risk that "remaining U.S. occupation forces might be destroyed or obliged to abandon Korea in the event of a major hostile attack, with serious damage to U.S. prestige in either case." Invoking the Joint Chiefs of Staff opinion that "the U.S. has little strategic interest in maintaining its present troops and bases in Korea," the report argued that, while preserving South Korea was worth some expenditure of foreign aid, it was not worth going to war.[80] The 7,500 troops remaining in Korea were withdrawn by the date set in NSC 8/2. The report remained official U.S. policy on Korea through August 1950, when the last of the semiannual progress reports on it acknowledged that it had been overtaken by events.[81]

Given official U.S. policy toward Korea, it makes no sense to treat the decision to intervene and the subsequent rearmament effort as unproblematic. Such a move by the North Koreans had long been considered a possibility, even if its exact timing came as a surprise.[82] The most puzzling aspect of the decision to intervene in Korea is the abrupt abandonment of the prior judgment about the value of South Korea in the face of a contingency that had been explicitly considered at the time that judgment was made. One can certainly argue that the decision to intervene accorded with the more general, global imperatives of Cold War national security policy, but this was equally true when NSC 8 and NSC 8/2 were written and approved. A decision to avoid the use of U.S. troops was not made in every case where a communist victory was considered a possibility. In Italy, for example, the use of force was contemplated even if communists took power by electoral means.[83] As I will discuss in greater detail in chapter 5, the Korean War undoubtedly facilitated passage of the rearmament program in Congress, something easily foreseen by those who made the decision to intervene. Like the other choices examined here, little can be said about the decision to intervene in Korea without some account of whose policy preferences were dominant in Washington. It certainly cannot be explained in terms of the strategic judgments of the United States as a unitary actor.

Conclusion

Given the issue it addressed and the institutional setting in which it was considered, the development of NSC 68 within the administration should be a strong case for realist and statist approaches. Despite some hesitation, the United States, as one of the two great powers in the international system, realized that in order to provide for its own security it had to devote a much greater share of its resources to defending its position in the system. Historical accounts like the ones presented by Leffler and Wells proceed from statist and realist premises. Indeed, several reviewers have noted the close correspondence between those historical accounts and neorealist theory.[84] Like neorealist theory, these historical accounts focus on the reactions of central state decision makers to events in the international system and begin with the premise that the requirements of defending core values or responding to the imperatives of the international system required the policy response that actually took place. In this case, these theoretical premises lead to several judgments—one could call them hypotheses—that are very difficult to sustain.

One such hypothesis is that policy choices depend on external events. If the position of the state in the international system or the need to defend core values drives policy, then external shocks provide the best way to explain how domestic disagreements over policy are resolved. In essence, this is what both Leffler and Wells seek to do in linking the development of NSC 68 to various international events. While international events and trends undoubtedly influenced individual decision makers' assessments of what should be done, the meaning of these external pressures depended on individual interests and priorities. The course of policy development, in turn, depended on the political fortunes of various policy currents within the administration—something not necessarily determined by external events. The connections usually made between external events and policy outcomes in this case are quite weak.

There is strong evidence that the administration was committed to NSC 68 before the Korean War and that this commitment was driven not by unambiguous external events, but by political changes in the executive branch. The notion that the major events of late 1949 explain the rearmament initiative is a mirage because these events were generally discounted when they happened and did not affect the September 1949 decision to cut the military budget. Once NSC 68 was completed, those who supported it were able to remove or neutralize the main proponents of a small defense budget very quickly and mobilize support for their own position. Confronted with this new balance of power within his administration, President Truman reversed his efforts to cut military spending and decided to proceed with rearmament. The attitudes of key members of Truman's White House staff, as well as the decision to bring Averell Harriman back from Europe to help coordinate and implement the plan, all indicate that NSC 68 was administration policy before the Korean War. Official approval of the report and a public announcement of the program awaited only final estimates from the Department of Defense.

There is, of course, no way to know if the rearmament program would have survived congressional scrutiny without a major international crisis. The Truman administration had an admirable record of success at getting its foreign policy initiatives through Congress, though, and administration officials evidently believed they could do it once again. They examined several different approaches before the war in Korea. Although it clearly affected the scope of the rearmament program, the Korean War will not suffice to explain the president's decision to reverse his earlier policy choice, because the decision to intervene is itself quite problematic. In committing troops to Korea, U.S. decision makers acted against their own considered policy. To treat the North Korean attack as if it interpreted itself and prescribed its own response requires some heroic assumptions about how decision makers understand the world. Accounts contending that intervention in Korea was an obvious response cannot explain the prior decision to avoid intervention in such a case.

Why must external events, rather than the policy interests of the dominant political faction in covering the dollar gap and making NATO a credible alliance, be used to account for the policy-making process in realist and statist accounts? One might argue, after all, that these general policy considerations are themselves driven by the position of the state in the international system. While foreign policy preferences are always linked to conditions in the international system, the problem confronting realist and statist approaches is that a given set of conditions may be linked to many different preferences. The international conditions that generate these often conflicting preferences do not resolve the domestic struggle over which of them will be enacted into policy. If a realist or statist account of foreign policy-making is to be sustained, the faction that wins the domestic political struggle must win because its view matches imperatives of the international system or the requirements of defending core values, not just because it is able to assemble a dominant domestic coalition. An external shock from the international system producing consensus around the "correct" view of the national interest is probably the only process these accounts of foreign policy can accommodate. This process does not match the evidence in this important case.

An account that stresses the demands of coalition building and maintenance in the context of conflicting interests in the domestic political economy provides a better explanation of policy-making, even at the highest levels of the state. Evidence concerning the development of NSC 68 supports the idea that the positions taken by executive branch officials are closely related to the ties they have to interests outside the executive branch. The interests of these groups do not change in response to particular events unless those events alter the underlying conditions in the international system. Neither the emergence of the People's Republic of China nor the development of the Soviet atomic bomb was such an event. For the State Department and its supporters in society, concern over the imminent end of the Marshall Plan and the viability of NATO as a genuine defense organization predates these events. Those opposed to larger defense budgets did not change their minds because of these events, either. Indeed, they achieved their greatest successes in the administration after these shocks took place. The debate in the administration was resolved not through the pressure of external events, but through the changing requirements of assembling a viable political coalition to support the president and his policies.

The failure of the international system to imply a single policy response is not only a problem for international relations theorists. It is a very practical issue for all accounts of foreign policy that begin, as Leffler's book does, by positing a set of core values or international imperatives that guide policy. Once this exogenous set of basic goals has been determined, the process that follows must be one in which policymakers learn what they must do. As in Leffler's book, this learning process may be a long and complicated one, with many obstacles and pitfalls preventing decision makers from coming to the correct conclusion immediately. However, events in the international system will intervene periodically to push decision makers in the direction of the policies required by the position of the state in the international system or the defense of core values. Neither Leffler nor Wells denies that there were some who opposed the rearmament program. Indeed, both occasionally allude to the existence of these opponents. What they cannot do without the *deus ex machina* of Korea, an event they assume implied but one policy response, is explain how the controversy over rearmament in the administration ended.

CHAPTER 4

The Political and Economic Sources of Divergent Foreign Policy Preferences in the Senate, 1949–51

> If we can . . . carry out only those agreements which can be ratified through Constitutional processes, I am quite sure that we not only can write a peace treaty, but it will provide the opportunity whereby we can put our financial house in order, reduce taxes, and keep off our back controls, regimentations, and directives issued by our Federal bureaus.
>
> —Kenneth Wherry, Senate Minority Leader

> It is imperative that this trend [of growing relative Soviet power] be reversed by a much more rapid and concerted build-up of actual strength of both the United States and the other nations of the free world. The analysis shows that this will be costly and will involve significant financial and economic adjustments.
>
> —NSC 68

Did congressional debates over the goals and priorities of U.S. foreign policy during the early Cold War era reflect cleavages in the American political economy? This chapter presents statistical evidence that they did. The international trade and investment interests of home-state firms and industries, mediated by the party system, strongly influenced senators' foreign policy preferences. In underscoring the need to take the opponents of U.S. foreign policy seriously, this statistical evidence sets the stage for the account of political conflict and bargaining between the administration and its opponents that follows. Congressional opposition to administration foreign policy cannot be treated as the product of individual idiosyncrasies, failure to understand the administration's goals, or mere political opportunism. It reflected systematic and lasting features of the American political economy. The problem facing the administration in its efforts to secure broad support for its foreign policy was not simply overcoming the misperception or myopia of its political opponents. It had to persuade them to accept a policy that simply did not serve their interests.

The attitudes of members of Congress are more amenable to statistical analysis than the views of executive policymakers discussed in the last two chapters. Roll call votes contain enough individual data points to make statistical inference possible. Because legislators can express their preferences on each issue in only a limited number of ways when they vote, the coding of each individual vote requires relatively little interpretation by the analyst. Reasonably good data exist about the economic structure of the United States and the international interests of large firms within it during the early postwar era. A statistical comparison of these economic data with the voting records of individual senators can reveal whether there are systematic relationships consistent with my theoretical argument about the influence of interests and the party system on foreign policy preferences.

While administration proponents of NSC 68 believed their vision of the global political and economic order would promote the interests of the United States as a whole, not everyone agreed. At the time, many parts of the United States had few ties to the international economy. While Dean Acheson and others found it hard to take their views seriously, members of Congress who came from such an environment saw little point in devoting enormous resources to the construction of a world order in which they had such a small stake. Other administration critics had international interests that called for an equally ambitious world order of a different sort. The administration's program was not intended to assert direct U.S. control over foreign territory, particularly in the Third World. These areas were understood in the administration primarily as an economic hinterland for the major industrial areas they sought to rebuild. As Frieden (1989; 1994) has pointed out, direct investors in extractive industries have strong incentives to favor direct colonial control of areas in which they have interests. Cumings (1990, 97–100) offers evidence that individuals linked to mineral industries were worried that the administration's brand of internationalism would not protect their interests. The administration's opponents worked assiduously to undermine its foreign policy and, indeed, to destroy politically those who had devised it. While the struggle between these interests is critical, the merit of the arguments they made need not concern us here. Even if one could show that either the administration or its critics were correct about the relative costs and benefits of their proposed courses of action, this evidence would reveal little about the policy-making process. Not only would such information have been unavailable at the time, but, in any event, policies are selected because those who favor them have political power, not because they are right.

The domestic political economy theory suggests a number of empirical relationships between the voting record of each senator, his or her party affiliation, region of origin, and the economic structure of his or her home state. Since the Truman administration's foreign policy was intended to establish and protect an international order open to U.S. trade and investment, firms and industries with a greater stake in this goal should favor it, while those without such a stake should oppose it. Politicians linked to these firms should reflect their interests. States with large import-competing sectors should produce senators less willing to support the costly foreign policy proposed by the Truman administration than senators from states with more export-oriented interests. Similarly, senators from states where more international lending was taking place should support the administration's foreign policy more than those from states without such activity. Senators from states where investors were more heavily involved in Third World extractive industries that would have benefited from a policy seeking direct control of these territories should also be more likely to oppose the program. Given the serious questions about the administration's commitment to preserving access to the Asian mainland after the fall of China, investors in that region should be another source of anti-administration sympathies.

Obviously, the influence of interests like these is not necessarily restricted by state borders. Nevertheless, it is reasonable to suggest that large firms and interests might have more political resources to offer to politicians in the regions where they are most active. Although it does not exhaust their potential influence, the balance of interests within each state should provide a rough test of whether or not economic interests really shape politicians' policy preferences. To the extent that these interests exercise influence across state lines, this influence should bias the results against finding significant relationships between policy preferences and economic structure. Rather than casting doubt on the statistical evidence presented here, this potential bias makes any statistically significant relationships even more striking.

Realist and statist accounts of the policy-making process treat basic policy goals as exogenous and cannot explain these differences over policy. It makes sense to treat basic policy goals as responses to objective threats in the international system, or efforts to defend consensual core values, when there is little political conflict or when political differences are caused by individual idiosyncrasies or mere partisan opportunism. Conflict rooted in lasting features of the domestic political economy is much more problematic, since it suggests that international conditions have different implications for differently situated groups and that the "core values" posited by state decision makers may be controversial. In effect, realist and statist accounts of the policy-making process furnish the null hypothesis in the quantitative analysis.

Measuring Support and Opposition to
Administration Policy

How can support for and opposition to the administration's foreign and domestic programs be measured? In order to develop an indicator of each senator's position on foreign policy and the Fair Deal, I examined all the votes taken in the Eighty-first Congress relevant to these two general issue areas. Of the more than 400 roll call votes taken in the Senate during the Eighty-first Congress, 153 pertained directly to some aspect of either the Fair Deal or foreign policy. I omitted some of these votes from the analysis for several reasons. Including near-unanimous votes on which less than 10 percent of the Senate voted in the minority would have understated the range of difference between senators. I also omitted votes on measures directed at a particular industry or special interest group, because they do not reflect positions on foreign policy or the Fair Deal. Finally, I excluded votes on civil rights measures, such as the antidiscrimination amendments proposed on public housing legislation. Although included in the Truman administration's legislative agenda, civil rights legislation was not part of the Fair Deal. The political divisions indicated by votes on these measures are not the same as those produced by votes on the Fair Deal, since they split the Democratic party and drew more Republican support than did Fair Deal measures. Civil rights–related amendments, such as antilynching measures and prohibitions on segregation in government-funded activities, were often proposed in an effort to kill the measure to which they were attached. In these cases, even some senators who usually supported civil rights measures usually voted against them.

Votes in each issue area were used to develop two scores for each senator, one indicating the level of support they gave the Fair Deal and the other indicating the level of support they gave the administration's foreign policy. Votes in favor of administration proposals were coded "1," while votes against such measures, or for initiatives designed to interfere with the administration's legislative efforts, were coded "–1." Mean scores between 1 and –1 were calculated for each senator across all the votes in each issue area. High scores indicate a greater propensity to support the administration's programs in these two areas. Those scoring higher on foreign policy are internationalists. Those scoring higher on the Fair Deal are liberals.

The 78 votes selected to represent the senators' positions on foreign policy concern not only military and security issues, but also commercial policy and foreign aid. Economic and political-military ends and means were inextricably linked in administration policy. Its framers intended the Marshall Plan to advance the security goal of rebuilding allies as well as the economic purpose of reconstructing U.S. trading partners. Similarly, the rearmament program associated with NSC 68 was to provide a source of dollars to cover the European balance-of-payments deficit as well as to arm American allies against the Soviet military threat. Aid, trade, and national security policy were also linked in the minds of the administration's conservative opponents. Lynn Eden (1984; 1985, 178) has demonstrated that the views of "business nationalists" were consistent on both foreign economic policy and military issues. These senators, who were mostly conservative Republicans, generally opposed both expensive military programs and trade liberalization. Eden presents statistical evidence of a uniform pattern on these two issues and classifies about 20 senators as business nationalists in 1948. These senators generally preferred a less costly strategy relying on air power for the defense of the United States. Eden's findings about the opponents of the Truman administration's foreign policy make sense in light of the close ties between economic and military issues in the administration's strategy. Although these issues may be disaggregated for some analytical purposes, they are closely related in practice and were linked to a common set of underlying policy goals during the early Cold War era.

Using these voting scores, it is possible to evaluate the extent of support for and opposition to the president's domestic and foreign policies in the Senate. While there was significant support for both sets of programs, neither could pass without the acquiescence of some of its opponents. An examination of the size of the various voting blocs in the Senate reveals the relative strength of the administration's supporters and opponents. The voting blocs presented here reflect both the voting scores and considerations of party and region. These groups also roughly correspond to the contemporary self-understandings of the actors indicated by other historical evidence.

Considering their views on both foreign policy and social welfare issues, the senators can be divided into five blocs. These are (1) Liberal Democrats, who were the administration's strongest supporters; (2) Western Democrats, who form a small but distinct group; (3) Southern Democrats, who were generally more conservative than other members of their party; (4) Internationalist Republicans, who generally supported the administration's foreign policy; and (5) Nationalist Republicans, who opposed the administration's foreign and domestic programs. The members of each of these blocs are listed in tables 1 and 2, along with the voting scores of each senator and the mean score for each bloc. A few senators whose voting behavior was especially unusual have been placed in voting blocs that do not accord with their region or apparent ideology. Three have been listed as outliers and are not included in any group.

I classified Democrats with Fair Deal and foreign policy voting scores above .75 as Liberal Democrats. This group includes Democrats from all regions as long as they voted in accordance with this pattern, although senators from the Northeast predominated. Five Southern Democrats who differed from others in their region were placed with the Liberals in table 1. Of these five, Frank Graham, Claude Pepper, and Estes Kefauver were among the most active liberal senators. Archival evidence indicates

TABLE 1.   Voting Scores of Democrats in the Eighty-first Congress

	Fair Deal Score	Foreign Policy Score		Fair Deal Score	Foreign Policy Score
Liberal Democrats			**Southern Democrats**		
Group Mean	*0.88*	*0.92*	*Group Mean*	*0.20*	*0.60*
Std. Deviation	*0.07*	*0.10*	*Std. Deviation*	*0.30*	*0.29*
Anderson (D-NM)	0.75	1.00	Chapman (D-KY)	0.23	0.81
Benton (D-CT)	1.00	1.00	Connally (D-TX)	0.16	1.00
Clements (D-KY)	1.00	1.00	Eastland (D-MS)	−0.24	0.41
Douglas (D-IL)	0.79	0.79	Ellender (D-LA)	0.14	0.47
Downey (D-CA)	0.85	1.00	Fulbright (D-AR)	0.26	0.82
Graham (D-NC)	0.85	0.97	George (D-GA)	−0.18	0.41
Green (D-RI)	0.88	0.97	Hoey (D-NC)	−0.04	0.75
Hill (D-AL)	0.84	0.86	Holland (D-FL)	0.00	0.66
Humphrey (D-MN)	0.92	0.97	Johnson, L. (D-TX)	0.38	0.95
Hunt (D-WY)	0.87	0.61	Johnston (D-SC)	0.68	0.18
Kefauver (D-TN)	0.90	0.93	Long (D-LA)	0.72	0.40
Kerr (D-OK)	0.75	0.90	McClellan (D-AR)	−0.15	−0.01
Kilgore (D-WV)	0.92	0.97	McKellar (D-TN)	0.53	0.68
Leahy (D-RI)	0.93	1.00	Maybank (D-SC)	0.64	0.55
Lehman (D-NY)	1.00	0.95	O'Conor (D-MD)	0.10	0.76
Lucas (D-IL)	0.86	0.97	Robertson (D-VA)	−0.18	0.76
McGrath (D-RI)	0.90	0.91	Russell (D-GA)	−0.04	0.05
McMahon (D-CT)	0.79	0.94	Smith, W. (D-NC)	0.33	1.00
Magnuson (D-WA)	0.87	0.79	Stennis (D-MS)	0.16	0.57
Miller (D-ID)	0.88	1.00	Tydings (D-MD)	0.06	0.84
Murray (D-MT)	0.92	1.00	Withers (D-KY)	0.68	0.93
Myers (D-PA)	0.92	0.95			
Neely (D-WV)	0.92	0.95	**Western Democrats**		
Pepper (D-FL)	0.94	0.89			
Sparkman (D-AL)	0.81	0.86	*Group Mean*	*0.50*	*0.44*
Thomas, E. (D-UT)	0.80	0.92	*Std. Deviation*	*0.19*	*0.37*
Thomas, J. (D-OK)	0.86	0.70	Chavez (D-NM)	0.68	0.75
Wagner (D-NY)	0.89	1.00	Gillette (D-IA)	0.36	0.47
			Hayden (D-AZ)	0.69	1.00
Outliers			Johnson, E. (D-CO)	0.29	−0.09
			McCarran (D-NV)	0.47	0.05
Byrd (D-VA)	−0.48	−0.31	McFarland (D-AZ)	0.55	0.84
Frear (D-DE)	0.53	0.39	O'Mahoney (D-WY)	0.73	0.83
Langer (R-ND)	0.77	−0.57	Taylor (D-ID)	0.91	0.42

that all three worked closely with liberals such as Hubert Humphrey, Harley Kilgore, Paul Douglas, and Herbert Lehman.[1] Graham, for example, was also one of only seven senators to vote against passage of the Internal Security Act. Kefauver joined Graham and eight others in the unsuccessful effort to sustain Truman's veto of the act three days later. Pepper had a similarly liberal reputation during his tenure in the Senate. Neither Pepper nor Graham survived the 1950 election, when both were defeated by candidates who made extensive use of their voting records to

TABLE 2. Voting Scores of Republicans in the Eighty-first Congress

	Fair Deal Score	Foreign Policy Score		Fair Deal Score	Foreign Policy Score
Internationalist Republicans			Nationalist Republicans		
Group Mean	*0.06*	*0.31*	*Group Mean*	*−0.56*	*−0.61*
Std. Deviation	*0.38*	*0.19*	*Std. Deviation*	*0.18*	*0.22*
Aiken (R-VT)	0.71	0.43	Brewster (R-ME)	−0.51	−0.67
Baldwin (R-CT)	−0.11	0.26	Bricker (R-OH)	−0.80	−0.75
Dulles (R-NY)	0.20	0.50	Bridges (R-NH)	−0.68	−0.63
Flanders (R-VT)	0.21	0.29	Butler (R-NE)	−0.81	−0.89
Gurney (R-SD)	−0.69	0.12	Cain (R-WA)	−0.70	−0.58
Ives (R-NY)	0.42	0.19	Capehart (R-IN)	−0.54	−0.82
Lodge (R-MA)	0.25	0.45	Carlson (R-KA)	−1.00	−0.60
Morse (R-OR)	0.61	0.53	Carlson (R-KA)	−0.64	−0.37
Reed (R-KA)	−0.59	0.04	Cordon (R-OR)	−0.64	−0.37
Saltonstall (R-MA)	−0.07	0.20	Darby (R-KA)	−0.36	−0.57
Smith, H. (R-NJ)	−0.07	0.44	Donnell (R-MO)	−0.30	−0.06
Smith, M. (R-ME)	0.23	0.43	Dworshak (R-ID)	−0.64	−0.68
Thye (R-MN)	0.15	0.17	Ecton (R-MT)	−0.70	−0.81
Tobey (R-NH)	0.27	0.12	Ferguson (R-MI)	−0.57	−0.41
Vandenburg (R-MI)	−0.27	0.72	Hendrickson (R-NJ)	−0.20	−0.18
Wiley (R-WI)	−0.35	0.04	Hickenlooper (R-IA)	−0.64	−0.33
			Jenner (R-IN)	−0.61	−0.94
			Kem (R-MO)	−0.69	−0.92
			Knowland (R-CA)	−0.46	−0.27
			McCarthy (R-WI)	−0.20	−0.48
			Malone (R-NV)	−0.39	−0.92
			Martin (R-PA)	−0.72	−0.72
			Millikin (R-CO)	−0.39	−0.38
			Mundt (R-SD)	−0.56	−0.49
			Nixon (R-CA)	−0.33	−0.60
			Schoeppel (R-KA)	−0.62	−0.63
			Taft (R-OH)	−0.53	−0.46
			Watkins (R-UT)	−0.49	−0.64
			Wherry (R-NE)	−0.70	−0.90
			Williams (R-DE)	−0.73	−0.76
			Young (R-ND)	−0.37	−0.70

portray them as "soft on communism" and as threats to white supremacy in the South.[2] Lister Hill and John Sparkman, the two senators from Alabama, were more loyal to the liberal priorities of the national Democratic party than most others from the South. Both were heavily involved in efforts to wrest control of the Alabama Democratic party from more conservative and independent Dixiecrats after 1948.[3] In general, these five senators fit the liberal pattern far better than the one set by the other Southern Democrats.

The Southern Democrats include all senators from the old Confederacy except the five just noted. (These states are Alabama, Arkansas, Florida, Georgia, Louisiana, Mississippi, North Carolina, South Carolina, Tennessee, Texas, and Virginia.) In addition, I included senators from the "border states" of Kentucky, Maryland, Oklahoma, and West Virginia if they did not meet the criteria set out for inclusion among the Liberal Democrats. This group was critical to the fate of the administration's foreign policy, and their positions on it varied widely. Seven have foreign policy voting scores below .50, and many of these were often sympathetic to the Nationalist Republican perspective on foreign policy.

The voting behavior of Harry Byrd (D-VA) was extremely anomalous. He had by far the lowest foreign policy voting score of any Democratic senator, which at −.31 was slightly more than three standard deviations from the mean for the rest of the Southern Democrats (.59). Byrd was also more consistent in his opposition to the Fair Deal than other Southern Democrats. His Fair Deal voting score of −.48 was, like his foreign policy voting score, more than two standard deviations from the mean for the rest of the South (.18).

I also placed J. Allen Frear (D-DE) with the outliers. Frear's voting behavior, while not nearly as extreme as Byrd's, is quite different from that of other non-Southern Democrats. He was much less supportive of both the Fair Deal and the administration's foreign policy than were his co-partisans. His foreign policy voting score (.39) is more than four standard deviations from the Liberal Democrats' mean (.90), and his Fair Deal score (.53) is nearly three standard deviations from the mean (.86). Republicans in the Senate viewed Frear as a potential conservative ally in 1950— the only non-Southern Democrat held in such esteem.[4] One possible explanation for Frear's anomalous behavior lies in the long-standing commitment of the largest corporation in his state, DuPont, to trade protection.[5] While confirming some connection between the interests of DuPont and the position taken by Frear would require additional research, it would not be surprising to find that the enormous role of DuPont in the economy of the state of Delaware had some effect.

The smallest group of senators I identified are the Western Democrats. With the exception of Guy Gillette (D-IA), these eight senators were all from the Mountain West, an area generally associated with isolationism. In her analysis of Senate voting during the Eightieth Congress, Eden (1985, 326–27) characterizes Edwin Johnson (D-CO), Glen Taylor (D-ID), and Dennis Chavez (D-NM) as business nationalists. She notes that Chavez and Taylor, while sharing some of the foreign policy preferences of conservative business nationalists such as Robert Taft (R-OH) and Kenneth Wherry (R-NE), held liberal views on domestic issues. Eden also lists William Langer (R-ND), who is included among the outliers here, as a liberal business nationalist. Langer and Johnson, a conservative business nationalist, are the only members of either party to support the Fair Deal but oppose the administration's foreign policy. The Republican Party Steering Committee considered Langer and all eight Western Democrats "incorrigible New Dealers," however, so the connection between Democratic and Republican business nationalists was probably attenuated in practice. The voting behavior of most of these Democrats is closer to that of the Liberal Democrats than to that of the Republican business nationalists.

Patrick McCarran (D-NV) merits some separate comment. While the Republican Party Steering Committee correctly noted that he voted against the Taft-Hartley Act in 1947 and Republican-sponsored amendments to it in 1949, it is hard to agree that he was an "incorrigible New Dealer" by 1950. The White House, which rated senators from 30 (very cooperative) to –30 (very uncooperative) based on votes on housing, natural resources, and foreign policy, gave McCarran a –5, the lowest score received by any of the Western Democrats and the only negative score received by any Democrat not from the South.[6] Although McCarran was relatively cooperative with the administration on the Fair Deal, his foreign policy voting score, .05, is the second lowest of any Democrat. McCarran was one of the leading members of the "China bloc" and was one of the chief inquisitors in the effort to discover "who lost China." Furthermore, McCarran's activities as chair of the Senate Internal Security Subcommittee and his sponsorship of the Internal Security Act mark him as one of the principal figures in the congressional attack on domestic communism. In these areas, McCarran behaved more like a Nationalist Republican than a Democrat.

The Internationalist Republican category includes all Republicans who had a positive foreign policy voting score. Although Internationalist Republicans had been able to nominate sympathetic presidential candidates in 1944 and 1948, they were an embattled minority in the Senate. During the Eighty-first Congress, Nationalist Republicans controlled nearly all major party leadership positions.[7] Furthermore, the staff of the

Republican Policy Committee was staunchly nationalist, with its director urging Republican senators to avoid the "trap" of bipartisanship on foreign policy, even during the Korean War.[8] Arthur Vandenberg (R-MI), the leading Internationalist Republican, was hospitalized with cancer in October 1949 and was never able to return to the Senate. Also, only a few months after being appointed to replace Robert Wagner, John Foster Dulles lost a New York special election to Herbert Lehman in November 1949, removing yet another major national figure from this group.

In addition to their leadership problems, the internationalists were divided on issues other than foreign policy. While the nationalists were fairly consistent in their opposition to the Fair Deal, the internationalists were not. Some, especially those from the Northeast, supported these programs, while others, especially those from the Midwest, opposed them. These domestic policy differences reduced the ability of the internationalists to form a united front against the nationalists within their party and posed a problem for the administration. Paul Nitze has noted that divisions within the Republican party played an important role in the administration's legislative strategy before 1950. "What we decided to do was to build up Senator Vandenberg, as opposed to Senator Taft, and create a split within the Republican Party, and then drive our policy in between these two poles in the Republican Party, and it worked."[9] Without Vandenberg's leadership, this strategy was no longer viable.

Although they all generally opposed the administration's foreign policy, not all the Nationalist Republicans were "isolationists." The range of views on foreign policy among opponents of the administration's foreign policy was wider than this term implies. Grimmett (1973), examining votes on foreign aid and trade policy, classifies as isolationists all of the senators I have described here as nationalists. As Eden (1985) and Cumings (1990) have made clear, however, the foreign policy outlook of most of these senators can best be described as "nationalist" or "expansionist." Few of them simply opposed all international involvement by the United States. Instead, they objected to multilateral entanglements on both economic and security issues, preferring trade relationships subject to unilateral American control, like those with Latin America, and security arrangements that preserved American freedom of action. Reliance on atomic weapons and air power, their preferred weapons systems, was also less expensive than maintaining a large conventional force in Europe. These nationalist attitudes were not confined to the Republican party. In addition to the Democrats Eden classifies as business nationalists, Grimmett lists Byrd (D-VA), Ellender (D-LA), Frear (D-DE), Johnson (D-CO), Long (D-LA), and McClellan (D-AR) as isolationists.

Some Nationalist Republicans stressed the threat of communism in

Asia rather than Europe. Koen (1974) lists nationalists Owen Brewster (R-ME), Styles Bridges (R-NH), Harry Cain (R-WA), Homer Ferguson (R-MI), Bourke Hickenlooper (R-IN), William Knowland (R-CA), and Joseph McCarthy (R-WI) as members of the "China bloc," along with H. Alexander Smith (R-NJ), an internationalist, and James Eastland (D-MS) and Patrick McCarran (D-NV), both Democrats. Although some of these senators, especially Bridges, Knowland, and McCarran, had ties to the Chinese Nationalist regime and its sympathizers in the United States, some adopted the issue simply because it offered an opportunity to attack the administration's foreign policy on its own terms. Others were concerned that U.S. inaction in China might imply that the U.S. would not support friendly regimes elsewhere in the Third World.

In order for the Nationalist Republicans to block administration policy initiatives, they had to gain the support of some combination of Southern and Western Democrats and internationalists from their own party. In fact, they were able to do this on some important votes, even after the beginning of the Korean War. As one confidential State Department memorandum put it, "[i]t is not exaggeration to say that the foreign policy barely got by in the 81st Congress."[10] As I will explain in greater detail later, on a critical vote to allow consideration of the Wherry amendment to the first supplemental appropriations bill, which would have effectively blocked aid to Britain, they received the support of all Republicans and 18 Democrats, mostly from the South and West. Passage of funding for rearmament was not guaranteed, in spite of the ongoing war in Korea.

Linking Domestic and Foreign Policy Preferences

Another important feature of congressional voting concerns the similarity of voting patterns on the two issue areas examined here. Senators who favored the administration's foreign policy tended also to favor the Fair Deal. In fact, the correlation between the two voting scores is .85. This is not surprising in light of the work of Keith Poole and Howard Rosenthal (1985; 1991) demonstrating that nearly all the variation in congressional voting patterns can be captured in one or two dimensions. This unified cleavage structure is both a nearly universal feature of congressional voting and an important source of support for the argument that domestic and foreign policy issues are not resolved in isolation from one another.

The similarities between the lines of political conflict in these two issue areas make linkages between them more likely. If the cleavage structure had been very different on the two issues, efforts to link them would have been greatly complicated. A bargain trading support for the administration's foreign policy for concessions on the Fair Deal might not have been acceptable if there had been a significant group that opposed the terms of such a bargain in both issue areas. The uniformity of the cleavage structure across issues meant that individuals holding this unhappy combination of positions did not exist in significant numbers. Indeed, there were only two senators whose voting scores indicate that they generally favored the Fair Deal and opposed the administration's foreign policy— William Langer (R-ND) and Edwin Johnson (D-CO). Although this combination of issue positions would be viewed more sympathetically in the wake of the Vietnam War, it found few influential listeners in 1950.

The Effects of Economic Structure, Party, and Region on Senate Voting

Were support for and opposition to the administration's foreign policy really influenced by ties to the domestic political economy? If so, there should be a systematic relationship between the structure of the economy and congressional voting on these issues. At least two general types of conflict among economic interests over the general outlines of foreign policy follow from the ways different firms and industries are linked to the international economy. First, some economic actors may benefit more than others from access to international markets and sites for investment. While foreign policy efforts to secure the interests of internationally oriented firms may not directly harm the interests of domestically oriented firms, groups that gain no clear benefits from these efforts nevertheless have to bear their potentially considerable costs. At the very least, the political representatives of firms and industries without important international interests should seek to keep the costs of these policies as low as possible. Second, there may be conflicting interests in the regional emphasis of foreign policy. Faced with limited resources, foreign-policy makers may choose to emphasize economic and security concerns in some regions over others. Clearly, firms whose most important investments or markets receive a lower priority should object to the prevailing foreign policy. The regression models presented here test hypotheses about both types of cleavages among commercial interests, direct investors, and portfolio investors during the 1949–51 period. Table 3 summarizes the hypothesized political effects of these interests.

First, since the Truman administration's foreign policy was intended to establish and preserve an open international trading system, the commercial policy interests of a senator's home state should influence their attitude toward it. Senators from states with a large import-competing sector should be less likely to support the Truman administration's foreign policy, and those from states with more export-oriented industries should be more likely to favor it. Using national aggregate data on trade and state-level data on manufacturing, mining and agriculture, I estimated the ratios of exports and imports to the total value added in each state. These ratios are a good indicator of the relative export orientation and import sensitivity of each state. The appendix offers a more detailed explanation of how I calculated these figures.

The administration's foreign policy was also intended to preserve a favorable climate for international lending, particularly in Europe. The State Department had more than its share of Wall Street veterans who understood these concerns, including Paul Nitze, the author of NSC 68. Their concerns about the future of investment in Europe fueled fears not only about potential Soviet domination of the continent, but also about the continuing European balance-of-payments deficit. The NSC 68 program was intended to deal with both of these problems. Senators from states whose banks were especially active in international lending, particularly to Europe, should support the administration's foreign policy. On the other hand, the administration was frequently criticized for failing to show the same level of concern about conditions in Asia that it did in Europe, particularly after the collapse of the Nationalist regime in China. Senators from states in which banks were more involved in lending to Asia should be less likely to support the administration's foreign policy.[11] Using data on international lending reported to the Federal Reserve by member

TABLE 3.   Economic Interests and the Truman Administration's Foreign Policy

	Support Administration Policy (Positive sign expected in regression analysis)	Oppose Administration Policy (Negative sign expected in regression analysis)
Trade interests	Export sector (especially exporters relying on European markets[a])	Import-competing sector Exporters relying mainly on Asian markets[a]
Portfolio investor interests	Banks with a relatively high proportion of international lending Banks lending to Europe	Banks with a relatively low proportion of international lending Banks lending to Asia
Director investor interests	Direct investors outside Western Hemisphere	Large firms with no direct investments outside Western Hemisphere Large firms with direct investments in Third World extractive industries

[a]These hypotheses are included for the sake of completeness, although the existing data do not allow them to be tested.

banks, I developed indicators of the level of international lending and its regional orientation by banks in each state.

Finally, not only banks lending to Europe, but also corporations with direct foreign investments outside the Western Hemisphere stood to benefit from the administration's foreign policy. Senators from states where a high proportion of the largest firms were internationally oriented should support the administration's foreign policy more readily than senators from states where most large corporations had no investments outside the United States. Since the administration's commitment to the physical security of Third World areas was in doubt after the fall of China, corporations with foreign direct investments in Third World extractive industries should also oppose the administration's foreign policy and pass these concerns along to their senators. Using data on the international activities of the 200 largest U.S. manufacturing, transportation, merchandising, and utility firms, I created aggregate indicators of the international interests of the largest corporations headquartered in each state.

It is worth emphasizing that my argument about economic structure does not directly concern campaign finance. Of course, to the extent that they made political contributions, officers and investors in these corporations probably used them to promote politicians who shared their policy views. Such contributions are not the only form of political influence, however. For example, their state's economy may decisively shape the attitudes of those with whom politicians discuss the issues of the day and form their ideas about "the national interest." The question addressed in these models is whether the pattern of policy preferences was consistent with the structure of economic interests in society, not how those interests actually influenced political leaders. This question is obviously important in its own right. Answering it would require a different research effort than the one undertaken here.

Finally, I will measure the effects of senators' home regions on their policy preferences. Of course, region is not exogenous to economic structure. Indeed, most discussions of regionalism in American politics treat region primarily as a proxy for economic structure.[12] Regional economies differ due to geographical features such as climate, soil quality, and the presence or absence of barriers to markets outside the region. These differences in economic structure lead to regional variations in political behavior. In short, variation in voting patterns captured by region is also rooted in economic structure. In principle, it should be possible to understand the effects of region simply by examining differences in economic structure. Even though regional differences are due primarily to variations in economic activity, region has some independent political effects that justify its inclusion in the models presented here.

The institutional structure of American politics privileges regional issues and makes them more likely than other political cleavages to become politically relevant. Legislative constituencies are formally defined in regional terms. Since every member of the House and Senate is elected from a territorially defined district, regional issues that unite the entire constituency are very attractive to political candidates. If Congress were elected through a nationwide system of proportional representation, by contrast, the incentives to appeal to regional issues would be fewer. While appeals to class, ideology, religion, or other factors are likely to alienate some voters, appeals that only divide voters in a given district from those in other districts are much less likely to do so. Efforts to bring federal projects into a member's district fall into this category, since they offer benefits to those in the area and disperse the cost over the entire country. Also, to the extent that their assets are tied to a particular region, economic interests may have more political resources at their disposal for political candidates in that region. Since the United States is a large country, the potential for regional variation is great. This variation encourages the emergence of sectional voting blocs in the Congress. These regional blocs may persist across issues, even when interests within the bloc differ on particular policy questions.

Furthermore, as Agnew (1987, 91) notes, although economic factors decisively shape regional political cultures, those political cultures change more slowly than does the economy. When economic change occurs rapidly and is accompanied by great uncertainty, as was the case during the immediate postwar period, these lag effects are likely to be more important. Uncertainty contributes to the lag since major economic actors may not be able to appreciate changes in their interests. A lag effect is also built into the careers of politicians. Individuals who achieve office with the support of a particular set of interests may remain there even after changing economic circumstances, such as a shift in international comparative advantage or the emergence of a new industry in their state, have greatly weakened those interests.[13] Lags resemble institutions in some respects, since they may preserve certain political outcomes in the absence of an ongoing base of political support.

Empirical Results

The tables below present the results of several different specifications of the relationship between economic structure, party, region, and senators' voting records. Because of the technical limitations of the available data, several slightly different models are necessary to test all the implications of theory. Table 4 presents descriptive statistics on the empirical indicators I used. The appendix presents more information on how the data for each variable were collected. Table 5 presents the results of five models evaluating the influence of economic structure, party, and region on each senator's foreign policy voting score.

The models in table 5 support the argument that regional variation in policy preferences is related to the influence of economic structure. Nearly all the economic structural variables are significant and have the predicted sign. Variables representing states in the South and Midwest were also significant in most of the models presented. When included in models with the economic structural variables, their effects were smaller than when they were used alone. Political party was significant in every case. I will address the effects of the various aspects of economic structure in turn.

TABLE 4.   Descriptive Statistics

Variable	Mean	Std. Dev.	Minimum	Maximum
Trade				
Ratio of . . .				
Exports to value added by				
industries in state	0.12	0.04	0.04	0.27
Imports to value added by				
industries in state	0.07	0.12	0.01	0.86
Portfolio Investment				
Proportion of total bank lending . . .				
To all non-U.S. borrowers	0.007	0.014	0.00	0.072
To Asia	0.003	0.014	0.00	0.033
To Europe	0.006	0.009	0.00	0.053
Direct Investment				
Proportion of 200 largest				
corporations headquartered in				
state with . . .				
Subsidiaries outside the				
Western Hemisphere	0.16	0.27	0.00	1.00
No foreign subsidiaries	0.76	0.33	0.00	1.00
Either no foreign subsidiaries				
or only in Third World				
extractive industries	0.85	0.25	0.00	1.00
Party and Region				
States in the Midwest or				
Mountain West	0.39	0.49	0.00	1.00
States in the South	0.31	0.47	0.00	1.00
Democratic party	0.57	0.50	0.00	1.00

TABLE 5. Economic Structure, Geography, Party, and Voting on National Security Policy

Variable	Model 1	Model 2	Model 3	Model 4
Trade				
Ratio of . . .				
Exports to value added				
by industries in state	–0.71	–0.53	–0.70	
	(0.86)	(0.86)	(0.86)	
Imports to value added				
by industries in state	–0.68**	–0.73**	–0.76**	
	(0.32)	(0.36)	(0.36)	
Portfolio Investment				
Proportion of total bank lending . . .				
To all non-U.S. borrowers	1.94			
	(3.20)			
To Asia		–126.3*	201.8***	
		(68.5)	(58.4)	
To Europe		81.7*	129.2***	
		(43.4)	(37.1)	
Direct Investment				
Proportion of 200 largest				
corporations headquartered in				
state with subsidiaries outside				
the Western Hemisphere	0.31**	0.28*	0.25*	
	(0.15)	(0.15)	(0.15)	
Party and Region				
States in the Midwest or				
Mountain West	–0.25	–0.20*		–0.34***
	(0.10)	(0.10)		(0.09)
States in the South	–0.28	–0.20		–0.31***
	(0.13)	(0.13)		(0.11)
Democratic party	1.11***	1.08***	1.04***	1.09***
	(0.09)	(0.09)	(0.07)	(0.09)
Intercept	–0.08	–0.17	–0.29	–0.10
	(0.14)	(0.14)	(0.13)	(0.08)
Adjusted *R*-squared	0.68	0.69	0.68	0.66

Note: The dependent variable is the foreign policy voting score for each senator, given in tables 1 and 2. The standard errors are in parentheses.

*p < .10   **p < .05   ***p < .01

Commercial Policy Interests

As expected, trade interests had important political effects. Senators from relatively import-sensitive states were more likely to oppose the administration's foreign policy than were senators from states with a lower ratio of imports to total value added. Although export orientation did not have the expected effect of boosting support for the administration's foreign policy, this finding accords with previous research. Baldwin (1985, 63–67) found that districts dominated by import-sensitive industries produced House members likely to vote in favor of trade protection.[14] As in the models presented here, Baldwin also found that the sign on his export sector variable was contrary to what he predicted and that it was not statistically significant. Baldwin points out that it is probably more difficult for firms in the export sector to overcome the collective-action problems inherent in organizing for political lobbying. Unlike import-competing firms, for which the costs and benefits of trade protection are immediately evident, exporters are not immediately affected, if they are affected at all, by domestic trade protection. The possibility of foreign retaliation against their products exists, of course, but this is only likely if the countries to which exports are sent are the same as those against whose goods tariffs are directed.

Although American exports greatly exceeded imports during the immediate postwar era, some industries nevertheless faced significant competition from imported goods. Table 6 lists the 13 most import-sensitive sectors of the U.S. economy and the states in which they were concentrated. In general, mining and primary-products manufacturing, such as sugar, wood products, textiles, and primary metals, were more likely to face foreign competition than more technologically advanced industries, such as fabricated metal, machinery, and transportation equipment. Import-competing industries like those in table 6 viewed the administration's efforts to reduce the European and Japanese balance-of-payments deficits by promoting imports with greater concern than did industries that faced less foreign competition. Many of the most import-sensitive industries were concentrated in the South and Mountain West, which tended to produce senators that were less supportive of the administration's foreign policy than senators from other areas of the country.[15]

Table 7 presents some information on the states where import-competing industries were most concentrated and clarifies several aspects of the statistical relationships presented in table 5. First, it should not be surprising that, even in the most import-sensitive states, many of the largest industries did not face serious foreign competition. Even Nevada and Arizona, where import-sensitive mining enterprises played a large role in the economy, other large industries in the state, such as cattle ranching, had few foreign competitors. Because the benefits of trade protection are concentrated, while its costs are dispersed among consumers throughout the country, import-competing industries can more easily organize themselves for political action. The influence of the import-competing sector was based more on its advantageous political position than on the aggregate interests of the whole state economy. Second, although the import sensitivity of industries in the state had a statistically significant effect on senators across all 48 states, this influence was not evident in every case. These eight states produced some of the most prominent administration opponents in the Senate, such as Patrick McCarran (D-NV), but other senators from these states were quite supportive of the administration. Although major features of their state's economic structure tended to influence senators' foreign policy preferences, they were obviously not decisive in every case.

TABLE 6. Most Import-Sensitive Industries

Industry or Agricultural Commodity	Ratio of Imports to Value Added in the Industry	States Where Greatest Value Added in Sector
Miscellaneous metal ores (SIC 109)	2.56	California, Colorado, Nevada
Wool, shorn	2.54	Texas, Wyoming, Montana, California
Sugar (SIC 206)	1.87	Louisiana, California, Colorado, New York
Miscellaneous nonmetallic mineral (SIC 149)	1.78	New York, North Carolina, Vermont, Nevada
Gum and wood chemicals (SIC 286)	1.02	Georgia, Mississippi, Florida, Louisiana
Bauxite (SIC 1051)	0.93	Arkansas
Primary nonferrous metals (SIC 333)	0.92	Texas, New Jersey, Illinois, Oklahoma
Ferro-alloy ores (SIC 106)	0.62	Nevada, California, North Carolina, Montana
Miscellaneous textile goods (SIC 229)	0.57	Pennsylvania, New York, Massachusetts, New Jersey
Meat, lard, and hides	0.50	Pennsylvania, Wisconsin, Ohio, Michigan, Illinois
Natural abrasives (SIC 146)	0.47	California
Pulp, paper, and paperboard (SIC 261)	0.42	Washington, Wisconsin, New York, Maine
Fur animals and pelts	0.41	Wisconsin, Texas, California, Minnesota

Source: Census of Manufacturers (1947), Census of Mineral Industries (1950), Census of Agriculture (1954), Schedule B. See the appendix for details on data collection and the calculation of import sensitivity.

TABLE 7. States with Largest Concentration of Import-Competing Industries

State (Ratio of imports to total value added in state)	Largest Industries in State (Ratio of imports to value added in the industry)	Senators (Party, foreign policy voting score)
Nevada (0.86)	Nonferrous metal mining, especially copper and silver (0.10–2.56) Cattle (0) Sheep and wool (0–2.54)	McCarran (D, 0.05) Malone (R, –0.92)
Montana (0.20)	Cattle (0) Grain (0.06) Petroleum and natural gas (0.02) Lumber and timber (0.11) Sheep and wool (0–2.54) Metal and mineral mining (0.11–1.78)	Ecton (R, –0.81) Murray (D, 1.00)
North Dakota (0.16)	Grain (0.06) Cattle (0) Hogs (0) Dairy farming (0) Sheep and wool (0–2.54)	Langer (R, –0.57) Young (R, –0.70)
South Dakota (0.14)	Cattle (0) Hogs (0) Grain (0.06) Other livestock, especially poutry, dairy cattle, and sheep (0.02–2.54) Meat packing (0) Gold mining (0)	Mundt (R, –0.49) Gurney (R, 0.12)
Arizona (0.12)	Copper mining (0.10) Cotton (0.03) Cattle (0) Metal refining, especially copper (0.92)	Chavez (D, 0.75) Hayden (D, 1.00)
Idaho (0.12)	Grain (0.06) Cattle (0) Other farm products, especially potatoes (0.01–0.02) Lumber and timber (0.11) Metal mining, especially lead, zinc, gold, and silver (0–0.11)	Dworshak (R, –0.68) Miller (D, 1.00) Taylor (D, 0.42)
Colorado (0.11)	Cattle (0) Petroleum and natural gas (0.02) Metal and mineral mining (0–2.56) Grain (0.06) Primary metal industries (0–0.92)	E. Johnson (D, –0.09) Millikin (R, –0.38)
Florida (0.10)	Fruits (0.12) Food processing, especially canning and preserving (0–0.17) Vegetables and horticultural specialties (0.03–0.05) Lumber and wood products (0–0.11) Crushed stone and mineral fertilizer mining (0)	Holland (D, 0.86) Pepper (D, 0.89)

Source: Census of Manufactures (1947), Census of Mineral Industries (1950), Census of Agriculture (1954), Schedule B, *Congressional Quarterly Almanac.* See the appendix for details on data collection and the calculation of import sensitivity and voting scores.

Portfolio Investor Interests

The models presented in table 5 also indicate that the interests of banks in their home state had a significant influence on the way senators voted. Because the variable for the overall level of international lending was not significant in model 1, the regional orientation of the banks' international activities is apparently more important. Models 2 and 3 indicate that senators from states where banks lent heavily to Asia tended to oppose the administration's foreign policy, while senators from states where banks lent heavily to Europe tended to favor it. The international lending variables are highly collinear with the Southern and Midwestern regional variables. As a result, the lending variables are more significant in model 3, when the regional variables are omitted.

Given the perceived weakness of the administration's commitment to preserving a favorable climate for investment in Asia and the corresponding strength of its commitment to Europe, the importance of banks' regional orientations makes sense. Moreover, the robust influence of these interests is particularly striking in view of the relatively small amounts of money involved. As table 8 indicates, even European lending was a tiny fraction of total bank activity. The volume of Asian lending was even smaller. Clearly, these internationally oriented elements of the financial sector had an influence on policy far out of proportion to their role in the U.S. economy.

When used in models like those in table 5, a variable representing lending to Latin America was not significant. This finding also fits the interpretation of foreign policy offered here. Although the total U.S. portfolio investment stake in Latin America was almost as large as that in Europe and was much larger than its stake in Asia, policy there was not as controversial as policy toward these regions. Latin America did not face the same threats of communist domination or incorporation into a potential autarkic European imperial trading area as other areas of the world in the late 1940s. No costly effort was required to maintain U.S. access to this region.

A wide range of other evidence also points to the importance of the international financial sector in this case. As I noted earlier, internationally oriented banking interests were well represented among the individuals making U.S. foreign policy. Paul Nitze, Robert Lovett, Averell Harriman, James Forrestal, and John McCloy were investment bankers in New York when they were not working in government. Dean Acheson, Thomas Finletter, and John Foster Dulles, among others, were lawyers for large firms in New York and Washington. These leading officials drew many of their subordinates from these same circles. Many were Republicans, but all shared a commitment to the idea that the United States should play an active role in promoting a liberal international economic order in order to preserve American access to trade and investment opportunities, especially in Europe. These same financial interests were directly involved in implementing the aid program. Through August 10, 1950, the Economic Cooperation Administration had issued letters of commitment to 59 U.S. banks for Marshall Plan aid funds, at the request of participating countries. The top 13 banks received more than 90 percent of the $4 billion these letters of commitment represented. All but one of these banks were based in New York, and the group included Brown Brothers Harriman, in which Averell Harriman and Robert Lovett were partners.[16]

There are good reasons to believe that the financial sector has significant influence over political action by business groups in general. Ferguson (1983, 16) notes that large financial institutions often play central roles in business organizations, partly due to their ability to exert leverage over other firms and thereby help overcome the collective-action problems inherent in building and maintaining such organizations. Along these same lines, McKeown (1994) presents statistical evidence that financial institutions played a significant role in political action committee formation during the 1975–84 period. The evidence presented here supports these earlier findings about the political influence of banks.

TABLE 8.   International Lending by U.S. Banks in 1950 (millions of dollars)

Federal Reserve City	Total Loans by Member Banks	Total Claims on Foreigners	Europe	Latin America	Asia
New York	13900.6	1002.7	410.6	343.2	81.4
San Francisco	6559.1	133.2	59.9	33.4	25.4
Chicago	6278.0	45.0	20.8	17.2	0.9
Philadelphia	4451.7	10.8	5.2	2.4	0.1
Boston	4056.0	49.0	12.2	29.2	0.1
Richmond	2405.3	0.2	0.0	0.1	0.0
Dallas	2263.2	9.6	2.0	7.1	0.0
Atlanta	2260.8	6.3	0.3	5.8	0.0
Cleveland	2042.0	24.0	11.5	11.2	0.3
St. Louis	2033.4	2.9	0.2	2.4	0.1
Kansas City	1667.6	0.0	0.0	0.0	0.0
Minneapolis	1226.0	0.5	0.1	0.1	0.0
Total	49143.7	1284.2	522.8	452.1	108.3

Source: Data on foreign lending are from B-2 reports submitted by Federal Reserve member banks and released to the author under the Freedom of Information Act. Data on total lending activity are from the *Statistical Abstract of the United States.*

Direct Investor Interests

The empirical results presented in table 5 indicate that the interests of large firms with foreign direct investments also influenced senators' voting patterns. The variable used in table 5 indicates that senators from states where corporations with direct investments outside the Western Hemisphere were headquartered were more likely to favor the administration's foreign policy. This finding makes sense because the policy was intended to develop a world order that would protect these investments. The results presented in table 9 also support the argument that the interests of large firms in their state influenced senators' foreign policy preferences. Model 2 indicates that senators from states where large corporations lacking foreign subsidiaries were headquartered tended to oppose the administration's foreign policy. These domestically oriented corporations had much less interest in the values this policy sought to protect. To them, the administration's proposals probably seemed excessively expensive.

The results of model 3 indicate that domestically oriented corporations and those with extractive investments in the Third World had complementary political effects. The fall of China appeared to indicate that the administration's foreign policy was not intended to insure direct territorial access or control in Third World countries. Frieden (1989; 1994) makes a compelling case that investors of this sort are the most likely to favor direct colonial rule. Kobrin (1980) has demonstrated that these investments are more likely to be expropriated by local governments than are direct investments in manufacturing, so the source of these interests is clear. Cumings (1990, 23–24, 97–100) has also noted that the opposition to the Truman administration's internationalist foreign policy came not only from isolationists, but from what he calls "expansionists" associated with extractive industries. These statistical results offer additional support for these arguments.

One final potentially important methodological issue deserves consideration here. Because the voting score cannot take on values higher than 1 or lower than –1, it may misrepresent support for or opposition to the administration's program among extremists on both sides. The observed voting score is bounded at 1 and –1, but the true unobservable levels of support and opposition to the administration's foreign policy are not bounded. There may be meaningful differences in support for the administration among senators who always voted either against or in favor of its policies. However, under the coded scheme used here, all of these senators receive voting scores of 1 or –1. In fact, although no senator voted against the administration's foreign policy in every case, 11 senators were perfect supporters of the administration, receiving scores of 1.

In order to assess the importance of this issue, I reestimated the models presented here using tobit regression, a method developed to model variables in which some observations are censored beyond some maximum or minimum value (Tobin 1958; King 1989, 208–13; Greene 1997, 962–65). The tobit model used here assumes that voting scores greater than 1 are censored, and that scores of 1 may actually represent some

TABLE 9.   Direct Investor Interests and National Security Policy Voting

Variable	Model 1	Model 2	Model 3
Trade			
Ratio of . . .			
Exports to value added by industries	—0.53	–0.38	–0.27
in state	(0.86)	(0.85)	(0.85)
Imports to value added by industries	–0.73**	–0.77**	–0.72**
in state	(0.36)	(0.36)	(0.36)
Portfolio Investment			
Proportion of total bank lending . . .			
To Asia	–126.3*	–127.4*	–130.0*
	(68.5)	(68.6)	(68.6)
To Europe	81.7*	83.1*	84.5*
	(43.4)	(43.4)	(43.4)
Direct Investment			
Proportion of 200 largest corporations			
headquartered in state within . . .			
subsidiaries outside the	0.31**		
Western hemisphere	(0.15)		
no subsidiaries outside		–0.21*	
the Western hemisphere		(0.12)	
no subsidiaries outside the			–0.26*
Western hemisphere, or			(0.15)
with subsidiaries in Third			
World extractive industries			
Party and Region			
States in the Midwest or	–0.20*	–0.21**	–0.21**
Mountain West	(0.10)	(0.10)	(0.10)
States in the South	–0.20	–0.20	–0.18
	(0.13)	(0.13)	(0.12)
Democratic party	1.08***	1.08***	1.09***
	(0.09)	(0.09)	(0.09)
Intercept	–0.17	0.02	0.06
	(0.14)	(0.17)	(0.19)
Adjusted R-squared	0.69	0.69	0.69

Note: The dependent variable is the foreign policy voting score for each senator, given in tables 1 and 2. The standard errors are in parentheses.
  *$p < .10$ **$p < .05$ ***$p < .01$

higher value in terms of true support for the administration's foreign policy. Strictly speaking, the voting scores are not censored, since the full range of values they could theoretically have is actually observed. However, one could argue that they are a censored representation of an unobserved latent variable capable of taking a much wider range of values. Table 10 presents tobit estimates corresponding to the least squares estimates presented in table 5.

TABLE 10. Tobit Estimates for the Models in Table 5

Variable	Model 1	Model 2	Model 3	Model 4
Trade				
Ratio of . . .				
Exports to value added by	−0.63	−0.43	−0.67	
industries in state	(0.90)	(0.89)	(0.90)	
Imports to value added by	−0.67**	−0.75**	−0.78**	
industries in state	(0.33)	(0.37)	(0.38)	
Portfolio Investment				
Proportion of total bank lending . . .				
To all non-U.S. borrowers	3.05			
	(3.51)			
To Asia		−160.3**	−244.9***	
		(74.6)	(65.3)	
To Europe		103.9**	157.5***	
		(47.2)	(41.4)	
Direct Investment				
Proportion of 200 largest	0.35**	0.33**	0.30*	
corporations headquartered	(0.16)	(0.15)	(0.16)	
in state with subsidiaries				
outside the Western hemisphere				
Party and Region				
States in the Midwest or	−0.26**	−0.20*	−0.37***	
Mountain West	(0.11)	(0.11)	(0.10)	
States in the South	−0.34**	−0.26*	−0.39***	
	(0.14)	(0.13)	(0.12)	
Democratic party	1.19***	1.17***	1.10***	1.18***
	(0.10)	(0.10)	(0.08)	(0.10)
Intercept	−0.01	−0.20	−0.31**	−0.08
	(0.14)	(0.14)	(0.13)	(0.08)
Log-likelihood	−50.67	−48.45	−50.88	−56.93

Note: The dependent variable is the foreign policy voting score for each senator, given in tables 1 and 2. Of the 106 observations, 11 are right-censored at 1.00. Because there are no observed values of −1.00, there is no left-censoring. The standard errors are in parentheses.
*p < .10   **p < .05   ***p < .01

A comparison of tables 5 and 10 shows that the tobit and least squares estimates are essentially identical. While the coefficients vary slightly, there are no substantively meaningful differences. All of the same variables are significant, the levels of significance are nearly the same, and all of the signs are in the same direction. Because the substantive interpretation of tobit coefficients should include an adjustment for the probability that an observation is censored, they cannot be interpreted in exactly the same way as least squares estimates. However, the precise magnitude of the effects is not very important in this case because the theoretical argument and corresponding interpretation of the statistical results offered here concern only the statistical significance and direction of the effects.

Conclusion

The goals of U.S. Cold War foreign policy extended far beyond the straightforward security interests of the United States. Policymakers in the Truman administration sought to establish and maintain an international order open to American trade and investment. The statistical evidence presented here suggests that, in order to understand who favored it, who opposed it, and why, it makes sense to frame the policy as an effort to shape the international political economy. While it was not always explained in these terms at the time, variations in economic interests help explain the politics of the policy-making process. Not all sectors of the U.S. economy had the same stake in this costly and ambitious policy, and politicians' ties to divergent economic interests in American society shaped their view of the administration's proposals. Senators from states with more import-competing industries, banks that were active in lending to Asia, and large firms with interests opposed to the administration's policies tended to oppose the administration's policy. Senators from states with fewer import-competing firms, banks active in lending to Europe, and large firms with interests outside the Western Hemisphere tended to favor it. Obviously, many idiosyncratic considerations not discussed here may influence the preferences of individual policymakers. My purpose is not to provide an exhaustive account of how each individual formed his or her preferences, but to present an empirically testable way to link these preferences to broader social forces, and to explain general tendencies. The statistical relationships indicated here strongly support this theoretical approach.

The evidence presented here suggests that the relationship between the underlying determinants of policy outcomes and the motives of individual policymakers is not necessarily a simple one. Factors that are never consciously considered by decision makers may nevertheless shape the political arena and strongly influence actual outcomes. In this case, many decision makers may have understood foreign policy primarily in terms of security goals. Whatever their thinking, though, the political coalitions that determined whether the policy would be implemented reflected divisions in the domestic political economy. The fact that particular foreign policy views coincided with the interests of influential groups in society made those views politically viable. Even if the socioeconomic origins of their political coalition were never fully understood by many policymakers, they were just as important in shaping outcomes as the considerations they actually discussed. This point is crucial for historical research on policy development because a theoretically uninformed reading of the archival record will not reveal the importance of these undiscussed socioeconomic factors.

Some historical accounts of the early Cold War period recognize that individual decision makers may fit into a larger structure in ways that they do not recognize. For example, Cumings (1990, 35–42) contends that economic considerations were fundamental to Cold War foreign policy, but also that much of the bureaucracy involved in carrying out this policy understood these considerations poorly. It is possible that many, if not most, U.S. policymakers failed to grasp the economic stakes in the political conflict over policy and instead understood the problem as a security threat. Their self-understanding is not the last word on the matter, however. Analyses of the policy-making process should do more than simply reiterate the policymakers' analyses of the international system. This account of the origins of political factions with different policy preferences sets the stage for the analysis of bargaining between these factions in the chapters that follow.

CHAPTER 5

The Conflictual Politics of Consensus Building I: Korea, Rearmament, and the End of the Fair Deal

[The rearmament program] would probably involve. . . . [r]eduction of federal expenditures for purposes other than defense and foreign assistance, if necessary by the deferment of certain desirable programs.
—NSC 68

[*Interviewer Jerry N.*] *HESS:* What's your opinion of Truman's legislative program?
[*Truman White House Special Counsel Charles*] *MURPHY:* Well, in the foreign policy field I think it was phenomenally successful, and in the domestic field, only moderately.

The statistical evidence presented in chapter 4 links divergent foreign policy preferences to the international interests of different domestic economic sectors. The evidence presented in chapters 2 and 3 indicates that the president's decision to increase the military budget was closely tied to political changes in his administration and his need to maintain the support of the internationalists who dominated the Democratic party. The next three chapters will present historical evidence that the administration's need to secure Republican acquiescence to its ambitious foreign policy eventually produced a tacit political bargain that linked this foreign policy to important parts of the Republicans' domestic agenda. Cold War foreign policy became politically viable because it was linked to the demise of the administration's social welfare proposals and to a campaign against domestic radicals in the labor movement, government, and other areas of American life.

It is tempting to explain the linkage between Cold War foreign policy and the domestic red scare in terms of a single, anticommunist ideological impulse. However, most of the major actors in the process sought either rearmament or an antiradical campaign and opposed the other. A bargaining process between the administration and Congress, rather than some substantive relationship between the policies, linked them together. While the administration sought to use the crisis created by the Korean War to secure congressional support for rearmament, its Republican opponents sought to link the crisis to their anticommunist domestic agenda. By linking the two policies together, both sides were able to secure their top policy priority.

The relative priority the administration and its Republican opponents accorded their domestic and foreign policy agendas set the stage for the trade-off across these two issue areas. Both the administration and its opponents made concessions on less salient issues in order to make gains in areas they believed were more important. The Truman administration placed a greater priority on achieving its goals in foreign policy than in domestic policy. While the advocates of a more ambitious national security policy strengthened their position in the administration in late 1949 and early 1950, the left wing of the party was increasingly excluded from the circle of decision makers surrounding President Truman. Truman's commitment to some elements of the Fair Deal, especially repeal of the Taft-Hartley Act, appears to have been largely rhetorical.

On the other hand, the dominant faction of the Republican party in the Senate had little use for the expensive national security program sought by the State Department. The foreign policy goals they expressed publicly and privately amounted to finding some way to reduce the distraction caused by international events. They had little stake in an open international trading system—indeed, most favored relatively high tariffs (Eden 1985, 185–99). When they demonstrated concern about the Soviet threat, they argued for the use of more economical means than those advocated by the administration. In terms of domestic labor and social welfare policy, however, they had much clearer objectives, revolving around their opposition to most of the social programs of the New Deal and their concern about the power of the labor movement.

The bargaining process began with policy proposals from both the administration and the Republican congressional leadership after U.S. intervention in Korea. The administration requested a $10.5 billion supplement to the fiscal 1951 defense budget on July 19. Five days later the president asked for an additional $4 billion in military aid funds. These requests, which would nearly double the defense budget and triple the size of the Mutual Defense Assistance Program, signaled that the administration's plans for the national security program were far beyond the scope of what had been proposed since the end of World War II. NSC 68 made it clear that relatively modest programs of the sort that had passed the Congress during the preceding five years would no longer suffice. At the same time, the Republican congressional leadership, which was dominated by conservative nationalists, quickly moved to end further progress on Fair Deal programs, something the administration readily conceded. At the same time, they argued that sweeping internal security legislation was also required under the conditions created by the war in Korea. They placed this legislation, which they had long sought, at the top of their agenda.

As in chapters 2 and 3, the next three chapters will compare an account of foreign policy stressing divergent interests rooted in the domestic political economy to realist and statist theoretical approaches. Realist and statist theories of foreign policy do not adequately account for much of the historical evidence about the policy-making process in this case. These theories stress the role of external events interpreted in light of consensual core values, or some objective set of international constraints and incentives. In this case, the influence of the Korean War is the principal explanatory device. The argument that the Korean War explains support for the administration's military spending proposal is plausible but incomplete. An alternative account of the policy-making process stressing bargaining among interests rooted in the domestic political economy has some important advantages.

While it is true, as Jervis (1980, 578) and others have argued, that Korea "changed the domestic political climate and so allowed statesmen to do what they wanted to do before," there is more to the story. First, accounts that stress the role of the Korean War must explain the decision to intervene after the North Korean attack. Historical evidence indicates that this was not an obvious choice. It is not easy to separate it from the administration's ongoing efforts to find a way to secure support for greater military spending. Second, an account stressing the bargaining process explains more about the behavior of the administration's opponents than does one assuming that the Korean War made support unproblematic. Although the war attached high domestic political costs to any effort to block the administration's military spending proposals, it did not change the opinions of major administration opponents. Nationalist Republicans continued to threaten the administration's foreign policy agenda after the war began, and they were able to attach some elements of their domestic agenda onto the crisis. Finally, focusing on domestic political bargaining explains several decisions and political outcomes not captured by accounts stressing the role of the Korean War. As I will explain in detail in the next three chapters, these include not only the demise of the Fair Deal and the expansion of the red scare, but also the conduct of the war.

This chapter addresses the initial stage of the bargaining process that followed the decision to intervene in Korea, focusing on the administration's initial proposal for increased military spending and corresponding conservative moves to put an end to the Fair Deal. Chapter 6 examines the development of a policy current linking the interests of business elites concerned about labor unrest, conservative members of Congress, and bureaucrats seeking an expanded internal security program before 1950. Chapter 7 examines how the bargaining over rearmament after the beginning of the Korean War contributed to the success of this policy current. As in the last two chapters, my goal is to test the ability of contrasting theoretical approaches to account for the details of the policy-making process rather than to extract broad themes or generalizations from the historical evidence.

"He suffered them, but he didn't believe in their movement"

Historians of the Truman era have long debated the reasons for the gap between the lofty rhetoric of the Fair Deal and the relatively meager achievements of the administration in the area of labor and social welfare policy. Harry Truman publicly stressed his commitment to the legacy of the New Deal. In late July of 1948, he called the Republican-controlled Eightieth Congress back into session and demanded that it pass a number of domestic social programs, including several popular measures just adopted as part of the Republican platform. Many of the programs that would later be included in the "Fair Deal" that Truman announced in his 1949 State of the Union address were proposed during the 1948 "Turnip Day" special session of Congress. They included a national health care program, rent controls, and federal aid to education. Truman used the predictable refusal of the Republicans to pass these programs to denounce the Republican party and the "do-nothing" Eightieth Congress during the fall election campaign.[1] During the campaign, Truman also called for the repeal of the Taft-Hartley Act, calling it a "slave labor law." In short, this social welfare agenda was central to Truman's 1948 reelection campaign and to his public rhetoric during the second term, beginning with the Fair Deal speech in 1949. Despite Truman's public commitment to this agenda, however, little of the Fair Deal was ever actually enacted.

The administration's poor domestic record has prompted some historians to raise questions about the sincerity of Truman's commitment to the Fair Deal. For example, Sitkoff (1974, 95–97) notes that the Housing Act of 1949 and the minimum wage law, among the few Fair Deal programs the Congress ultimately passed, were weak compared to the administration's original proposals. The Housing Act authorized the construction of 810,000 new units of public housing, many fewer than had been included in the 1946 Housing Act. The administration did not even pursue the construction of the units authorized, building only 60,000 units during Truman's second term. Congress raised the minimum wage to 75 cents an hour, but only after excluding many previously included categories of workers from coverage under the new law. Similarly, Bernstein (1970, 269–314) has argued that the administration's rhetorical commitment to civil rights was not always matched by strong actions.[2]

The administration's performance in the area of labor law is perhaps the clearest example of the gap between the rhetoric and the reality of the Truman domestic program. Despite Truman's professed opposition to the Taft-Hartley Act, passed over his veto in 1947, the president invoked its injunction provisions to stop strikes eight times in 1948 alone—more than Eisenhower did during his entire presidency (Sitkoff 1974, 93). Charles Murphy, who succeeded Clark Clifford as Truman's special counsel in 1949, recalled that Truman's views on Taft-Hartley were not as unsympathetic as his public position indicated. "[A]s time went on and he considered it more, why, he became more and more of that view."[3] Despite his private views, Truman felt obligated to keep up appearances. When discussing his 1950 legislative agenda with the White House staff, he told them, "We must push [Taft-Hartley repeal]. Our record's got to be clean."[4]

The administration's lukewarm commitment to the labor relations aspects of the Fair Deal makes political sense in light of the position of the labor movement in the Democratic party. Organized labor was strongly tied to the Democratic party and could not credibly threaten to withdraw its support. Unlike money, the loyalties of the blocks of voters represented by organized labor could not easily be switched to the other party if its public policy goals were not met. The president appears to have been more concerned about his public image as an ally of the labor movement than with actual policy outcomes that benefited labor. The failure to achieve these outcomes could always be explained in terms of Republican opposition. Indeed, this was precisely what Truman had done so successfully in 1948. As long as the record of administration actions was clean, there was little the labor movement could do, or threaten to do, that could influence the administration.

The 1948 election exacerbated the weaknesses of the left wing of the Democratic party. Henry Wallace's disastrous third-party campaign for the presidency had attracted many liberal activists who might otherwise have remained within the Democratic party. Wallace's support for liberal social programs and his advocacy of peaceful accommodation with the Soviet Union were attractive to like-minded groups, such as the Progressive Citizens of America, and to left-wing elements of the labor movement.[5] The administration's strategy for dealing with the Progressive party challenge was an all-out campaign to demonstrate that it was dominated by communists and that its supporters were, at best, communist dupes.

Organizations supporting the Wallace campaign sometimes found themselves on the attorney general's list of subversive organizations, a situation that most often resulted in dissolution due to the flight of members concerned about their reputations, as well as difficulties in raising funds or finding meeting places. The criteria for placement on the list were written to be "elastic and flexible," and it was freely used against foreign policy dissenters.[6] The decision by some unions in the Congress of Industrial Organizations (CIO) to endorse the Wallace candidacy created serious conflict within the leadership of the CIO. All the unions that had endorsed Wallace were ultimately expelled from the organization in 1949 and 1950. Few of them survived.[7]

Individuals who had actively supported the Wallace campaign were also subject to various forms of official harassment, whether from the FBI, which kept a close eye on the activities of the Wallace campaign, or because of their association with groups on the attorney general's list of subversive organizations, which made government employment impossible. FBI reports on the Wallace campaign's strategy and the identity of its supporters were periodically sent to the White House. These reports also helped fill the individual files maintained by the Bureau, which were used in security clearance proceedings for government employees and were sometimes also furnished to private employers.[8] In general, supporters of the Wallace campaign were politically marginalized and without influence in either party.

While a hunt for domestic communists now seems naturally linked to Cold War foreign policy, it was not the only logical or possible domestic corollary to the international confrontation with the Soviet Union. A push for greater achievements in domestic social policy might have been presented as a way to demonstrate that communism was not the best alternative open to workers. Indeed, this was roughly the course of action Wallace and most of his supporters advocated. As Theoharis (1971), Freeland (1972), and others have argued, by ruling out this way of linking domestic and foreign policy and stigmatizing those who had advocated these policies, the administration made it easier for its Republican opponents to argue that the fight against international communism demanded a similar offensive at home. This conceptual issue linkage—made by both the administration and its Republicans opponents—can be understood as the ideological result of efforts to remove their common opponents from the political arena.

While they did not face the political repression directed against the Progressive party, major anticommunist liberals also earned the enmity of the administration during the 1948 campaign. Although they had opposed Henry Wallace and even participated in the red-baiting of the Progressive party, the leadership of the Americans for Democratic Action (ADA) had also opposed Truman's renomination bid. The ADA leadership worked to draft Dwight Eisenhower or William O. Douglas as the party's candidate prior to the Democratic convention. These efforts did not pass unnoticed by Truman and his political advisers. Truman's appointments secretary and political gatekeeper, Matthew Connelly, recalled that "he suffered them, but he didn't believe in their movement."[9] In 1948, the financially troubled Truman campaign turned instead to conservatives like Louis Johnson, who became Truman's chief fund-raiser.[10] The fund-raising group headed by Louis Johnson had a decidedly small-business flavor and included Francis Matthews, a Nebraska lawyer and a key figure in the anticommunist campaign waged by the United States Chamber of Commerce. Matthews became secretary of the navy when Johnson was named secretary of defense. Always suspicious of the liberals in his party, Truman was even more ill-disposed toward them after the 1948 campaign.

Truman's poor relationship with the liberals and his weak attachment to their policy agenda were paralleled by the gradual disappearance of major liberal figures from his administration. Truman replaced most of Roosevelt's cabinet with individuals less closely associated with the New Deal. Harold Ickes and Henry Wallace, held over from the Roosevelt administration as secretaries of the interior and commerce, were among the few well-known liberals who remained in his cabinet after 1945.[11] Both departed under unpleasant circumstances in 1946. The lack of such people in the administration was a continuing source of concern to liberals outside the administration and contributed to their tepid support for Truman in 1948.

In contrast to the administration's ambivalence toward the domestic legacy of the New Deal, it did not turn away from the Roosevelt administration's internationalist foreign policy. Most major Truman administration foreign-policy makers had also served in the Roosevelt administration. In contrast to his treatment of New Deal domestic policy elite, Truman retained and promoted many Roosevelt administration holdovers in the area of foreign policy. For example, Averell Harriman initially came to Truman's attention as ambassador to the Soviet Union, but he was appointed secretary of commerce in 1946 and held a series of other key positions afterward. Similarly, Truman promoted State Department officials who had served in the Roosevelt administration to high positions there, while he often brought in political allies from outside the government to fill such positions in other departments. Lacking experience in this area, Truman frequently deferred to the judgment of foreign policy experts in his administration. George Elsey recalled that "[t]o the President, the Secretary of State was number one. The State Department was the senior department."[12] Matthew Connelly commented that Truman liked and trusted Acheson, although Connelly himself viewed the secretary of state as "an egghead, not a practical administrator, and not a man who represented the opinion of America, or of the people of America."[13]

In sum, the administration's commitment to its national security policy was much stronger than its commitment to the Fair Deal. Although the administration proposed these programs, and Truman would probably have signed them into law if they had reached his desk, the priority placed on getting them through Congress was not high. They were secondary considerations compared to the administration's foreign policy agenda. In contrast to the domestic programs of the Fair Deal, there is no evidence of ambivalence in Truman's commitment to his administration's foreign policy goals. When domestic and international priorities conflicted, foreign policy considerations usually took precedence. In the executive branch debate over rearmament, the expectation that such a policy would require cuts in domestic social programs was a minor consideration. This debate centered not around the effects of rearmament on the Fair Deal, but on its implications for fiscal policy.

"I would reverse this policy"

Given the prevailing mood of the Congress in the spring of 1950, the proponents of NSC 68 had good reason to worry about how the program would fare. There were indications that Congress might cut even the much smaller military spending proposals contemplated in the fiscal 1951 budget. News reports on the administration's proposed budget stressed the desire of many in Congress to cut it further. *U.S. News and World Report* noted in December 1949 that Senator Harry Byrd (D-VA) had prepared an alternative to the president's budget that would reduce the proposed $13.5 billion military budget to $10 billion. When the president's budget message was released in January 1950, *Time* reported that

> [i]n both Houses one of the warmest debates would come over taxes and the new budget, which was giving concern even to some staunch Administration Democrats. Majority Leader Scott Lucas hopefully predicted a cut of $1 billion in foreign aid and $2 billion in military spending. Illinois' rising Freshman Senator Paul Douglas, a Fair Dealer, wanted to trim the budget by $4.5 billion.

When the House Appropriations Committee reported the budget out in April, it contained $1 billion in reductions from the president's original proposals. Critics demanded additional cuts, especially in foreign aid.[14]

Except in the columns of Joseph and Stewart Alsop, there is little evidence in the contemporary press of the sense of crisis mentioned by Wells (1979, 117). Indeed, Acheson privately commented in March that "the American people have a false sense of security and do not realize the world situation."[15] Leffler (1992, 358–59) differs from Wells on this particular point, arguing that the military threat was not sufficient to make the call for more military spending in NSC 68 very compelling. Getting the rearmament program through the Congress promised to be a difficult task.

The administration's staunchest opponents, the Nationalist Republicans, were the main obstacle to the rearmament program. They were especially strong in the Senate. Although they made up slightly less than one-third of the Senate, they were able to draw on the support of conservative Democrats against some administration initiatives. Given the general consensus in favor of cuts in military spending, they might well have blocked the rearmament program in the absence of an administration strategy to prevent them from doing so. Indeed, as I will explain later, the possibility that they would block the program remained even after the beginning of the Korean War. Liberal Democrats might grumble about inaction on the Fair Deal, but only the Nationalist Republicans could assemble a coalition to block the rearmament program.

The Nationalist Republicans in the Senate were probably more powerful at the beginning of 1950 than at any time since the Democrats had regained control of the House and Senate in the 1948 elections. Republican internationalists were largely leaderless in Vandenberg's absence, and the nationalists controlled nearly all Senate leadership positions. The effectiveness of Nationalist Republican opposition to the administration's foreign policy grew after the Communist revolution in China. After the August 1949 release of the State Department's white paper acknowledging the effective control of China by the Communists, a small but vocal group of senators with ties to the Chinese Nationalist regime began loudly attacking U.S. foreign policy in the Far East, charging that communist sympathizers in the State Department had helped bring the Chinese Communists to power. Since some of the members of the "China bloc," especially William Knowland (R-CA), Styles Bridges (R-NH), and H. Alexander Smith (R-NJ), had previously been considered internationalists, their opposition made the position of the administration's foreign policy more precarious than before. Patrick McCarran's (D-NV) central role in the China bloc—as well as the efforts of Joseph McCarthy (R-WI), which began in February 1950—added to the erosion of support.

Both the goals and the priorities of the Nationalist Republicans differed from those prevailing in the administration. While they opposed the administration's national security program, most Nationalist Republicans were less concerned about its specifics than were the members of the China bloc. Most viewed it simply as an especially extravagant line item in a federal budget they believed was too large. While Acheson and others had an ambitious vision for the world role of the United States and sought a correspondingly ambitious foreign policy, the Nationalist Republican leadership had much more modest goals and viewed much of the national security program as an unnecessary expense. In January 1950, Kenneth Wherry wrote to the publisher of the *World Herald* in Omaha, stating that he hoped for an agreement with the Soviets that "will provide the opportunity whereby we can put our financial house in order, reduce taxes, and keep off our backs controls, regimentations and directives issued by our Federal bureaus."[16] Robert Taft expressed similar sentiments in a handwritten note outlining remarks he made to the Republican Policy Committee.

> President Truman places all importance on foreign policy, & domestic economy must be sound to support it. I would reverse this policy. The welfare of the people of the U.S. is the aim of our govt. Foreign policy is only incidental to it—to preserve the freedom of our people from attack & threat of attack.[17]

In contrast to their foreign policy preferences, the domestic policy goals of the Nationalist Republicans were more salient and clearly defined. Since the 1930s, conservative Republicans had been especially interested in reducing the size and scope of government involvement in the economy. These themes continued to loom large in their policy agenda during the postwar era, sometimes to the virtual exclusion of foreign policy issues. The personal papers of individual Nationalist Republicans are filled with evidence of their commitment to these policies. A document summarizing the "General Program of Republican Congress," found in the papers of Styles Bridges, lists reductions in the scope of federal regulations, the number of federal agencies, the size of the federal budget, and the amount of federal taxes as the top four goals. Foreign policy is not mentioned.[18] During the 1950 campaign, Kenneth Wherry ridiculed the administration's social welfare agenda, referring to it as the "fare-well deal" and arguing that it was "the Administration's blueprint for socialism."[19] Robert Taft had risen to prominence on the basis of his opposition to the New Deal and to most subsequent social welfare programs.[20] While their international goals were minimal and generally defined in negative terms, their domestic agenda was more ambitious.

The division of authority between Taft and Vandenberg prior to Vandenberg's illness also indicates that nationalists placed a higher priority on domestic than on foreign policy. Taft was willing to follow Vandenberg's lead in foreign policy—even voting for programs he had publicly opposed—in return for similar support from Vandenberg in the domestic arena.[21] While this arrangement irritated some less accommodating nationalists, it did not erode their support for Taft's leadership. Patterson (1972, 339) quotes Kenneth Wherry telling a reporter, "I like him, goddamit, even if we have had a hell of a time keeping him from climbing in Claude Pepper's lap." In general, the party was more united in its opposition to the Fair Deal than in its opposition to administration foreign policy. The data presented in the last chapter indicate that 16 of the 46 Republicans had voting scores indicating some support for the administration's foreign policy, while only nine had scores indicating support for the Fair Deal.

An important part of the Republicans' attempt to reverse various aspects of the New Deal was their effort to reduce the power of labor unions. When the staff of the nationalist-dominated Senate Republican Policy Committee examined senators' voting records in search of potential allies, they used only votes on the Taft-Hartley Act and efforts to repeal it. Based on these votes, they ranked senators from "reliable conservatives" through "incorrigible New Dealers."[22] Among Robert Taft's major legislative accomplishments was the passage of the Taft-Hartley Act in 1947 and its subsequent defense against Democratic efforts to repeal or weaken it. Many conservatives viewed the labor movement as the backbone of their liberal opponents and were especially worried about its potential electoral influence. Taft's 1950 reelection effort reflected serious concern about the labor movement's effort to defeat him. The Taft campaign kept a close watch on the CIO's media campaign, devising special written materials designed to counter the charges made against the senator. They also organized a "Labor League for Taft" in an effort to publicize worker support for him. (Its organizer, Eugene Carr, reported that he had trouble producing "actual union members" at rallies and had to rely on "leading industrialists" to encourage their workers to attend.) In his responses to congratulatory letters from political allies after winning the election, Taft made a point of expressing his pleasure at receiving the votes of 40 percent of union members.[23]

Taft was by no means alone among Senate Republicans in his concerns about the political clout of the labor movement. The Republican National Committee prepared a special report on labor's contributions to Democratic senators. Kenneth Wherry also received anxious reports about the activities of the labor movement in his state. Before the 1950 election, one supporter wrote with alarm that the CIO had been raising money in Nebraska for use against Republican candidates. Although it probably did little to assuage Wherry's concerns, he added hopefully that a CIO fund-raiser had assured him it would be used against "only those who they know positively are representing selfish interests for the benefit of industry."[24]

"From then on we explained it in terms of the Korean problem"

For those seeking a way to get the rearmament program through a hostile Congress, Korea provided a tremendous opportunity. As I noted in the last chapter, the use of the Korean War to secure passage of the rearmament program in Congress inevitably raises questions about the real motives for U.S. intervention there. Did President Truman commit troops simply to get his program through Congress? Although the answer to this question is not really necessary to support the argument made here, a brief consideration of the issue is useful because it addresses the misgivings many readers have about explanations of national security policy that stress domestic politics.

Most people have serious normative qualms about the use of force for domestic political purposes. Particularly for those who believe that foreign policy reflects the national interest, the contention that decisions about the use of military force were made to serve other ends implies a sinister conspiracy on the part of the decision makers. Arguments about the use of international incidents for domestic purposes are more widely heard and accepted when the moral character of the actors involved is either believed to be low or is unimportant to the audience. Discussion of the domestic sources of German foreign policy before World War I, for example, is less likely to raise the ire of an American audience than is a comparable discussion of U.S. foreign policy. Similarly, arguments about the importance of domestic politics are more commonly made and are more widely accepted with respect to the Vietnam era, since beliefs about the depravity—or at least the error-prone worldviews—of major decision makers are relatively widespread. The suggestion that a well-regarded historical figure such as Harry S. Truman was involved in such sordid activity is viscerally unacceptable to many people.[25]

These concerns miss the point of my argument. While I contend that the notion of the national interest has very limited usefulness as an explanatory concept, the theory I have presented here is quite compatible with the argument that all decision makers act on their sincere beliefs about the national interest at all times. My claim is that regardless of decision makers' beliefs about the national interest, any policy serves the interests of some segments of society and harms the interests of others. Decision makers tend to prefer policies that serve their own interests and those of others with whom they have political, social, economic, or other ties. The way the decision makers understood these policies and rationalized them to the public may be interesting for some purposes, but it is irrelevant to my argument about the socioeconomic sources of foreign policy.

With this caveat in mind, some informed speculation—for accounts of individual motives can never be much more—about the motives of the major players in the decision to commit U.S. forces to Korea is possible based on the available evidence. Cumings (1990, 408–38) presents a convincing argument and substantial evidence that Dean Acheson was awaiting some sort of action by the Soviets or Chinese that would allow him to secure policies he believed were necessary and important. The remarks he made to Christian Herter, quoted at length in chapter 3, are perhaps the secretary of state's clearest statement on the subject. Truman's motives, on the other hand, are less clear. Because he was looking for other ways to get the rearmament program through Congress, he may not have believed such a crisis was necessary. Since Truman relied heavily on his advisers in foreign policy matters, Acheson was able to present the Korean crisis to the president in a way that made Truman more likely to intervene.

Evidence about the decision-making process supports this interpretation. Acheson suggested all of the initial moves in the crisis to Truman and interpreted the North Korean attack as a direct Soviet challenge to American credibility, rather than as the culmination of a local civil war or an independent initiative by North Korea. Acheson had framed events in China, where he opposed intervention, very differently. Cumings (1990, 625) notes that Acheson instructed John Hickerson, the under secretary of state for United Nations affairs, to ask the secretary-general to call a meeting of the Security Council on Korea before consulting the president. At the administration's meetings on the Korean situation, between June 25 and June 28, Acheson spoke first, summarizing the situation and offering proposals that were eventually accepted by everyone.[26] Cumings (1990, 627) also points out that Acheson apparently also drafted the statement on Korea that was eventually issued by the president on June 27.

Acheson's account (1969, 405) of the decisions following the North Korean attack treats the U.S. troop commitment as inevitable. "When I set off to meet the President [on June 25], I had no plan, but my mind was pretty clear on where the course we were about to recommend would lead and why it was necessary that we follow that course." Acheson did not share his sense of the situation with other administration decision makers, however, even when they sought to limit U.S. involvement. Truman was initially hesitant to commit ground forces to Korea, stating on June 26 that "I don't want to go to war," but Acheson continued to stress the need for action. The secretary of state initially agreed to postpone the question of committing ground forces at the June 26 meeting, when sentiment among military chiefs present at the meeting was running strongly against this course of action. Two days later, when these skeptical military advisers were not present, Acheson was less guarded in his advice, steering the president toward further intervention.

> SECRETARY ACHESON pointed to the serious nature of the situation if the difficulties in Korea increased instead of our meeting with quick success.
> THE PRESIDENT said he didn't intend to back out unless there should develop a military situation which we had to meet elsewhere.
> SECRETARY ACHESON suggested that the President might wish the Military Establishment to review United States forces available in the Far East in case the President should decide later that he wished to act.
> THE PRESIDENT said that was right.[27]

Predictably, Truman did not back down from a crisis presented to him in this way, nor did he bother to consult prior policy as a basis for his judgment about the strategic importance of Korea. Although the president made the decision to commit the first ground troops on June 30 without first consulting the secretary of state or anyone else, Acheson (1969, 412) later noted that "[t]he request from the front and the President's response came as no surprise for me."

The commitment of U.S. forces to the defense of South Korea was facilitated by the knowledge that a case would soon have to be made for rearmament and that military action of this sort would make this task much easier. At the time, of course, no one knew that intervention would lead to a long and costly war. Despite the military situation on the ground in Korea, administration decision makers had great faith in their ability to defeat North Korean forces militarily. Since they had presided over the absolute defeat of Germany and Japan just a few years before, this confidence is understandable. Cumings (1990, 709–10) and Foot (1985, 72–73) report that by July 1, just a few days after troops were committed and with U.S. and South Korean forces struggling to maintain a foothold at the southern tip of the peninsula, plans for an occupation of North Korea were already being discussed. Korea promised both domestic and international success to U.S. decision makers. The problems it would bring lay hidden in the future.

In any event, prior policy toward Korea was abruptly cast aside after

June 25. As noted in chapter 3, the standing policy expressed in NSC 8/2 was to send aid to South Korea but to avoid direct military involvement there. However, officials from the State Department and the National Security Council staff who might have been expected to refer to NSC 8/2 as a basis for decision making in the wake of the North Korean attack were all deeply involved in the planning of the rearmament program. At the meetings in the days following the North Korean attack, they supported Acheson's dire definition of the situation and the options open to the president. Examining the summaries of these meetings, one might think that the NSC had never discussed policy toward Korea before. Military intervention solved serious and important domestic political problems for the decision makers. This realization can only have given them an added incentive to play along with the inherent drama of the situation and allow the president to seize the opportunity for them.

While Acheson's account of the decision-making process lends it an air of inevitability, not everyone involved in the decisions shared his sense of where the process was leading. Those not already committed to rearmament were considerably more cautious about the appropriate response to events in Korea. At the June 25 meeting, Louis Johnson and Frank Pace—participating in his new capacity as secretary of the army—both opposed the commitment of ground forces. Johnson sought corresponding restrictions on the orders given to General MacArthur. The chairman of the Joint Chiefs of Staff, Omar Bradley, also "questioned the advisability of putting in ground units particularly if large numbers were involved." Johnson and Bradley both appeared to be at least as concerned about Taiwan as about Korea, suggesting that action be taken to deter an attack there. Reversing his previous position, Acheson agreed and suggested that the Seventh Fleet be sent to the waters between Taiwan and China.[28]

The decision to intervene may have come as a surprise to some outside the administration as well. As James Hershberg (1993, 493) notes in his biography of James Conant, although they quickly fell in line once the decision had been made, many administration supporters thought that the Third World in general and Korea in particular were not especially important. The *Washington Post* had editorialized on May 25 that "[t]he moral commitment to Korea is fast running out, as the House has recognized, and, strategically, Korea is another Bataan. The only justification for continued aid is results, and here the utmost realism is necessary in assessing American interests."[29] Even the Democratic chair of the Senate Foreign Relations Committee, Tom Connally, commented that the defense of South Korea was not a major priority in May 1950.[30] Immediately after the attack, most press discussion noted that the United States would probably avoid any troop commitment.[31] Louis Johnson predicted a South Korean victory and promised to keep cutting the military budget.[32]

In contrast to the positions they would take after ground forces had been committed, even Dulles and MacArthur also initially advocated caution. Returning to the United States from a tour of Japan and Korea, Dulles argued strongly against the commitment of ground forces. "I mentioned that General MacArthur had remarked to me at the Haneda airport, just before I left at 12 o'clock Tuesday, June 27th (Japan time), that anyone who advocated [the commitment of ground forces in Korea] ought to have his head examined."[33] Dulles acknowledged in a letter to Walter Lippmann that he had publicly called on the administration to do "something" after the North Korean offensive began, but he stressed his surprise at the ultimate outcome.

> It could have been economic sanctions, blockade, air cover to the Republic of Korea's army, or all-out war by air, sea and land. I did not, myself, anticipate the latter, even after the attack occurred. . . . The decision to use U.S. ground forces on the mainland was wholly a decision by the Defense Establishment itself and it was not, in this respect, under the compulsion of any prior political commitment.

Lippmann shared Dulles's doubts. "We have given hostages to fortune which we would have been much stronger without."[34] The eventual commitment of ground forces may have been the obvious next step for Acheson, for whom rearmament was a high priority, but it was not obvious to others who did not share this goal.

Whatever its view before the fact, the White House had no trouble seeing the domestic political advantages of the Korean War after committing ground forces. The White House and the State Department soon sought to use the situation to secure approval for the military buildup envisioned in NSC 68. After a few days of confusion, the commitment of ground forces set off a rushed effort to assemble a large request for additional spending. Charles Murphy recalled in his oral history interview that

> from then on we explained it in terms of the Korean problem, which I think was permissible. It got kind of muddied, but we had in mind, I think, a clear belief that the general necessities, so far as defense was concerned, required a large increase in our defense strength as well as the Korean fighting. So I expect that you'll find in Presidential documents all during that period, sort of an effort to explain this in a twofold fashion, maybe with a particular emphasis on the Korean part of it.[35]

The administration used the Korean War to secure congressional approval for new expenditures that exceeded all previous postwar programs. Through three supplemental appropriations bills, the fiscal 1951 budget for the Department of Defense nearly quadrupled, rising from $13.3 billion to $44.26 billion.[36] An additional $4 billion was added to the $1.4 billion already requested for MDAP. The Marshall Plan, by contrast, had only amounted to about $12 billion over four years. Little of the additional money was actually slated for use in Korea. Huntington (1963, 55) notes that only $4.5 billion of the $10.5 billion in the first supplemental appropriation was designated for Korea and that the proportion declined in the later supplemental requests. Condit (1988, 224–40) notes that planning for both the fiscal 1951 supplemental budget requests and the fiscal 1952 budget proceeded under assumptions limiting the amount allocated to the fighting in Korea to a relatively small fraction of the budget. Republicans were well aware that the new spending was not going entirely to Korea. General Bonner Fellers, serving as a military consultant to the Republican National Committee, informed Robert Taft that the Joint Chiefs of Staff believed that the war in Korea would cost only $2 billion. The rest of the sum requested by Truman, he argued, would be "wasted."[37]

From the time troops were committed, discussion of the Korean War before Congress was closely linked to plans to gain approval for large new military and foreign aid appropriations. Initially, there was some disagreement on the details of the political strategy, since Acheson apparently wanted to move more quickly than Truman. On July 3, the cabinet and Democratic congressional leaders met to discuss the State Department's proposed request for a congressional resolution in support of the decision to send troops to Korea. Scott Lucas (D-IL), the Senate majority leader, and most of the rest of the cabinet opposed any request for congressional approval because the administration already had extensive support and had nothing to gain by a debate over such a resolution. Although there was general agreement on the need for a message to Congress on events in Korea, most of those at the meeting believed that it should not be a request for congressional authorization of actions already taken. In spite of the contrary views of Acheson, Harriman, and others, the president decided to take no action until after meeting with the "Big Four" Democratic congressional leaders on July 10.[38]

Although no records were kept of Truman's regular Monday meetings with the Big Four, there is some evidence that a decision was reached on July 10 simply to ask Congress for additional military appropriations instead of approval for the military action in Korea. Acheson conferred with the president after the July 10 Big Four meeting, noting afterward that the president would not deliver a message on Korea until it could be coupled with an appropriations request. Acheson wanted more immediate congressional action and chafed at Truman's unwillingness to tell him more.[39] The delay was very brief, though. Preparations began immediately, and the president sent a message to Congress containing a request for $10.5 billion in supplemental defense spending on July 19. Truman's decision to wait until the appropriations request was ready probably reflected his understanding of how best to present the program to Congress, based on his conversations with the Big Four. Acheson was not privy to these discussions. While Truman accepted Acheson's judgments regarding international events, he kept his own counsel on the more familiar topic of legislative strategy. In any event, the differences between the White House and the State Department were purely tactical. Their goals were the same.[40]

Charles Murphy and others in the White House apparently wrote the bulk of the speech and probably even decided on the final spending figure, since firm estimates from the Department of Defense did not become available in time. Not surprisingly, much of the executive bureaucracy expressed an interest in the deliberations on Korea. Murphy later recalled that, while representatives of all the relevant departments were routinely invited to participate in such speech-drafting sessions, "this one got to be the largest group I ever had." Unable to get firm cost estimates from the Department of Defense, "I took the biggest number that I had heard anybody mention and I wrote it in."[41]

Murphy's recollection is supported by other archival evidence. As noted in the last chapter, the White House had been pressing the Pentagon to offer some preliminary estimates since May, anticipating a presidential announcement on the subject in early June. These estimates were still not ready in early July. Preliminary spending figures of $5–6 billion were produced on July 12 and were increased to $10.5 billion by July 19, when the president's message was finally delivered. Reviewing his handwritten notes on the July 15 discussions, George Elsey wrote with amazement that "[n]ote only $5 to $6 Billion estimated to this date; by July 19 it was $10 billion!!"[42] Stuart Symington, then heading the National Security Resources Board, wrote that "[i]n order to carry out what is essential to maintain the President's position, should we not now recommend erring if anywhere on the 'too much' side instead of 'too little'?"[43] Acheson echoed Symington's recommendation at the July 14 cabinet meeting called to discuss the message to Congress. "[The president] must ask for money, and if it is a question of asking for too little or too much, he should ask for too much."[44]

Although Acheson was excluded from Truman's meetings with congressional leaders, he had a strong influence on the message Truman ultimately sent. He elicited assurances from Louis Johnson on July 13 that defense spending figures were being prepared as quickly as possible.[45] When the Defense Department finally produced its portion of the president's speech after the July 14 cabinet meeting, however, Acheson found it unacceptable and suggested major changes. The message ultimately sent to Congress closely followed the points of emphasis Acheson urged.[46]

The message itself explicitly links Korea and rearmament. It begins with a long summary of the events in Korea, concluding that "[t]he attack upon the Republic of Korea makes it plain beyond all doubt that the international communist movement is prepared to use armed invasion to conquer independent nations." All of the actions called for in the message, including the increased military appropriations and the limited controls imposed on the economy to prevent inflation, were framed in terms of the Korean conflict. The president also delivered a radio and television address to the nation the same day outlining the program. As if to underscore the political consequences of opposing these programs, the address concludes with the following remark: "I know that our people are willing to do their part to support our soldiers and sailors and airmen who are fighting in Korea. I know that our fighting men can count on each and every one of you." Although the speech was directed to the country in general, the White House certainly knew that members of Congress, whose support was most important for the proposed program, were also listening.[47]

"I never would have thought we ought to fight for Korea"

What was the effect of the administration's effort to make opposition to its defense program politically impossible? Opponents of larger military budgets in the Senate, chiefly the Nationalist Republicans, were fully aware of the administration's strategy, but they could do little to stop it. The outbreak of war in Korea forced the Nationalist Republicans to accept the administration's foreign and defense program, at least temporarily, but it did not change their underlying opposition to it. Instead, a gap emerged between the public and private positions taken by Robert Taft and other Republican leaders on Korea. While they publicly supported the war, they kept open the option of turning against it by charging that it was the result of the administration's foreign policy blunders and by maintaining contacts with others who questioned the wisdom of intervention.

Two aspects of the Korean War played a role in forcing the grudging acceptance of rearmament by Nationalist Republicans. First, it occurred during an election year. With major nationalist figures including Robert Taft facing reelection less than five months after the commitment of U.S.

ground forces, opposition to such a popular and highly visible action by the president was politically dangerous. Second, because the war occurred in Asia and raised the U.S. level of commitment in that part of the world, Nationalist Republicans with close ties to the Chinese Nationalists on Taiwan supported the war as a way to force a change in the administration's policy toward China. Since the release of the China White Paper in the summer of 1949, members of the China bloc such as Styles Bridges and William Knowland had been among the administration's harshest critics. Other Nationalist Republicans had opportunistically joined in the attacks on the administration's China policy even though they did not share the China bloc's genuine commitment to using U.S. resources to fight communism in Asia.

Although nearly all Nationalist Republicans publicly expressed support for the war, even these remarks sometimes revealed their ambivalence. On June 28, Robert Taft stated that he would vote in favor of a resolution approving the president's actions in Korea if one were proposed, but he added that Korea was "not vitally important to the United States." Taft further qualified his endorsement of administration policy, commenting that, while a line had to be drawn somewhere, "[w]hether the President has chosen the right time or the right place to declare this policy may be open to question. He has information which I do not have." Taft also questioned the legal authority of the president to involve the United States in a "de facto war" without congressional approval.[48]

Two days later, Kenneth Wherry, in announcing his intention to vote in favor of the increase in MDAP funds requested before the beginning of the Korean War, expressed similar uneasiness about supporting administration policy. He stressed the administration's failure to prevent the Chinese revolution, adding that "[t]hese terrible, ghastly failures cannot now be swallowed up with a show of flag-waving and cries of emergency, hurry up, and do not question this or that." Wherry did not abandon his preference for a smaller military budget.

> Mr. President, the resources of the United States, great as they are, are simply not sufficient to arm and support half the world. The United States cannot build and maintain ground forces, navies, and air cover for every freedom-loving country on earth. We must not spread out defense dollars so thinly around the world that our defenses will not be adequate anywhere. We should tailor our defenses to fit our resources.

He suggested that funding for the Air Force be emphasized as a way of providing a more economical defense.[49]

Some Nationalist Republicans hinted that the administration might be using the crisis in Korea to force the Congress to accept rearmament. The president's July 19 request confirmed their worst fears. Senator George Malone (R-NV) charged that administration foreign policy was "part of a deliberately designed plot to advance Communism." Reciting a veritable catalog of Nationalist Republican policy positions, Malone argued that "'spend and elect' theories of welfare-statism," trade liberalization, and communists in the State Department had put the country in its current position.

> Unless there is a complete reversal in Washington's mood, this armed outbreak will be the occasion for more reckless spending, further demands for power, and more of all the same trappings which have accompanied this country to its present plight. There will be bigger request for all sorts of things that can in some way be tied to the label "national defense."[50]

Malone's public comments about the administration's use of the crisis were unusual, however. Most nationalists publicly adhered to the line that the war was an unfortunate necessity brought on by administration policy failures. Kepley (1988, 88) notes that only Malone, James Kem (R-MO), and Arthur Watkins (R-UT) openly questioned the wisdom of the decision to commit U.S. forces to Korea.

Privately, Taft, Wherry, and others were less guarded in their assessments of the Korean War. Taft reportedly told Senate Republicans immediately after the invasion that they "shouldn't be stampeded into war."[51] Taft and Robert R. McCormick, publisher of the *Chicago Tribune,* shared their mutual skepticism about U.S. involvement in Korea.[52] Curiously, Kenneth Wherry chose to preserve in his papers only those constituent letters that condemned his support for the war. An excerpt from Wherry's response to one of these letters underlines his grudging acceptance of administration policy, as well as his lamentable prose:

> It is of little moment to blame the other fellow for a situation into which we find ourselves already drawn, and I submit we stand committed today to extricate ourselves from Korea by as prompt as possible a subduing of the conflict to which we were committed in name by President Truman himself, and in truth through a long series of tragic blunders of the weak—and in some cases—treasonable handling of our foreign policy by subversive aides and advisors in the Department of State.[53]

There is some evidence that a coalition between conservatives like Taft and liberals concerned about damage to social programs was possible. Harold Ickes, a prominent liberal who had served as secretary of the interior from 1933 through 1946, wrote Taft on July 28 to express his views on the administration's decision to defend Taiwan and South Korea.

> I am in favor of keeping as far away from Formosa and China as we can. I also think that if it was not necessary a few weeks ago to fight for Korea, in order to carry out our policy of containment of communism, it was not necessary to fight when we undertook to do so with bare hands.

Taft wrote back a few days later and generally agreed with Ickes.

> It seemed to me that Formosa was an easy part of the world to defend, and in principle I never would have thought we ought to fight for Korea. After the President committed us to that job, however, there was nothing to do except back up the Army which had been sent there.

Ickes wrote Taft again on August 9 to reaffirm his opposition to the war and to express some additional concerns about overcommitment that Taft almost certainly shared.

> I just do not see where the United States is to get enough men and money, rich as we are, to fight all over the world. War is so expensive these days; with too many wars in too many spots over too long a time, it is bound to reach the end of the longest purse.[54]

The reality of a large commitment of U.S. resources in Asia and the possibility of a war with China appear to have inspired second thoughts even among some members of the China bloc, despite their vigorous public support for the effort. In particular, Styles Bridges's real sentiments on Korea are difficult to determine and may be better explained by political opportunism than his commitment to the China bloc. Bridges and others met privately with Hamilton Long, an isolationist activist, in August to discuss possible avenues of attack on the administration's foreign policy. Long argued that aid to Europe would only contribute to the Soviets' war potential because they could seize Western Europe quickly and use its resources against the United States.[55] Bridges also stepped up his efforts to undermine the position of Dean Acheson and the State Department, despite the fact that they had moved closer to his position on China.

Other members of the China bloc, especially internationalists such as William F. Knowland (R-CA) and H. Alexander Smith (R-NJ), were less ambivalent in their enthusiasm for the war in Korea. They succeeded in linking the defense of Korea to that of Taiwan and urged acceptance of a Chinese Nationalist offer to send 30,000 troops. As Cumings (1990, 713) has noted, throughout the summer of 1950, virtually everyone argued for stronger military action against the North Koreans and even the Chinese. Those who had sought to change U.S. foreign policy toward Asia and other Third World areas were joined by those who, like Dulles and MacArthur, had initially questioned the wisdom of intervening with ground forces. Dulles's initial opposition to the war, as well as Mac-Arthur's opinion that anyone who wanted to commit ground troops "ought to have his head examined," quickly faded from the minds of those few who had known about them. Once confronted with the crisis in Korea, Nationalist Republicans sought to turn it to their own ends, particularly their domestic priorities.

"A holding operation"

Although it placed tremendous pressure on them to accept a national security program about which they had serious doubts, the crisis created by the Korean War also presented opportunities for the Nationalist Republicans. Rearmament was not the only policy that could be conceptually linked to Korea, and the Republicans moved quickly to establish their own wartime agenda. They sought to use wartime budgetary stringency to eliminate the Fair Deal, and wartime repressive measures to eliminate radicals from the labor movement. As noted earlier, these policy goals were closely related in the Nationalist Republican political agenda, since both the labor law reforms and the social welfare programs of the Fair Deal were believed to promote the political agenda of domestic radicals in the government and the labor movement. Ending the Fair Deal and curbing the power of its supporters were two aspects of the same set of policy goals.

While Republicans had pursued these policy objectives before the Korean War, the administration's effort to secure approval for rearmament changed the bargaining situation and increased their chances of gaining administration acquiescence. In spite of the war in Korea, Republicans and conservative Democrats from the South and West could have made cuts or imposed crippling restrictions on vital portions of the administration's appropriations requests not directly related to the war. The military aid the State Department considered vital to alleviate the balance-of-payments problem and make NATO an effective military alliance was especially vulnerable. Indeed, as I will explain later, Republicans demonstrated their ability to attach unacceptable provisions to the supplemental appropriations bills by actually doing so when it appeared likely that the president would block the Internal Security Act in September.

The Fair Deal was among the early casualties of the Korean War. As the military budget increased, funding for other programs was cut. The Senate opened floor debate on the omnibus appropriations bill for fiscal 1951 on July 11, a little more than a week before Truman submitted his message on Korea calling for an additional $10.5 billion for defense. This initial request was followed by another for an additional $4 billion in military aid funds on August 1. On August 3, Harry Byrd (D-VA) and Styles Bridges (R-NH) proposed an amendment to the appropriations bill calling for a 10 percent cut in all nondefense spending. After amending the proposal to exempt foreign economic aid, the Senate passed the Byrd-Bridges amendment by a vote of 55 to 31. Once it was reconciled with a somewhat different measure proposed by the House, the final appropriations bill called on the Bureau of the Budget to cut $550 million from programs not related to national defense.[56]

These cuts cannot be understood entirely in terms of a budget constraint imposed by rearmament spending. They constituted only a small fraction of the amount requested for defense and foreign aid in the supplemental appropriation bill then before the Congress. If balancing the huge increases in the national security budget had been the goal, much larger cuts would have been required. A more important effect of the cuts was to remove from the agenda the remaining spending programs of the Fair Deal, including the national health insurance program and agricultural subsidies. Virtually all of the policy initiatives of the Fair Deal disappeared after the beginning of the Korean War and were not revived again during the Truman administration. As Richard Neustadt (1974, 34) has noted, after the beginning of the Korean War, "[a]ll along the line, Fair Deal proposals were permanently shelved or set aside, as Congress worked on measures for defense." Stephen Spingarn also noted the contrast between the administration's legislative success on foreign policy issues and its failures on domestic policy. "Truman's record on foreign policy was tremendous, but when you look at his record on domestic policy, it was more of a holding operation."[57] Contemporary observers also remarked on the eclipse of the Fair Deal. Robert C. Albright, one of the primary political reporters for the *Washington Post,* noted on September 3 that "'The Welfare State' that was to have been this session's theme was eased out of the legislative picture by seeming tacit agreement, without any formal burial."[58]

The disappearance of the Fair Deal from the political agenda in mid-1950 is paralleled by the disappearance of any further discussion of it from most historical accounts of the Truman presidency. Most general accounts of the Truman administration virtually drop domestic policy from their narrative after they reach June 25, 1950.[59] In one respect, this omission is understandable, since there are almost no serious domestic policy initiatives to discuss apart from those connected to rearmament. However, considering the administration's rhetoric and its previous record of proposing—if not always passing—major domestic policy initiatives, the absence of such proposals after the beginning of the Korean war demands a more careful explanation.

Most accounts of the end of the Fair Deal focus on the political atmosphere in the United States, understood in very general terms, or the specific distraction of Korea. Alonzo Hamby (1973, 311), who spends more time than most on the fate of the Fair Deal after the beginning of the Korean War, argues that "McCarthyism and the Korean War together would in the end overwhelm the Fair Deal." Hamby credits the efforts of the liberal "vital center" for what he argues are considerable domestic achievements before Korea. He appeals to the irrationality of human nature and the pressure of external events to explain both the end of the Fair Deal and the administration's participation in some of the most unsavory aspects of the red scare, which intensified after Korea.

> The rise of the vital center made it impossible to smear the liberal movement until external events—the fall of China, the Soviet atomic bomb, the espionage cases, and especially the Korean War—created an irrational climate of hysteria and frustration. (507)

While this appeal to the political atmosphere of the time is superficially plausible, it begs questions about how the atmosphere was created and how it actually influenced policy choices. Viewed from a distance, the political climate of 1950 indeed appears "irrational." An internationalist and anticommunist foreign policy was adopted while its architects were vilified as communist sympathizers. However, the apparent irrationality of political outcomes like this one does not necessarily imply that the individual actors involved behaved irrationally in terms of their own objectives. On closer examination, the decisions and actions of individual actors can be understood as steps toward long-standing goals, rather than simply expressions of "hysteria and frustration." Hamby's appeal to external events does not explain how the climate developed unless one believes that these events could evoke only one response. This is precisely the position taken by statists and realists, and it suffers from the theoretical and empirical problems plaguing Wells's and Leffler's explanations of rearmament. As with those arguments, Hamby's requires some account of why the events he mentioned evoked the particular response they did.

In terms of the amount of time it consumed, congressional work on Korea and rearmament does not explain the end of the Fair Deal either. While the wide range of programs connected to rearmament were certainly time-consuming for Congress, the body found time to deal with many matters not directly connected to these issues. For example, while the administration's proposals for agricultural subsidies went nowhere, Congress expanded and restructured the Commodity Credit Corporation, the agency charged with administering agricultural price supports. It also made a variety of changes in the tax code, only some of which involved tax increases to offset the cost of the rearmament program. There was also sufficient time to deal with a wide range of less important issues after the beginning of the Korean War; not every committee in the Congress was concerned with Korea or rearmament. Time constraints simply do not explain the demise of the Fair Deal.[60]

A budget constraint might provide a more plausible explanation for the demise of the Fair Deal after Korea, but it suffers from serious shortcomings. Indeed, as was noted earlier, because the cuts made in domestic programs amounted to only a tiny fraction of the increase in the budget for defense and foreign aid, it may not be meaningful to speak of a budget constraint at all in this case. Furthermore, even Fair Deal initiatives that did not involve government spending, such as the repeal of the Taft-Hartley Act, disappeared after Korea. Above all, the mere existence of a budget constraint does not explain choices made within it. International events did not compel the administration to act in any particular way. Even if budgetary considerations created by rearmament had compelled the sacrifice of the Fair Deal, the decision to proceed with this program was a choice, not an externally imposed necessity. Because of the priorities of the faction that had prevailed in the struggle over the military budget within the administration, alternative courses of action were not seriously considered. Alternatives did exist, however. In determining why the administration abandoned the Fair Deal and pursued rearmament instead, the central issues are those addressed in chapters 2 and 3: how the dominant group's priorities developed and why they were accepted as the basis for policy.

The logic of the bargaining process after the beginning of the Korean War suggests the abandonment of the Fair Deal as a likely outcome. Once the Fair Deal had been discarded, the administration made other concessions to the Nationalist Republican domestic agenda through the internal security program. As was already noted, the end of the Fair Deal was not the only domestic objective of the Nationalist Republicans. The internal security program eroded the political basis for additional liberal reforms by attacking left-liberals in the bureaucracy and radicals in the labor movement. These may not have been the objectives of the program as it was understood in most of the executive branch, but they were the program's actual effects, and they corresponded to the interests of its supporters in Congress. In any event, as I will explain in the next chapter, the internal security program was not entirely under the effective control of the Truman White House but was instead administered by bureaucratic entities with independent political agendas and bases of support.

The bargaining process was dominated by the interests of the administration and the Nationalist Republicans. Each of these groups was in a position to secure the acquiescence of more reluctant factions of their own party. As was noted earlier, the Nationalist Republicans dominated their party in the Senate. The administration was in an equally good position to gain Democratic cooperation. Truman met with the Democratic leadership on a weekly basis, and the Democratic party rarely fielded policy initiatives that did not originate in the White House. This is simply an institutional feature of American politics. While individual members of the administration's party may oppose the White House on particular issues, the party leadership in Congress rarely develops policy on its own. In any event, the specific concessions made by the White House to the Nationalist Republicans did not require much congressional action. The administration simply stopped asking Congress for further action on most Fair Deal programs and took actions in the internal security field on its own.

The process is best understood as one of tacit bargaining that does not imply a formal understanding between the administration and its Nationalist Republican critics. As I noted earlier, there were several unsuccessful efforts in the spring of 1950 to work out a consultation arrangement between the administration and the Republican leadership to build support for rearmament. Given the extreme distrust between the administration and the Nationalist Republicans and the harshness of their public rhetoric against each other, explicit cooperation may have been impossible. While the Nationalist Republicans argued that the State Department was riddled with communist sympathizers bent on sabotaging U.S. policy, the White House sought to use the Internal Revenue Service to investigate and embarrass members of the China lobby.[61] In the atmosphere of mutual suspicion prevailing between the administration and the Nationalist Republicans, it is difficult to imagine either side trusting the other to carry out the terms of a secret bargain in good faith. The arrangement that emerged was probably stronger for not being the product of such an agreement.

Rather than relying on a negotiated arrangement with congressional

Republicans, the administration used the crisis brought on by U.S. intervention in Korea to force them to accept rearmament. Opposition to military spending measures would have constituted a failure to support U.S. troops in a wartime situation, something no one wanted to do, especially less than six months before an election. The administration had given up attempting to force the Fair Deal through the Congress by the spring of 1950 because only a very asymmetrical bargain could have compelled the Nationalist Republicans to accept both sets of programs. Once the Korean War began, the decision to make these concessions still made sense because it offered a way to attract some Republican support and to reduce the chance that they would turn against intervention in Korea and attempt to forge a coalition with others who might have opposed the rearmament program. Instead, the administration allowed the Nationalist Republicans and their allies to launch an all-out attack on the gains made by New Deal constituencies during the preceding 15 years.

CHAPTER 6

The Conflictual Politics of Consensus Building II: The Development of the Internal Security Program

I have read as carefully as time allows the proposed report of the Committee on Socialism and Communism. . . . I am particularly in agreement with the emphasis placed on Communistic influences in connection with labor.

—Emerson Schmidt, United States Chamber of Commerce

At some later stage of the proceeding you might [have a problem] with the matter the Major mentioned a short time ago, namely, developing a suspected subversive character who is merely a militant union man and probably persuading the investigator without too much effort, I gather.

—John Fanning, Munitions Board
Industrial Labor Relations Committee

This chapter steps back from the political bargaining process that followed U.S. intervention in Korea and examines the constellation of business elites, bureaucracies, and members of Congress that supported the effort to remove the influence of radicals from American life. This policy current and the internal security program it sought provided an institutional linkage between antilabor and antiradical domestic policies and Cold War national security policy. It made these domestic policies part of the national security policy planning process and gave effective control over them to conservative bureaucracies with links to sympathetic members of Congress and interested groups outside the government. In short, it gave the otherwise skeptical American right a stake in the Cold War.

The internal security program predated NSC 68 and the Korean War by several years, but it remained a relatively small operation until mid-1950. Without the conditions outlined in this chapter, the linkage between anticommunist domestic and foreign policies might not have emerged and persisted after 1950. By the time of the Korean War, antilabor elements of the business community knew that an industrial security program run by the Department of Defense could be helpful to them. Similarly, the FBI, an organization closely tied to conservative members of Congress, had been able to establish itself as the principal government bureaucracy concerned with internal security and to make its agenda a component of the overall national security program. This arrangement greatly facilitated the efforts of Nationalist Republicans in the Congress to link the internal security program to the rearmament effort after the beginning of the Korean War.

"Russia abroad and labor at home"

American business leaders were increasingly concerned about the growing power of the labor movement after World War II.[1] While labor activism had long been a concern of business, the issue became increasingly salient in the immediate postwar era. As unions sought to regain ground they believed they had lost under the wartime strike prohibition, 1946 saw more workers involved in job actions than in any previous year—and a higher proportion of the total workforce than in any year since 1919.[2] Business reaction to the increased labor militancy varied, but it eventually converged around an effort to secure legislation reducing the power of the labor movement. McQuaid (1982, 140–49) notes that the major business organizations, including the National Association of Manufacturers, the Council for Economic Development, the Business Roundtable, and the United States Chamber of Commerce, generally adopted a pragmatic course of action seeking to contain the labor movement rather than to abolish it. The success of this strategy formed the basis for what Charles Maier (1977, 611–18) terms the "politics of productivity," in which an ostensibly apolitical focus on economic growth superseded concerns about the distribution of wealth in society.

Like the acceptance of Cold War foreign policy, the acceptance of the politics of productivity was not unproblematic.[3] Some in the leadership of the labor movement—especially in the Congress of Industrial Organizations (CIO)—remained committed to further redistributive social change. Among these labor radicals were a small but significant number of communists. While Kampelman's estimate (1957, 14–23) that communists had "control or effective control" of up to 40 percent of CIO unions may be somewhat overstated, the influence of communists and other leftists in the labor movement is undeniable. For example, Len De Caux, the editor of the *CIO News,* and Lee Pressman, the organization's general counsel, were party members.

There had been conflict within the CIO over the role of communists since the organization's founding. After World War II, this conflict increasingly centered on issues of foreign policy, as anticommunist labor leaders attacked leftist opposition to the Truman administration's increasing hostility toward the Soviet Union. By contrast, domestic policy was not a major source of tension, because the various political factions within the CIO were united on most domestic issues, such as their opposition to the Taft-Hartley Act. While many noncommunist labor leaders also opposed much of the administration's foreign policy at least through 1946, a serious split developed in 1947 when many union leftists, including the communists, began backing the Progressive party.[4]

While there were also internal reasons for the conflict between communists and anticommunists within the labor movement, the political environment outside the unions was critical. Anticommunist union officers were able to use popular anticommunism to advance within their organizations. For example, Levenstein (1981, 196–207) notes that Walter Reuther stressed the support given by union communists to his rivals within the United Automobile Workers (UAW) in his successful effort to gain the presidency of the union in 1946. Anticommunist union leaders could usually count on local newspapers, the Catholic Church, and sometimes direct government intervention for support in removing communists from leadership positions in union locals. Given these advantages, it is not surprising that the leadership of the CIO became increasingly anticommunist over time. Ultimately, in 1949 and 1950, the CIO board voted to expel 11 member unions it alleged to be "communist-dominated." Rosswurm (1992, 2) points out that these unions constituted between 17 and 20 percent of the CIO's total membership.[5]

Business conservatives heavily promoted broad public concerns about domestic communism. The United States Chamber of Commerce (USCC) was especially active in this respect, initiating an anticommunist publicity campaign in 1946 focusing on the government and the labor movement. Under the direction of Francis Matthews and Emerson Schmidt, and with assistance from the FBI and the Catholic Church, the Chamber published three widely circulated reports on communism in the United States in 1946 and 1947. Its report "Communists within the Labor Movement" included a confidential appendix sent to other business groups listing the unions and locals considered to be most seriously influenced by communists and suggesting some possible tactics for eliminating them.[6] Schmidt testified before the House Committee on Un-American Activities that the labor movement was a "key point for [Communist] penetration" and suggested the basic outlines of what later became the Internal Security Act of 1950.[7]

Even business liberals who accepted most of the New Deal agenda, such as those running the Council for Economic Development (CED), were concerned about the threat of labor militancy. Speaking to the Business Council in 1946, former CED head Averell Harriman noted that he could not speak openly of the growing hostility between the United States and the Soviet Union, because communist sympathizers in the CIO would attack him for doing so. Henry Wallace, who was present at the meeting, noted that after Harriman made this remark, "there was considerable discussion then on how important it was to fight any organization that had any commies in it."[8] Harriman also later assisted the National Industrial Conference Board in developing a study titled "Controlling Communism and Sabotage in Industry," writing letters of introduction for researchers sent to inquire about methods used to deal with this problem in Europe.[9] The resulting study suggested that suspected subversives could be fired even if there was not enough evidence to sustain their removal for security reasons.

> Security personnel maintain, however, that in the long run, with vigilance and careful "bookkeeping" of the actions, comings and goings, absences, vacation leaves and any violations of these and other company rules, management will be able to get rid of some of its security risks.[10]

While business liberals like Harriman were more willing than the extremists in the USCC to accept the existence of unions, both sought to limit the power and the political goals of the labor movement. To the extent that they helped get rid of union militants, the virulent anticommunism and antiunion orientation of business conservatives played a role in setting up the "politics of productivity" usually associated with more moderate members of the business community.

Labor militancy, whether led by communists or not, was a serious concern not only for business in the heavily industrialized northeastern quadrant of the country, but also in the West and South, where the unions were trying to increase their membership. Before the war, some of the strongest efforts to link the New Deal to domestic communist influence came not from Republicans, but from Southern Democrats like Representative Martin Dies (D-TX), who chaired the Special House Committee on Un-American Activities from 1938 until 1944. According to Lichtenstein (1989, 143), the American Federation of Labor (AFL) and the CIO added roughly 800,000 new members in the South during World War II. The CIO sought to build on this trend after the war, launching "Operation Dixie" to unionize the Southern textile and tobacco industries. This effort, which was by all accounts a failure, was met by an intense counterattack stressing the influence of African-Americans and communists in the CIO.[11]

Southern conservative Democrats provided the Nationalist Republicans with an important set of allies on important elements of their domestic agenda. If these Democrats voted with the Republicans on any given issue, they could deprive their party of its majority in the Senate.

The labor movement was not the only target of those concerned with domestic communism, of course. They also charged that communists and other radicals had infiltrated the executive branch during the New Deal era. A purge of the bureaucracy was attractive not only to Nationalist Republicans, who had opposed its expansion during the 1930s, but also to some in the Democratic party. Truman and conservative members of his staff were concerned about the reliability of New Deal bureaucrats whose first loyalty was to the promotion of social reform, rather than the administration. J. Edgar Hoover fed these suspicions by passing along information about the political activities of liberals in the bureaucracy. A typical example is Hoover's March 1946 report to Truman's military aide, Harry Vaughan, that there was an effort under way "to infiltrate the National Housing Administration and its housing program with so-called 'liberal elements' presently in Washington." Hoover enclosed a transcript of a phone conversation between two National Housing Administration officials, Harry Magdoff and Norton Long, praising Secretary of Commerce Henry Wallace, then one of Truman's major liberal intraparty rivals. Magdoff later ran into trouble with the Federal Employee Loyalty Program, and copies of a polygraph test administered to him found their way into the hands of Senator Styles Bridges.[12]

"We have been under constant pressure"

Business efforts to link the labor movement and the communist threat were not confined to public relations efforts. Business sought to use the military's industrial security program to attack militant labor leaders and unions in their industries. A government-run program to investigate the workforce helped reduce the legal liability of employers who fired suspected subversives, possibly violating union contracts and local labor relations laws. It also provided them with an additional source of information on the identity of politically suspicious individuals in their workforce. Industry representatives who participated in the development of the industrial security program recognized its usefulness against militant unionists and pressed for its expansion on this basis.

Antilabor elements of the business community and the Munitions Board, the agency in charge of procurement-related issues in the Office of the Secretary of Defense, had a common interest in expanding the scope of the industrial security program. In the early stages of the program, Munitions Board officials sought to extend its jurisdiction to plants that might be important to national security but were not actually under government contract. They were also anxious to determine the motive for strikes in such plants. As one military participant in the board's internal security planning process commented,

> I think we have some responsibility, too, of looking into the situation where communists or subversive elements are promoting unwarranted labor strife. They may be responsible for a strike at a certain plant. We may be able to straighten it out if we can put the proper agency on the communists.[13]

Despite these aspirations, the resources available to the internal security program in 1948 were simply too small to allow its extension to plants not under contract to the government, a situation lamented by the program's advocates in both business and government.

Before 1949, the role of business in developing the program was mainly indirect, since business representatives were not invited to participate directly in the formulation of policy. This indirect influence nevertheless produced results. Members of the Munitions Board's Industrial Labor Relations Committee (ILRC), which planned the industrial security program, felt pressure from employers' organizations to act against militant unions. During a 1948 waterfront strike on the West Coast, the representative of the Department of the Army told the committee:

> We have been under constant pressure during the period of the 80-day injunction from the Seattle Chamber of Commerce and everybody else to go to the Attorney General and get him to investigate the slowdown, and certain parts of the National Military Establishment even approached us with what appeared to be similar pressure.[14]

At the suggestion of the Chamber of Commerce, the Army eventually agreed to hire nonunion workers to load and unload military shipments during the strike. (Employers had refused to accept a union offer to unload these military items during this strike.) The International Longshoremen's and Warehousemen's Union (ILWU) retaliated by picketing Army employment offices, bringing the union into direct conflict with the military, which was quick to see communist influence behind the confrontation. At a subsequent meeting of the ILRC, the Army representative argued that the ILWU should not be allowed to control military hiring practices on the docks because it had not fully complied with the provision of the Taft-Hartley Act requiring all union officers to provide affidavits stating that they were not members of the Communist party. The Navy representative, Rear Admiral Charles W. Fox, went a step further, arguing that the military should refuse to deal with any union that had not complied with the Taft-Hartley Act. Fox added that he particularly distrusted Harry Bridges, head of the ILWU. He added indignantly that Bridges had "called me a popular American name to my face."[15]

Business use of the program was not limited to requests for action in the case of a strike. Although background investigations were conducted by the military services, they were initiated by requests from government contractors. In late 1948, the ILRC had an enormous backlog of requests for security clearances. The Army and Air Force complained that they had some 50,000 cases pending and that the FBI refused to assist them. Committee members suspected that some investigations had been requested because of union activity rather than genuine security concerns. The Army representative complained that security inspectors were "get[ting] themselves compromised with management to the point that the government is put on the spot and charged with the removal of individuals whose only offense has been labor activity and who are therefore troublesome to management."[16] Committee members were well aware that union and National Labor Relations Board rules about firing employees were easier to evade when responsibility for removing the worker rested with the military instead of the employer. According to Caute (1978, 365–66), the long delay occasioned by the backlog of security investigations was itself sometimes enough to cost employees their jobs. Although the committee eventually complained to the Munitions Board about procedures encouraging employers to initiate investigations of union activists, there is no evidence these procedures were changed.[17]

Beginning in 1949, representatives of major military contractors were directly included in the planning and implementation of the internal security program. Although much of the program was secret, industry representatives were in a position to understand its details as well as the implications of expanding it. When the charter of the Industrial Employment Review Board (IERB), the body designed to handle the appeals of individuals denied a security clearance, was completed in late 1949, the vice president for labor relations of RCA, Edward McGrady, was called in to review the document. McGrady, who had worked in the War Department during World War II, was especially interested in these procedures because they were expected to be used extensively against the United Electrical Workers (UE), RCA's principal union. When John Fanning, who chaired the ILRC during its first year of existence, announced McGrady's approval of the IERB charter to the committee, he also noted that there had been no time to consult any representative of the labor movement.[18]

In April 1949, an Industrial Advisory Committee (IAC) was created to consult with industry representatives concerning loyalty and security procedures.[19] As was generally the case with the military's internal security program, the proceedings of the committee were secret, and no labor representatives were included. The IAC met only four times in 1949 and 1950, but it provided an occasion for industry representatives to learn its details and influence its development. The legal staff from each of the corporations with representatives on the IAC even reviewed the proposed security clearance regulations before they were promulgated.[20] Industry representatives urged expansion of the effort to remove labor radicals and sought to have the government assume more of the legal responsibility for firing these individuals.

Industry representatives on the IAC urged the expansion of both the range of plants covered by the program and the scope of workers subject to investigation. In 1949, they recommended that all employees in facilities listed as "vital" or "critical" be investigated, not just those working on classified projects.[21] The Munitions Board representative countered that the program lacked the resources to investigate workers in all these facilities and noted that not all of them were working on contracts for the government. The expansion of the program after 1950 solved this problem, however, and by 1953 all of the 3,282 plants on the key facilities list were covered by the industrial security program, although only 30 percent were working on government contracts.[22] Industry representatives hoped to use the internal security program against union radicals in their facilities. David Prince of General Electric was especially eager to have all employees at GE's large plant in Schenectady, New York, investigated. While nearly all the industry representatives agreed that the scope of investigations should be extended as far as possible, Prince had an additional motive for focusing on security at Schenectady, since it was the jurisdiction of UE Local 301, the largest union local in the entire industry.[23]

Industry representatives also wanted to review the results of investigations of their employees. Several IAC members noted that many military security officers provided this information on their own initiative, even though it was illegal to do so. IAC members wanted to establish legal access to information not only on employees working on classified contracts, but on prospective employees as well.

And there is where we like to do our work, not after they get in there, but before they get in there we like to screen them. Well, if you have enough to be cautious about the fellow and yet you want to check some more, you exhaust your resources, and then it would be very nice if you could call up the ONI or G-2 or the OSI and say, "How about this fellow? Do you have anything on him? He is going to be an engineer in our company and he is going to be a key figure. Can you find out something about him?"

At its meeting on July 12, 1950, the committee decided to recommend that investigating government agencies be asked to "advise and counsel" management, although they decided not to insist that "actual findings" be provided, since the FBI and other intelligence agencies were unwilling to relinquish control of their files.[24]

In addition to expanding the scope of the program, industry representatives on the IAC sought to have the government assume more of the legal responsibility for firing politically unreliable employees. While everyone agreed that "suspected saboteurs" should be fired, the Munitions Board representatives argued that the government lacked the legal authority to order the firing of any employee; they could only prevent them from having access to classified material. If the government were given the power to direct the firing of individuals, employers would be relieved of legal responsibility but would also lose control over their workforce. The IAC was divided between industries confident of their ability to fire suspected employees and those more concerned about the limits union work rules and local labor laws imposed on loyalty investigations.

Mr. Howard [*of Standard Oil of New Jersey*]: What it really comes down to, putting the cards right on the table, you'd like to get rid of them but you don't think you can and, therefore, you want the government to do it for you.

Mr. Miller [*of Consolidated Vultee Aircraft*]: If the management could do it without law suits from the labor unions they'd do it. We feel exactly like you do. We don't want the government or anybody else with hands in our business.[25]

The dilemma of whether to give the government the power to order employees fired was partially resolved by the passage of the Internal Security Act in September 1950. Afterwards, arbitrators generally ruled that Communist party membership, failure to secure a government security clearance, or refusal to testify before a congressional committee on Fifth Amendment grounds were all just causes for dismissal. Stein (1963, 103) notes that the Internal Security Act helped change the legal status of being a communist, making it possible for employers to dismiss them as such. These effects of the legislation were anticipated in the IAC.

It's an omnibus bill. It has got about everything in there you can think of, that without making it illegal to be a Communist, every time he moves he has to say so, and that would have a tendency—I mean this is the nearest thing that has come out in peacetime to correct the thing that you are referring to [i.e., the problem of being unable to find out who was a Communist, or to fire that person as a result].[26]

Concerns about internal security were not applied with equal vigor on all the matters facing the IAC. In fact, nearly all measures not pertaining to the labor movement were viewed with suspicion. At the first meeting of the IAC, industry representatives objected to proposed restrictions on the export of sensitive technologies. Arguing that these restrictions would disrupt international business activity, they unanimously recommended avoiding any such regulations.[27] They also objected to rules limiting the use of classified technologies on unclassified projects.[28] Since organized labor was not invited to participate in the development of the internal security program, it is not surprising that the burden of the program fell on workers.

Aside from labor's lack of representation in the development of the military internal security program, there were other reasons to expect it to take on a distinct antilabor cast. Historically, relations between the military establishment and the labor movement were poor. Morris Janowitz (1960, 248) noted in his study of social attitudes among military officers that they were generally hostile to trade unions and tended to blame them for problems in the economy. John Ohly, who handled labor relations problems in the War Department during World War II, had noted at that time that the military's internal security program tended to move in antilabor directions.

Specific instructions, however, had to be issued to prevent some local War Department representatives from using the program to secure investigations of active labor elements who were disrupting production. The Provost Marshall General constantly emphasized that normal labor activities were not matters of interest to the Key Personnel Security Program or Removal of Subversives Program. Similarly, local War Department security representatives were often over-zealous in the employment of the information received from the investigation.

Ohly characterized the internal security activities of Army Intelligence (G-2) as "nothing more than the promulgation of anti-administration, anti-labor propaganda within the Army."[29]

Although it predated rearmament, the conflict between labor and the military was exacerbated by the fact that the military's interest in expediting production often conflicted with labor's interest in maintaining its ability to strike. Civilians handling military procurement shared the military services' interests on this issue. As rearmament placed greater demands on the American economy and on bureaucrats in the Department of Defense, their bad relationship with labor grew worse. In effect, rearmament added another set of interests to the constituency backing an antilabor internal security program. The importance of these interests would become apparent as the pace of rearmament quickened.

"Edgar Hoover's organization would make a good start toward a citizen spy system"[30]

The most important executive bureaucracy in the internal security program was not the Department of Defense but the Federal Bureau of Investigation. The FBI played a key role in establishing and maintaining the linkage between an antilabor, antiradical domestic agenda and rearmament. Under the leadership of J. Edgar Hoover, the bureau's director since 1924, the FBI was a bureaucratic juggernaut with political connections to important members of Congress, conservative interests in society, and other parts of the executive branch charged with coordinating the internal security effort. Hoover used these political connections to keep the FBI at the center of the internal security program. While much has been made of Hoover's personal role in building the power of the FBI, he would never have been able to accomplish what he did without consistent support from Congress and sympathetic interests in society. While Hoover may have had his own reasons for involving the FBI so deeply in the campaign against domestic radicalism, his supporters served their own interests by backing him.

J. Edgar Hoover's crusade against domestic communism served both his personal goals and the organizational interests of the FBI. The surveillance and harassment of domestic radicals had been the focus of Hoover's career since he first joined the Department of Justice in 1917 as a clerk in the enemy alien registration program. He helped organize the mass arrests of members of the Industrial Workers of the World (IWW) and other radicals during and after World War I. He personally arranged the highly publicized deportation of 249 alleged anarchists, including Emma Goldman, to the Soviet Union in 1919. During his early years at the Justice Department, he also began developing a filing system to store information on suspected subversives.[31] Even if Hoover's personal anticommunist convictions had not been so strong, however, the campaign against domestic radicalism would still have served an important purpose for the bureau as an organization. During World War II, the FBI grew from a force of 898 agents to 4,886, with a corresponding increase in its budget. In order to maintain this large force after the war, Hoover actively promoted the threat of domestic communism.[32]

The antilabor slant of the FBI's campaigns against domestic radicals dated from Hoover's involvement in the campaign against the IWW. Hoover continued to view unions with great suspicion after World War II. Soon after it ended, he sent White House aide Harry Vaughan a memo arguing that the Communist party was planning a major effort to infiltrate the labor movement and noting that the FBI planned to keep a close eye on developments there. He also argued that the CIO was dominated by a Soviet spy ring led by "Communist key individuals." Hoover followed up these charges with a series of memoranda alleging communist involvement in various labor disturbances in 1946 and in the effort to prevent passage of the Taft-Hartley Act in 1947.[33]

The FBI also cultivated sympathetic elements of the news media and conservative groups in society. Through its Crime Records Division, the bureau provided useful information on crime and subversion, especially to Hearst-owned newspapers throughout the country. The FBI—and Hoover himself—also maintained close relationships with some of the major columnists and radio personalities of the period, including Walter Winchell, Drew Pearson, George Sokolsky, Fulton Lewis, and others. Not surprisingly, given the political orientation of most of Hoover's support- ers, the FBI's relations with media figures associated with internationalism in foreign policy, such as Joseph Alsop and Walter Lippmann, were poor.[34] The FBI also regularly contacted more than 62,000 members of the American Legion, both to assist in monitoring suspected subversives throughout the country and to provide a network of grassroots political support for the bureau. Although the program was supposed to have stopped at the end of World War II, progress reports on the internal secu- rity program submitted to the NSC indicate that it continued.[35]

Hoover's most powerful allies in Congress were also eager to see the FBI pursue a campaign against domestic communists. Even if Hoover had preferred a different rationale for maintaining a large force of agents after World War II, the FBI might not have been able to maintain the support of key members of Congress without involving itself in an attack on domestic radicalism. During the war, some members of Congress sought to reduce the size of the FBI and limit its autonomy, particularly in its hir- ing practices. Among Hoover's strongest defenders against these attacks were Senators Patrick McCarran (D-NV) and Styles Bridges (R-NH). McCarran was already a member of the Senate Appropriations Committee in 1940, and Bridges soon joined him. Theoharis and Cox (1988, 166) note that

> on 24 July 1944, Bridges contacted Hoover's office to express renewed concern over "the Communist situation" and his continuing belief that the Bureau "is the only one to handle this matter." Pointing out to the Director that he "could be of decided help to the Bureau if he changed over [his membership on] one of the subcommittees on Army and Navy Appropriations to the sub-committee on State and Justice Appropriations," the Senator wondered "whether the Bureau would like him to seek this transfer."

After securing the reassignment, Bridges helped to block proposed cuts in the FBI budget, beginning in 1945. Bridges's papers contain ample indication of the senator's service and of Hoover's gratitude.[36] Hoover, of course, continued to attend to "the Communist situation."

The FBI's relationship with Bridges was extremely broad and eventually extended to other nationalists on the Republican Policy Committee. Hoover sent Bridges reports on the senator's political opponents and business associates, always requesting that the source of the information be kept confidential.[37] The FBI also provided Bridges with lists of suspected Communist party members and sympathizers living in New Hampshire, many of which Bridges passed along to the conservative publisher of the Manchester *Union Leader* for publication. Clippings in the Bridges Papers indicate that his office followed the unhappy fates of the New Hampshire communists after their names were published in the *Union Leader.* Some of the clippings date from as late as 1960, the year Bridges died.[38]

On Hoover's recommendation, Bridges hired a former FBI agent, R. W. Scott McLeod, to serve as a direct contact with the bureau. McLeod worked closely with Maurice Joyce, the Republican Policy Committee staff member charged with handling allegations about communists in the government.[39] Both men made use of information that probably came from the FBI, since the reports they used strongly resemble others Bridges received from the bureau with accompanying letters from J. Edgar Hoover. Through its contacts with Joyce, McLeod, and Bridges, the FBI was able to use the Republican Policy Committee as a conduit for furnishing useful information to Senate Republicans interested in pressuring the administration for action on internal security policy. According to Theoharis and Cox (1988, 261–62), the FBI also leaked information directly to many other conservative members of Congress for the same purpose.

The FBI also had ties to other parts of the executive branch, especially the staffs of the White House and the NSC. As noted earlier, Hoover corresponded with Harry Vaughan, Truman's military aide, and with Matthew Connelly, the president's appointments secretary, furnishing political intelligence gathered by the bureau. The FBI's most important connections for influencing the development of the internal security program were probably on the NSC, however. J. Patrick Coyne, the 31-year-old chief of the Internal Security Division of the FBI, was appointed NSC Representative for Internal Security in 1948. After leaving the FBI, Coyne remained close to Hoover, who sought to promote Coyne's career in the NSC by praising his work to NSC officials.[40] Hoover also had a close relationship with Sidney Souers, the executive secretary of the NSC until January 1950. More generally, the FBI was responsible for checking the background of all NSC employees and determining their eligibility to handle classified material.[41] These connections proved useful to Hoover in his efforts to maintain the FBI's central position in the growing internal security program contemplated by the NSC.

"The United States is not secure internally at the present time"

The internal security program was not simply a set of independent initiatives taken by the FBI and the Defense Department, although pressure from these sources played a major role in its development. The program was planned in the National Security Council, and its development parallels that of the rearmament program in some respects. In 1948 and 1949, the NSC adopted policies on internal security that integrated it into the national security policy planning process while leaving the FBI with substantial control over most aspects of it. When the program expanded along with other aspects of national security policy after the beginning of the Korean War, it did so under the auspices of a very conservative bureaucracy with ties to similarly conservative interests in Congress.

Domestic communism had been a source of concern for some conservatives since before the New Deal, and the subject of administration policy since the president's March 1947 Executive Order on Employee Loyalty. The integration of these concerns into national security policy planning did not really begin until 1948, though. The role of domestic subversives in a potential Soviet campaign against the United States was mentioned in NSC 7, discussed by the National Security Council on March 30, 1948. The report called on the government to

> urgently develop and execute a firm and coordinated program (to include legislation if necessary) designed to suppress the communist menace in the United States in order to safeguard the United States

against the disruptive and dangerous subversive activities of communism.[42]

Other NSC and Defense Department memoranda from 1948 also indicate some concern about domestic communism, although they are generally vague about the policies their authors envisioned.

A few days after the discussion of NSC 7, Souers hired Coyne to prepare a report on internal security with policy recommendations. Souers proposed the Coyne study to the NSC on his own authority but may have been prompted by his friend Hoover, who had a long-standing interest in expanding and protecting his authority in this area.[43] Other intelligence agencies may have feared an expansion of FBI influence due to Coyne's appointment. The Office of Naval Intelligence (ONI), for one, expressed concern that the NSC report might interfere with its ongoing study of port security. ONI's concerns about possible domination of the study by the FBI are understandable, because the bureau had been at odds with the military intelligence agencies over jurisdictional issues since before World War II. These jurisdictional disputes had been formally resolved in the June 5, 1940, delimitation agreement giving the FBI jurisdiction over most internal security matters and setting up an Interdepartmental Intelligence Conference (IIC) to coordinate the operations of these organizations. This arrangement did not fully settle the issue, however, and tension between the members of the IIC persisted. Coyne reassured ONI that the NSC's role would be "coordinating, consultative, and advisory" and promised to avoid any actions that would "put the damper on" other projects related to internal security.[44]

Coyne's report, designated NSC 17, was submitted to the council on June 28, 1948. Although couched in language designed to appeal to others in the executive branch, the report represented the FBI's interests in internal security policy. It began with the ominous warning that "the United States is not adequately secure internally at the present time" and concluded that communism was the greatest threat to the internal security of the United States. Echoing Hoover's public remarks about the ability of each communist to control ten sympathizers outside the party, Coyne's report argued that "the strength of communism in the United States as elsewhere is cleverly concealed and organized on different levels." Casting its net broadly, the report argued that the Communist party planned to use nonmembers as the principal basis for its influence, noting that the internal security threat included "confused liberals" and those "unknowingly supporting communist 'front' organizations and mass movements." Monitoring such individuals and organizations was to be a concern of the internal security program.

The report's conclusions would have expanded the scope of the legal actions open to the FBI. Even though it concluded that most internal security problems were "interdepartmental" in nature, its proposed solutions most often called for FBI action. The FBI was already taking many of the policy actions the report recommended, in some cases without legal authority. In addition to investigating subversive individuals and organizations under the Smith Act and other existing laws, the FBI had also developed a list of aliens and U.S. citizens to be detained in the event of an emergency, and it was searching the baggage of suspected subversives leaving the United States. The report also criticized the State Department and other agencies for having permitting a group of Soviet civil engineers to visit the United States over FBI protests.[45]

The central recommendation of the report was that the NSC hire a Special Assistant on Internal Security to coordinate the internal security program, although this individual was to have no authority over the agencies involved. The report specifically rejected "the committee mechanism, comprised of representatives from many interested agencies," stating that it would be excessively cumbersome. It also warned that such a committee might undertake operations, rather than simply coordinate the functions of the existing agencies, encroaching on the authority of these other organizations.[46] All of these qualifications addressed FBI concerns about its bureaucratic autonomy. Since Coyne, the author of the report, was the obvious candidate for the position of special assistant, his appointment would have an FBI loyalist in the position of coordinating all internal security activities, giving Hoover a voice in national security policy planning without sacrificing any of his autonomy and authority.

Unfortunately for Hoover, Coyne's recommendations did not meet with immediate approval. While the initial response to NSC 17 was favorable, the program soon encountered resistance from other departments and became mired in the bureaucratic procedure of the NSC. On August 20, 1948, the NSC discussed the recommendation that a special adviser on internal security be appointed instead of establishing a new agency or interagency committee. Secretary of the Army Kenneth Royall contended that the special adviser would have insufficient authority to insure effective coordination. Royall's objections may have been prompted by the concerns of Army counterintelligence about the potential increase in FBI power implied by NSC 17. In any event, after some discussion, Souers offered to have the State-Army-Navy-Air Coordinating Committee (SANACC) review the matter, and the council agreed.[47] Souers requested that SANACC include representatives from other agencies concerned with internal security and appointed Patrick Coyne to represent the NSC in the discussions.[48]

The FBI had no interest in a reexamination of internal security policy that it could not control, and Hoover moved aggressively to prevent SANACC from doing anything that would erode the position of the bureau. Since the FBI was not directly represented in these deliberations, it had to work through the Department of Justice. As the White House staff member most closely involved with the formulation of internal security policy later recalled, however, in this area "the Attorney General's recommendations always came from the FBI."[49] Probably at Hoover's behest, Attorney General Tom Clark argued that SANACC's reconsideration of internal security policy was not necessary. He suggested instead that the White House reissue Franklin Roosevelt's statement asking all government bodies, as well as "all patriotic organizations and individuals," to report any subversive activities or other internal security matters to the FBI. Coyne strongly endorsed this suggestion in a letter to Sidney Souers.[50] Such a statement would have reconfirmed the authority of the FBI in internal security matters. The White House, however, declined to issue it.

The FBI had well-founded fears about the potential erosion of its authority and autonomy in the course of the SANACC reconsideration of internal security policy. Although the Department of Justice was invited to participate in the process, the basis for the SANACC discussion was a memorandum for the president written by Secretary of Defense James Forrestal. The memo argued for the establishment of "one individual or agency deriving its authority from the President" in the area of internal security, much as the CIA did in the intelligence field.[51] The new agency, the Interdepartmental Committee on Internal Security (ICIS), would have had the authority to review and supervise the activities of the FBI. This outcome, which had been explicitly rejected in Coyne's NSC 17, was precisely what Hoover wanted most to avoid.

Adding to its problems at this point, the FBI also had opponents on the White House staff. Although the staff's involvement in the deliberations of the NSC and SANACC was usually minimal, Truman referred Forrestal's memorandum to Stephen Spingarn, the member of the White House staff who usually dealt with internal security matters, before it was discussed by SANACC. While Spingarn argued that a new oversight body like the one Forrestal recommended was not necessary to coordinate all internal security matters, he was quite critical of the FBI.

In my opinion the most important and useful job that could be done in the internal security field would be to send a task force of competent experts into the FBI with a charter giving them complete access to all its records and all its information and the assignment of appraising the effectiveness of its internal security policies and work from the ground up. Such a survey should result in restoring control of the FBI to the Department of Justice and the Executive Branch where it belongs. Among other benefits, this would have the effect of suppressing further leakage of FBI reports to Congressional Committees in search of scare headlines, a practice which has adversely affected internal security most seriously by keeping the country disturbed about Communism on the basis of stale information which has already been acted upon by the proper authorities.[52]

Throughout his tenure in the White House, Spingarn expressed concern about the impact of internal security legislation on individual rights, although he also appears to have learned few additional details of the actual internal security program approved by the NSC after his comments on Forrestal's memorandum.

When the SANACC Ad Hoc Committee on Internal Security discussed Forrestal's recommendations, the Justice Department representative, reflecting the interests of the FBI, refused to accept the report. In his written dissent, he argued that his department was already carrying out the most effective elements of current internal security policy and rejected greater supervision of its activities.

The representative of the Department of Justice does not propose to abandon this highly successful policy nor to jeopardize the Department's traditional efficiency as an investigative and law enforcement agency by subscribing to a conclusion that the foregoing coordination must be placed on a compulsory basis, whereby an agency or person other than the Attorney General would be cloaked with the authority to monitor, supervise, or otherwise direct the functions of the Department of Justice in the field of internal security. Such a conclusion is as untenable as it is unnecessary.[53]

The Justice Department recommended instead that the coordination function be assigned to the IIC. Attorney General Clark repeated this recommendation in a letter to the president.[54] Rather disingenuously, the Justice Department then voted to approve the Forrestal recommendations provided that they were not interpreted to conflict with current Justice Department policy. Since this reservation amounted to a refusal to cooperate, the SANACC Ad Hoc Committee decided to send a set of documents to the NSC detailing its deliberations instead of formal recommendations.[55]

Although the report of the SANACC Ad Hoc Committee was circulated to the National Security Council as NSC 17/3, it did not recommend any clear course of action, and the council did not immediately discuss it.[56] Instead, the NSC awaited the outcome of informal negotiations between the FBI and the secretary of defense. John Ohly and Najeeb Halaby, who were then handling internal security matters for the Office of the Secretary of Defense, began drafting a new proposal, which they asked Patrick Coyne to review. The proposal would have established a somewhat less powerful Central Internal Security Subcommittee with most of the oversight powers envisioned by Forrestal. Coyne objected to this provision, arguing that it might evolve into a "new agency, or at least a semi-agency." He also argued that the CIA should be excluded from the IIC, because its charter prohibited any domestic activities, and that any new committee be expressly prohibited from examining the files of any existing agency without permission of that agency's head. Coyne kept Souers (and almost certainly Hoover as well) informed of these negotiations, which were to lay the groundwork for a meeting between Hoover and Forrestal in early 1949.[57]

When Forrestal, Hoover, and the attorney general met in January 1949, they adopted the FBI's position on most of the issues that separated them. As Forrestal had wanted, an Interdepartmental Committee on Internal Security was formed including representatives from the Departments of State, Treasury, and Justice and the National Military Establishment. However, it was limited to voluntary coordination rather than authoritative oversight, and it was prohibited from handling issues already under the jurisdiction of the IIC, which included most operational matters. Although the final agreement did not mention protecting the files of existing agencies, as Coyne had suggested, the CIA was excluded from the IIC. Finally, an NSC Representative on Internal Security was to be appointed to serve as a liaison between the two coordinating committees and submit semiannual reports to the National Security Council.[58] Forrestal and Hoover agreed that Coyne should occupy this position.[59]

Once Hoover and Forrestal had come to agreement, the NSC quickly ratified the arrangement. After several minor revisions, a joint memo from Forrestal, Hoover, and the attorney general was discussed by the NSC on March 23, 1949. The only dissent came from Secretary of the Army Kenneth Royall, who argued that dividing responsibility among two committees would not produce better coordination and would preclude any further action to do so. Forrestal probably shared Royall's concern, but he also knew this arrangement was the most the FBI could be persuaded to accept. He argued that the new arrangement was "a step forward, which must be monitored and pushed."[60] A directive authorizing the formation of the ICIS was promptly approved by the president as NSC 17/4. The charters of the IIC and the ICIS, which gave the IIC primary responsibility for the operational aspects of the internal security program, were drafted and approved by the president as NSC 17/6 on July 18, 1949.[61]

In addition to preventing the establishment of an executive body to oversee the internal security activities of the FBI, the arrangement embodied in NSC 17/6 preserved many of the advantages for the FBI contained in NSC 17. Its authority within the IIC was increased by the new charter. Hoover was elected to chair the conference, a position he occupied through the rest of the Truman administration. He also furnished the IIC with its permanent secretary, who selected the rest of its staff.[62] The ICIS elected Raymond P. Whearty, the representative of the Department of Justice, as its chair and set up its offices in the Department of Justice. Finally, as anticipated, Patrick Coyne was appointed NSC Representative on Internal Security, giving the FBI a permanent presence in the NSC staff.[63] Since the final outcome amounted to a nearly complete victory for the FBI, Defense Department advocates of a centralized internal security agency hinted that Louis Johnson might reject the agreement when he replaced James Forrestal as secretary of defense a few months later. When he failed to do so, the battle was effectively over.[64]

Although the approval of NSC 17/4 and 17/6 did not signal an immediate burst of activity in the field of internal security, it made the matter a formal part of overall national security policy planning in the NSC and insured that policy in this area would be dominated by the FBI. When it came, the expansion of the overall national security program would imply a concomitant expansion of internal security activities controlled by Hoover. Future NSC reports on the general topic of national security policy—including NSC 68—contained annexes on internal security drafted by the IIC and ICIS, just as they did on more conventional areas of national security policy. When NSC 68 was submitted to the council by the president so that the programs it suggested could be planned and their costs estimated, the IIC and ICIS drafted a set of goals for the internal security program. After the beginning of the Korean War, the achievement of these goals, which had been slated for 1954, was moved ahead to 1952.[65] As the rearmament program developed, the IIC and ICIS helped solidify the linkage between rearmament and a domestic agenda associated with the interests of the Nationalist Republicans and their bureaucratic and societal allies.

CHAPTER 7

The Conflictual Politics of Consensus Building III: Rearmament and the Red Scare

Mr. President, I think it is time for this Congress and for the 152,000,000 normal American people to serve notice that we can successfully fight a war abroad and at the same time can dispose of the traitorous filth and Red vermin which have accumulated at home.

—Joseph McCarthy

It is often said that the Truman administration and, particularly, the Secretary of State were "unpopular" and had trouble with Congress. It is true that many uncomplimentary things were said, but in Washington it is better to get what one wants than to be loved.

—Dean Acheson

This chapter presents historical evidence concerning the implementation of the trade-off between the rearmament program and the campaign against domestic radicalism. The last chapter examined the identity and institutional position of the conservative bureaucracies, business elites, and members of Congress backing this domestic agenda. A theoretical approach stressing bargaining between coalitions of interests rooted in the domestic political economy accounts for more of the historical evidence about the policy-making process than does the realist-statist approach, with its emphasis on state actions to defend core values or conform to the constraints and incentives of the international system. Statists and realists correctly point to events in Korea as an important force behind congressional approval of the rearmament program. However, they cannot explain interests and policy goals of the most important actors in the process. These interests shaped the response of the administration's opponents to the crisis in Korea and meant that the administration's pursuit of the rearmament program would have important consequences in other policy areas. Furthermore, historical evidence suggests that the bargaining process even influenced the conduct of the war in Korea.

Because the war would have required some increase in the military budget even in the absence of a broader rearmament program, the connection between the Korean War and rearmament was easy for the administration to establish. The linkage between the internal security program and the war was less obvious. It developed because it served the interests of both the administration and the Nationalist Republicans. The process through which the linkage developed was complex. With considerable help from their allies in the executive branch, the Nationalist Republicans took the initiative in engineering it, using the domestic red scare inaccurately remembered as "McCarthyism" as their principal weapon. Confronted with the administration's efforts to use the Korean War to induce them to accept rearmament, they sought to use the crisis to achieve some of their own political goals. Efforts to link a foreign threat to domestic radicalism were not new, but they enjoyed unusual success after the beginning of the rearmament. Although they may look like "hysteria and frustration" in retrospect, the tactics employed to implement the issue linkage make sense in terms of the actors' goals. The process-tracing analysis in this chapter will clarify the advantages of the domestic political economy model by demonstrating its ability to capture more of the details of the policy-making process.

"It would alert every employer in America"

Congressional action helped those in the executive branch seeking to expand the internal security program. Congressional hearings put pressure on the administration to act in certain cases, legitimized actions already under way in others, and helped create an atmosphere in which the FBI and the military internal security bureaucrats could pursue their own agendas unchecked by the doubts about their actions that persisted in the rest of the administration. As the administration sought congressional approval for the rearmament program, its Republican opponents prepared their own wartime agenda, which included antisubversive legislation that they had been seeking for some time but had been unable to enact.

Congressional action against the left in general and labor in particular was not new in 1950. During the 1930s, conservatives had often sought to link the New Deal to communist influence in the administration. These efforts culminated in the creation of the Special House Committee on Un-American Activities in 1938. Martin Dies (D-TX), who chaired the committee, was rabidly antilabor and had called for an investigation of the CIO's use of the sit-down strike. In August 1938, the Dies Committee charged 640 organizations and 438 newspapers with being communist-controlled and named 284 labor organizers and about 1,000 other individuals as members of the Communist party. Dies continued his activities along these lines through 1944, with significant help from the FBI. Although Dies's ill-advised efforts to force Hoover into even greater cooperation eventually contributed to his political downfall, the methods used by the Dies Committee were resurrected a few years later when the House Committee on Un-American Activities was reestablished.[1]

The most important domestic anticommunist action taken by Congress in 1950 was the passage of the Internal Security Act. Too often dismissed as an empty gesture to appease anticommunist hysteria, this legislation actually served an important purpose in the antilabor and antiradical campaign of the Nationalist Republicans. Its passage is also closely linked to congressional approval of the rearmament program. Also known as the McCarran Act, the measure included two titles, a Subversive Activities Control Act and an Emergency Detention Act. The first and most important title required all "communist" or "communist-front" organizations and their members to register with the attorney general. It authorized the formation of a Subversive Activities Control Board (SACB) to investigate suspected organizations that failed to register. The act also imposed a variety of penalties and restrictions on covered organizations, including the denial of tax-exempt status to the organizations and passports to their members. Title II of the act authorized the arrest and detention of suspected subversives in the event of an "internal security emergency."

Some parts of the Internal Security Act were never actually carried out, and the entire measure was eventually overturned by the courts or repealed by the Congress. As Fried (1990, 187) notes, the Supreme Court ruled in 1965 that the registration requirement violated the Fifth Amendment protection against self-incrimination. Richard Nixon, an early supporter of the measure while a member of the House of Representatives, abolished the Subversive Activities Control Board in 1973 after the Senate refused to broaden its duties. The emergency detention provisions were repealed by Congress in 1971. The future of the law was unknown in 1950, though. Its supporters expected it to become a lasting part of American law and to serve as a political signaling device, providing cover to the bureaucratic proponents of the internal security program by demonstrating the strength of its supporters.

The only part of the legislation that was probably not seriously intended was the Emergency Detention Act. This section, which led Truman to label the entire measure a "concentration camp bill," was actually written as a liberal alternative to the registration provisions contained in Title I and was opposed by many of those involved in developing the original McCarran bill. Indeed, they argued that it was unconstitutional.[2]

Believing that they could not stop the registration bill without providing an alternative, a group of liberal senators wrote the emergency detention measure in order to present an alternative that sounded tougher but omitted what they believed were the most harmful aspects of the McCarran bill. The emergency detention measures would have no practical effect unless the president declared a state of internal security emergency. On the other hand, liberals worried that the registration provisions would effectively blacklist liberal organizations with radical ties, particularly unions. The liberals were themselves quite anticommunist, but they worried about the consequences of a government program to rid unions and other organizations of communists. Recalling the red scare that had followed World War I, William Langer (R-ND) argued that supporters of the McCarran bill were attempting to re-create it in 1950. "We saw what happened the other day on the floor of the Senate. The senior senator from New Hampshire [Styles Bridges] rose and called members of the Farmers Union and their leaders Communists." Langer filibustered the bill until he collapsed and had to be carried from the Senate floor.[3]

Langer's concerns were well founded. In the context of existing law, the registration provisions were expected to eliminate radicals and communists from labor organizations and other groups. The Subversive Activities Control Act was part of a continuing legislative effort to achieve this goal. The Taft-Hartley Act had required the officers of labor organizations appearing before the National Labor Relations Board (NLRB) to file statements affirming that they were not members or supporters of the Communist party. In a 1948 speech stressing the threat of communism in the unions, Robert Taft proudly quoted the administrator of the NLRB: "the most potent weapon for fighting the Communist menace in America is the anti-red clause of the Taft-Hartley Act."[4]

Much to the irritation of its supporters, however, the affidavit provision was not especially effective in purging communists from the leadership of unions in which they were deeply rooted. Some unions and their officers simply refused to comply with the law, while others resigned from the party under protest, stating publicly that they did so only to comply with the law. Above all, Nationalist Republicans and their supporters worried that some who signed the affidavits secretly remained communists or "fellow travelers." For example, Robert Taft was especially concerned about the case of Maurice Travis, the secretary of the International Union of Mine, Mill and Smelter Workers, who had resigned from the Communist party on August 15, 1949, while affirming his belief that "good Communists are good trade unionists." Under the Taft-Hartley Act, no special mechanism existed to investigate the affidavits signed by union officials.[5]

Investigations by the SACB were expected to settle the question of who was a communist.

The Subversive Activities Control Act expanded the definition of a subversive organization. The law ordered registration not only of "Communist-action organizations," a term intended to apply to the Communist party itself, but also of "communist-front organizations." This broad category included organizations with communists or communist sympathizers among their leaders. This new definition raised liberal fears. Herbert Lehman (D-NY) argued that the discussion of communist-front organizations was "so broad that they can include almost every liberal in America. They can include labor organizations, church groups, social welfare groups, and even fraternal groups."[6]

The Internal Security Act provided other weapons for use against labor radicals. By requiring the registration of individual members as well as organizations, the law would publicly identify these people and make it easy for employers to fire them. The registration lists were to be available to the public. Karl Mundt, the Senate sponsor of the original measure, asserted that this was one of the bill's central purposes. "What would registration do? It would alert every college president. It would alert every employer in America."[7] There was little doubt about how this information would be used. Caute (1978, 153–55) reports that membership in any group on the attorney general's list of subversive organizations was a legally sustainable cause for dismissal. Even appealing to the Fifth Amendment protection against self-incrimination before a congressional committee was a sufficient basis for dismissing an employee. Caute (1978, 358–59) notes that congressional committees had been using hearings to influence the outcome of union elections and facilitate the firing of radical workers since 1947.

If most employers could be expected to fire suspected members of communist-connected organizations, "defense facilities" were legally required to do so. The Internal Security Act made it illegal for a member of any communist-action organization "to engage in any employment in any defense facility." "Defense facility" was defined very broadly under the act, and the secretary of defense was required to produce a list of them. Although the Department of Defense never actually published the list, the management of individual plants on it knew they were included, because each of them was assigned a security officer by the military. As noted earlier, members of the Industrial Advisory Committee of the Munitions Board followed the progress of these sections of the Internal Security Act through Congress, anticipating that it would facilitate the gathering of information on their employees by the FBI and military intelligence organizations. Employers with union contracts limiting their ability to fire suspected radicals also expressed hope the McCarran Act would provide a way of avoiding these restrictions by having the government assume legal responsibility for the dismissal.[8] In fact, Stein (1963, 103) reports that the legal standards applied in arbitration hearings changed, due in part to the influence of the McCarran Act, making it easier to dismiss suspected employees than it had been before.

While these aspects of the law were expected to have practical significance, the most important role played by the Internal Security Act was probably political rather than legal. Most of the programs mandated by the act already existed in the executive branch in embryonic form. For its Nationalist Republican sponsors in the Congress, the Internal Security Act was an attempt to institutionalize these programs and prevent the administration from curtailing them in response to liberal pressure. It demonstrated to the administration the political power of those backing the internal security program and provided the basis for further pressure if the administration had sought to back away from the program. There was no great protest from the supporters of the measure when certain aspects of it, especially the announcement of a list of defense facilities, were not carried out as stated in the act, because these programs were already in progress under the control of sympathetic elements of the executive bureaucracy. In short, the Internal Security Act provided political cover for the executive branch allies of the Nationalist Republicans.

The role of those allies, especially the FBI, in the development of the Internal Security Act is unclear. The Interdepartmental Committee on Internal Security and the Justice Department had suggested certain measures that were incorporated into the law, such as an amendment to the Espionage Act of 1917 lengthening the statute of limitations for espionage from three to ten years; nevertheless, J. Edgar Hoover refused to take any public position on the legislation. To the chagrin of the White House, however, he testified before the Judiciary Committee in the hearings on the bill, giving an alarmist view of the threat posed by domestic communism.[9] Both sides scrambled to appropriate Hoover's statements to support their position. Estes Kefauver (D-TN) repeatedly invoked Hoover's name in opposition to the bill, citing the FBI director's admonition against driving the Communist party underground. Explaining his support for the emergency detention bill as a substitute for registration, Kefauver contended that "[i]t means that I am ready to put all Communists and internal enemies of the United States behind bars anytime the FBI and the men who know Communists best say the word."[10] Senator Herbert O'Conor (D-MD) countered with more references to Hoover's wishes. "The McCarran bill follows the desire of J. Edgar Hoover, FBI Director, who has given us assurances that the primary thing in which the FBI is interested is in knowing the identity of all Communists in the United States."[11]

Despite Hoover's public silence, there are indications that he supported most elements of the Internal Security Act. Patrick McCarran had close ties to the FBI, and the law held important benefits for the bureau. O'Reilly (1983, 213–14) notes that the provisions of the law removing tax-exempt status from communist-action or communist-front organizations provided the bureau with another tool to use in the legal assault on these groups. The FBI furnished information on this subject to the House Special Committee to Investigate Tax-Exempt Foundations beginning in 1952. The act also tightened the rules governing the behavior of aliens and naturalized U.S. citizens, authorizing the deportation of those who engaged in various prohibited forms of political action. Most of the law simply legitimized ongoing FBI activities, something Hoover frequently sought to do by securing presidential orders. The registration provisions gave the FBI a broad rationale for investigating any group that arguably might have to register with the attorney general. The Internal Security Act gave the attorney general the authority to ask the SACB to hold hearings to determine whether an organization should be ordered to register. Theoharis (1978, 134–35) and O'Reilly (1983, 261) note that the FBI was often the source of these requests.

By contrast, the liberals' emergency detention measures were not helpful to the FBI. The bureau already had a list of persons to be detained in the event of an emergency. Title II of the Internal Security Act used a different set of standards for its emergency detention program, posing some difficulties for the bureau. Ironically, as Fried (1990, 196) points out, Senator Paul Douglas (D-IL), one of the coauthors of the Emergency Detention Act, was on the FBI's list of those to be detained. Theoharis (1978, 48–52) notes that, although the FBI sought to fit its preexisting program into the Title II criteria in various ways, Attorney General J. Howard McGrath instructed the bureau to proceed with its previously developed program after the act passed.

The Justice Department, which usually reflected the position of the FBI on internal security matters, maintained an ambiguous position on the registration requirement long after it was clear that the president opposed it. Justice ignored instructions from the White House on this issue. In May, White House Special Counsel Charles Murphy and Stephen Spingarn, the staff member who handled most internal security matters, wrote a memo to Truman criticizing the Department of Justice for its approach to internal security, arguing that it ignored individual rights. Truman sent Spingarn to tell the attorney general to follow the White House line on these issues. Although Spingarn spent "the better part of an hour" discussing the matter with McGrath, Deputy Attorney General Peyton Ford nevertheless continued to argue in favor of a registration requirement.[12] When the Korean War began, the White House staff feared consulting the Justice Department about changes in the "urgent list" of proposed legislation, expecting them to place additional antisubversive measures on it.[13]

"An action of moral appeasement on a matter of highest principle"

While the major provisions of the Subversive Activities Control Act had been before the Congress for several years, they remained stalled there until the beginning of the Korean War. Indeed, some expected the measure to die without a vote in 1950.[14] Much as it did for the administration, the political situation that developed after the beginning of the war provided Nationalist Republicans with a new opportunity to pursue a preexisting agenda. Republicans had long blamed subversives in the administration for the New Deal and communists in the unions for postwar labor unrest. According to a report prepared by the Republican National Committee in 1946, "[t]here is still no question that the present Democratic Administration, like its predecessor, is still harboring a dangerous number of Communists and Communist-sympathizers on the Federal payroll."[15] The centerpiece of the Internal Security Act, the registration requirement, was first introduced by Representative Karl Mundt (R-SD) in July 1947. It was reported out of the House Committee on Un-American Activities in April 1948 with the cosponsorship of Representative Richard Nixon (R-CA). The Mundt-Nixon bill was quickly passed by the House, 319 to 58, but failed due to Senate inaction. Although hearings were scheduled for the bill before the Korean War began, it faced an uncertain future with the Democratic leadership committed to blocking it. Once the war began, the Republican Policy Committee placed the bill on its "must list."[16]

After the beginning of the Korean War, the Nationalist Republicans sought to link the revised Mundt-Nixon bill, now under the sponsorship of Patrick McCarran, to the ongoing international crisis, which even the administration portrayed as part of a larger international communist agenda. Republican efforts to promote this legislation did not consist entirely of ideological appeals, however. Circumstantial evidence indicates that they may have threatened to delay the supplemental defense appropriations requested by the administration in order to ease passage of the Internal Security Act. The search for communists in the State Department, exemplified by Joseph McCarthy's highly publicized antics, is best understood as part of an effort by the Nationalist Republicans to raise the costs of obstructing the internal security program in both Congress and the executive branch, just as the Korean War raised the costs of obstructing rearmament. Failing to take action on internal security under such circumstances would have been politically embarrassing to the administration. Since internal security policy was effectively controlled by elements of the bureaucracy with strong ties to Nationalist Republicans, administration action in this area was likely to further the Republican agenda. Republican threats to the administration's appropriations request were a coercive bargaining device used to increase the chances that the administration would choose to cooperate with them by accepting their interpretation of the domestic requirements of the Cold War.

While McCarthy lent his name to the red scare, his activities were only one aspect of the political machinery that sustained it. His efforts were abetted by the Nationalist Republican leadership, which provided him with both political support and some of the information needed to make his allegations. Although Robert Taft apparently had serious doubts about McCarthy's reckless charges, "which may be embarrassing before we get through," he nevertheless encouraged them, arguing that he "should keep talking and if one case doesn't work out he should proceed with another one" (Patterson 1972, 446). The fact that Taft was then engaged in a difficult reelection battle, confronted with an all-out effort by both the AFL and the CIO to defeat the principal author of the Taft-Hartley Act, probably added to his anticommunist vehemence. As was generally the case, the demands of the political situation took priority over private intellectual misgivings.

The Republican party in the Senate provided McCarthy with additional support. A little more than a month after McCarthy first asserted that he had a list of communists in the State Department, Taft's Republican Policy Committee hired a special staff member, Maurice Joyce, for the sole purpose of investigating additional cases of subversive influence in the government. Joyce developed an informant in the State Department who provided the names of employees about whom loyalty investigations had turned up some derogatory information. He then passed these names along to McCarthy, Bridges, and others who charged publicly that these people were communist sympathizers or Soviet spies.[17] Joyce also helped plan the timing of charges made on the Senate floor about communists in the State Department and suggested that Republicans launch "a careful well planned offensive against the administration's deliberate 'whitewash' of the 1945 Amerasia case," stressing the role of Owen Lattimore. Within a month, Lattimore became one of McCarthy's principal targets.[18]

McCarthy also received assistance from the FBI, both directly and through the Republican Policy Committee. Theoharis and Cox (1988,

280–81) note that McCarthy had been on friendly personal terms with Hoover since his arrival in Washington in 1947 and that Hoover even agreed to a radio interview with McCarthy in April 1949. By all accounts, Hoover and his lieutenants provided McCarthy with evidence to help substantiate his charges and suggested new angles of attack on the State Department and other targets. This arrangement, which began in March 1950 and lasted until Hoover severed relations with McCarthy in July 1953, was concealed from the attorney general when he sought to find out how McCarthy obtained FBI information.

Without the support of Senate Republicans and the FBI, McCarthy might not have been able to sustain his effort as long as he did. After the election of Eisenhower in 1952, both Senate Republicans and the FBI withdrew their support and assistance, contributing to McCarthy's Waterloo at the 1954 Army-McCarthy hearings and his subsequent censure by the Senate. McCarthy, of course, was never part of the Republican leadership and had his own motives for continuing his assault on alleged communists in the government and the society. Without their support and that of the FBI, however, McCarthy's power quickly waned. The timing of their withdrawal of support sheds light on the motives of those who had assisted him earlier. With a Republican in the White House, there was no longer any reason for the Republican congressional leadership or the FBI to bring pressure of this sort on the administration.[19]

For several reasons, the State Department was an especially inviting target for Nationalist Republicans seeking to bring pressure on the administration to act aggressively against domestic radicals. Foreign policy was the administration's highest priority, so threats against the State Department, the principal agency charged with carrying out that policy, were likely to get the administration's attention. As early as 1947, Nationalist Republicans were using the State Department as a way to get the administration to take action against domestic communism. As chair of the Senate Appropriations Committee during the Republican-controlled Eightieth Congress, Styles Bridges had the means to command the attention of major State Department officials. He raised the issue of communists in the CIO with Robert Lovett and John Puerifoy during the course of discussions on the State Department's budget.[20] Although it is not clear if any action resulted from this particular request, it is significant that Bridges chose to raise the matter with the State Department rather than an agency more directly concerned with such matters. Attacking the State Department served a similar purpose after the Republicans lost control of both houses of Congress in 1948: threats to the administration's highest priority were most likely to wring concessions from it.

Attacking the State Department was also an attractive strategy because Nationalist Republicans opposed most aspects of the administration's foreign policy anyway. No understanding of the bargaining value of putting pressure on the administration was required to motivate the Nationalist Republican rank and file to act on this issue. Undermining the State Department's effectiveness in carrying out the administration's foreign policy was itself a goal they and their societal constituency could support. Although not all Nationalist Republicans had identical foreign policy preferences, they were all united in their opposition to the administration's European-oriented internationalism. The specific goals attributed to the alleged conspiracies in the State Department, from supporting state socialism in Britain to selling out anticommunist forces in China, differed depending on who was making the charges. The target of the charges, however, remained the same. The search for communists in the State Department promoted unity among the administration's Republican opponents.

During the crisis surrounding U.S. intervention in Korea, attacks on the State Department were an especially advantageous way to link the domestic goals of the Nationalist Republicans to the administration's efforts to secure support for rearmament. Since the administration was using the ongoing crisis as a means of insuring support for rearmament, administration officials were very reluctant to argue that the Republicans were exaggerating the seriousness of the situation. By focusing on the State Department, the Republicans linked their allegations about domestic communism to the war in Korea. However, the policies they proposed, especially the Internal Security Act, were the same ones they had been seeking since the end of World War II. As Korea had done for the administration, the red scare provided a convenient vehicle for Republicans to build support for their preexisting policy agenda. The administration had been having trouble handling the charges made against the State Department throughout the spring of 1950. After the beginning of the Korean War, with the administration itself stressing the threat of a global communist conspiracy, these problems became even more serious. Nationalist Republicans hammered away at the need to attack the domestic manifestations of the global communist conspiracy the administration identified as the cause of the war in Korea and the reason for rearmament. Homer Capehart, the Nationalist Republican senator from Indiana, put succinctly the predicament facing the administration and congressional liberals opposed to the Internal Security Act: "I cannot conceive of anyone who would be opposed to passing the legislation necessary to control the Communists within our own ranks, particularly at a time when we are at war."[21]

Proponents of the Internal Security Act had more political assets with which to pressure the administration than simply the rhetorical connection between communism and the Korean War. There is significant circumstantial evidence that Nationalist Republicans and their Southern Democratic allies may have threatened to sabotage the first supplemental appropriations bill if the president had made a serious effort to prevent passage of the McCarran bill. The timing of legislative action on the two measures, the circumstances surrounding the president's veto of the McCarran bill, and the removal of Stephen Spingarn from the White House staff immediately after these events took place all suggest that there was some connection between them. While an explicit bargain between the administration and congressional supporters of the McCarran bill is unlikely, there are good reasons to believe that the administration and its Republican opponents understood the connection between that piece of legislation and the rearmament budget.

The first supplemental appropriations bill and the McCarran bill were dealt with by the Senate almost simultaneously. On September 14, when the Senate approved the first supplemental appropriations bill, it attached an amendment proposed by Kenneth Wherry (R-NE) that would have banned all nonmilitary aid to any country exporting to the Soviet Union any commodity that could be used for military purposes. Among other countries, Wherry made it clear that Britain was a target.

> All one has to do is read the newspapers if he does not want to take the argument of the Senator from Nebraska. . . . There was a statement by Winston Churchill condemning his own country for shipping $2,000,000 worth of machine tools straight to Russia last year. These tools process other tools, the very tools that make the tanks and make the wire used by the enemy in Korea this afternoon.[22]

Even if Britain had not been excluded from economic assistance, the imposition of congressionally mandated restrictions on European exports would have seriously hampered administration efforts to maximize European foreign exchange earnings.

On September 20, the same day the House and Senate passed the final version of the McCarran bill, Truman appealed to the conference committee to drop the Wherry amendment, an action he said was "of grave importance."

> The amendment applies not only to arms and armaments, but to any articles that could be used for the production of military materiel. Since almost all goods and commodities can be used for the production of military materiel in one way or another, the amendment, if effective, would require a substantially complete embargo between

Eastern and Western Europe. . . . To cut this trade off suddenly would bring about dislocations in the Western nations that would more than offset any advantages that might be gained.[23]

Two days later, Truman vetoed the McCarran bill, and both houses immediately voted to override his veto. The same day, the Senate agreed to a House proposal to substitute a measure calling upon the NSC to determine the countries that should lose their foreign aid for shipping goods to the Soviet Union.

At first glance, Truman's veto of the McCarran bill seems to rule out any possibility of a trade-off between it and the rearmament budget. On closer examination, however, the circumstances surrounding the veto raise serious questions about his intentions. Since Congress was expected to adjourn very soon after it passed the McCarran bill, it seemed likely before September 21 that Truman might block the legislation through a "pocket veto," simply by refusing to sign it. Once Congress adjourned, the measure would have died without presidential action in ten days. The president's comments on the legislation raised this possibility.[24] The Democratic congressional leadership evidently raised the issue of a pocket veto with the president at their regular Monday meeting with him on September 18. The "Big Four" Democratic congressional leaders wanted Truman to sign the bill. While he would not agree to do so, Truman promised to take action on the bill promptly, foreclosing the option of a pocket veto.[25] In fact, the veto message was prepared in such haste that the Bureau of the Budget was unable to secure the usual formal agency recommendations on which such messages were usually based. Only a few oral comments could be solicited.[26] Truman also rejected the idea of appointing a Presidential Commission on Internal Security and Individual Rights, something his staff believed might help sustain the veto, because of opposition from the Big Four.[27] With its outcome a foregone conclusion, both houses voted to override Truman's veto only hours after the president acted.

The pending vote on the Wherry amendment offers a good explanation for the president's action on the McCarran Act. Truman told his staff that all of the Democratic congressional leaders had urged him to sign the bill when it reached his desk. Although the actual content of their discussion with Truman cannot be known, because no records of these meetings were kept, they almost certainly discussed the status of the critically important first supplemental appropriations bill, then under consideration by a conference committee. The Wherry amendment was still attached to the bill at that point, and Truman and the leadership probably believed they would have a more difficult time persuading the Senate to agree to its removal if Truman took action to kill the McCarran Act.

The circumstances under which the Wherry amendment had been approved by the Senate gave cause for concern. Eighteen Democrats, mostly from the South and West, had voted to suspend the rules and allow the voice vote that passed the Wherry amendment on September 14.[28] Combined with the Senate Republicans, all of whom had supported the voice vote, these defections raised the possibility that the measure might actually pass on a final vote if the president antagonized these conservative Democrats, all but one of whom supported the McCarran Act. Truman's agreement to act quickly on the McCarran Act so that his veto could be overridden before the Senate considered whether to retain the Wherry amendment makes sense in light of this concern. The Big Four may have argued that a pocket veto would endanger the more important appropriations bill. When the Wherry amendment was reconsidered on September 23, the day after the Senate passed the McCarran Act over Truman's veto, only two of the Democrats who had previously supported the measure voted in favor of it.[29]

Given Truman's concern about the Wherry amendment, why did he not simply sign the McCarran bill into law, as the Big Four had urged? Such an action would have created serious problems not only with the Democratic party's liberal and labor constituencies, which uniformly opposed the bill, but also within the White House staff, where Charles Murphy and Stephen Spingarn had devoted enormous effort to defeating the measure. Spingarn argued that signing the bill "would represent an action of moral appeasement on a matter of highest principle."[30] At the urging of Murphy and Spingarn, the president had already stated his opposition to the measure, although somewhat obliquely, in his August 8 message to the nation on internal security. Liberal senators who had voted against the measure also contacted the White House to express their concern that "they would be out on a limb if the president did not veto the bill." Spingarn assured them that the president had always intended to veto it, although he acknowledged that the Department of Justice had drafted a signing statement as well.[31] The veto message, written under Spingarn's direction, brought Truman enormous praise from liberals, who had become increasingly alienated from the party, without any real cost to the administration. Hamby (1973, 414) quotes a number of effusive liberal commentaries on Truman's veto message, calling it "magnificent" and "a new Magna Carta of human and civil rights."

Shortly after the passage of the Internal Security Act, Stephen Spingarn was removed from the White House staff and appointed to the Federal Trade Commission. The move came as a surprise to Spingarn, who was extremely unhappy at being "kicked upstairs" and was never able to find out why it happened.[32] Although Spingarn is not an important figure in his own right, his removal is important because it marks a change in White House handling of internal security matters. Spingarn had a reputation for being overbearing, which is the usual reason given for his removal.[33] While his personality certainly played a role, it does not fully explain his transfer. Spingarn had worked in the White House for two years and had even been assigned there for a trial period before officially joining the staff in 1948, so there had been ample opportunity to assess his personality before he was permanently hired.

The events surrounding Truman's veto of the McCarran bill furnish some missing pieces in the explanation for Spingarn's removal. While there is no indication that Spingarn's personality changed during his tenure at the White House, there is ample evidence that the importance of internal security policy did. Given the pressures of the bargaining situation and the likelihood that further compromises on the issue would be necessary, Truman probably felt a need to be more flexible about internal security policy. Spingarn's commitment to limiting the internal security program, coupled with his inability to keep a low profile, posed an increasingly serious problem in late 1950. There was also a growing gap between the actual internal security program and Spingarn's knowledge of it. Like the rest of the White House staff, Spingarn was rarely privy to the deliberations of the NSC, and there is no reason to think he knew the scope of the internal security program it supervised. In any event, his rhetoric on internal security would have made little sense if he had known what was actually going on. Progress reports submitted to the NSC in early 1951 by the NSC Representative on Internal Security indicate that the FBI already had drawn up plans to detain over 14,000 people in the event of an emergency and was busily recruiting informants in defense plants.[34] Spingarn's frequently expressed ideological commitments and ties to the Americans for Democratic Action and other liberal groups might have created problems for the White House had he learned what it was willing to tolerate.[35]

Spingarn's difficulties with the conservatives who now dominated internal security policy were also a growing problem. His bad relationship with the FBI has already been mentioned. Spingarn's relations with other conservative figures was similarly strained during the struggle over the Internal Security Act. His effort to "explain the defects" in the legislation to a group of Democratic senators offended Herbert O'Conor (D-MD), who especially supported the antialien provisions of the legislation and believed the president did also.[36] When Spingarn told him he was mistaken, O'Conor walked out of the meeting. Others who stayed behind may also have been irritated. Spingarn also recalled offending Vice President Alben Barkley, one of the members of the Big Four who urged Truman to sign the McCarran bill.[37] These incidents no doubt underlined the president's concerns about Spingarn's handling of this increasingly sensitive issue.

"This is an outrageous condition in connection with loyalty investigations"

Despite the concerns of many in the administration, including the president, little was done to discredit Nationalist Republicans' alarmist version of the threat posed by domestic communism or to limit the corresponding escalation of the internal security program. The administration's record during the months following its decision to proceed with rearmament and to commit troops to Korea is filled with missed opportunities to take action against Joseph McCarthy and others in Congress. Instead, the White House actually facilitated the efforts of the FBI to expand its authority over the internal security program. The administration's concurrent effort to build support for the rearmament program and the bargaining situation it faced with its Republican opponents are crucial in explaining why it placed so few obstacles in the way of the developing internal security program.

Throughout 1950, the White House reacted passively to the internal security legislation developing on Capitol Hill. The appointment of a Presidential Commission on Internal Security and Individual Rights was repeatedly postponed, although the White House staff unanimously believed it would be useful in preventing the passage of the bill. Beginning in June, before the development of the McCarran bill was very far advanced, some White House staffers urged the appointment of a presidential commission to balance internal security concerns with the protection of individual rights. The White House was becoming increasingly disillusioned with the work of the Tydings Committee in the Senate, which had originally been set up to examine McCarthy's charges. Staff memoranda maintained that the committee had become more a public platform for McCarthy than a tool for exposing the absurdity of his charges. A presidential commission might keep the investigation under closer White House control and afford McCarthy fewer opportunities for making spectacular public charges.[38] On June 19, Spingarn drafted a proposed executive order establishing the commission and a letter to potential members. Three days later, the president called a meeting of congressional leaders, the White House staff, and the attorney general concerning the proposed commission. While the staff and the State Department favored the proposal, the attorney general and most of the congressional leadership opposed it. The president took no action.[39]

Support for a presidential commission remained strong within the

White House staff, but the president took no action in time to make a difference. The plan was again considered for incorporation into the August 8 message on internal security and later into the veto message on the Internal Security Act, but it was rejected in both cases. Before the veto message was drafted, Truman told the staff he was favorably disposed toward the plan, which they believed might help sustain a veto. While the announcement of a presidential commission was included in the first three drafts of the message, it was deleted from the final version at the attorney general's request. During discussion of candidates for the Subversive Activities Control Board, Spingarn raised the issue yet again.[40] When the passage of the Internal Security Act failed to end congressional agitation on domestic communism—and with all the supplemental appropriations bills safely passed—Truman finally appointed a Commission on Internal Security and Individual Rights under the direction of Admiral Chester Nimitz in January 1951. However, the panel was never able to begin work, because Patrick McCarran refused to report out of the Judiciary Committee a bill exempting commission members from conflict-of-interest statutes. No further initiatives of this sort were undertaken.[41]

While the president opposed the McCarran Act in discussions with the White House staff, his public rhetoric on the matter was ambiguous. The August 8 message on internal security argued that some action had to be taken "to keep our freedom secure against internal as well as external attack, without at the same time unduly limiting individual rights and liberties." While the message criticized some pending legislation as being "so broad and vague as to endanger the freedoms of speech, press, and assembly protected by the First Amendment," it did not mention the McCarran bill or attack any specific provision of the proposed legislation.[42] Above all, the address did not attempt to diminish the sense of crisis that had prevailed since the Korean War and made opposition to the McCarran Act politically difficult for liberal members of Congress. If anything, the August 8 message lent credibility to the linkage between the international communist threat and radicalism at home by stressing the need for action against the threat of domestic communism. Because the White House was using this crisis to promote the rearmament program, and because the cooperation of the McCarran bill's supporters was needed to get the program through Congress, the decision not to attack the bill directly or diminish the importance of internal security is not very surprising.

The White House did even less to limit the internal security bureaucracy's freedom of action and much more to facilitate its activities. On July 24, Truman released a statement affirming the FBI's authority in the area of "espionage, sabotage, and subversive activities" and calling on all organizations and individuals with information on internal security matters to refer them to the FBI.[43] The IIC, which Hoover chaired, proposed that the president issue such a statement on July 5. The administration may have intended this measure to undercut congressional action. In 1948, Spingarn had suggested to then–Special Counsel Clark Clifford that such a statement be issued "to spike vigilante activity in the internal security field."[44]

For the FBI, however, the president's July 24 statement had a rather different meaning. As Theoharis (1978, 75–81) points out, the prevailing directive, issued by President Roosevelt on January 8, 1943, had avoided the mention of subversive activities, addressing instead only "espionage, sabotage, and violations of the neutrality regulations." This statement had marked a specific change from the September 6, 1939, statement, which had included the handling of information on "subversive activities" in the scope of the FBI's authority. Ever since the issuance of the altered 1943 statement, Hoover had been concerned about its implications both for the FBI's bureaucratic turf and for its legal authorization to monitor domestic radicals. At Hoover's request, the attorney general had requested a new presidential directive to reaffirm the FBI's authority to investigate subversive activities in 1948. As noted earlier, the White House had rejected this request at the time. Because of pressure from Hoover's congressional allies, and perhaps some measure of White House inattention, the FBI director was able to get the authorization he sought in 1950.

The White House also succumbed to pressure to increase the breadth of the government employee loyalty program. Despite the fact that the Loyalty Review Board was headed by a Republican, Seth Richardson, it was harshly criticized by Republicans for alleged leniency and for refusing to permit an independent review of the loyalty cases it had dismissed.[45] Theoharis (1971, 256–57) notes that in 1949, the Loyalty Review Board asked the president to revise the standard for dismissal from government service to toughen the loyalty test for employment. Congressional pressure and administration concern that McCarthy and others might find more politically damaging cases strengthened the case for tougher loyalty standards. In February 1951, the Loyalty Board again asked that the president revise the standard for dismissal from "reasonable grounds exist to believe that the person involved is disloyal" to "reasonable doubt exists as to the loyalty of the person involved." Following the failure of his attempt to appoint a presidential commission to review loyalty procedures and other internal security measures, the president implemented the new standard by executive order in April 1951. Not only did it reverse the burden of proof, placing it on the employee rather than the government, it also required a new investigation of previously closed loyalty cases and set the stage for a new round of resignations and dismissals.[46]

There are good reasons to believe that, by this time, Truman was acting more out of a sense of political necessity than from his anticommunist
convictions. While there is no doubt about the president's anticommunism, his ideological convictions do not explain why he accepted programs
he doubted and placed them in the hands of bureaucracies he mistrusted.
Truman had long been suspicious of Hoover's promotion of the threat of
domestic communism. The president privately compared the FBI to the
"NKVD or Gestapo" and had initially decided not to assign it the task of
investigating federal employees in 1947.[47] On a memo from Clark Clifford
suggesting this course of action, Truman wrote: "Clark: You have prop-
erly diagnosed the case. But J. Edgar will in all probability get this back-
ward looking Congress to give him what he wants. It's dangerous."[48]
Much of Truman's staff appear to have shared his suspicions about the
bureau.[49] These misgivings about the internal security program did not
disappear after 1950. Donovan (1982, 367–68) quotes Matthew Connelly's
notes on Truman's comments at the August 10, 1951, cabinet meeting:
"This is an outrageous condition in connection with loyalty investigations.
People are being persecuted without cause. [Truman] urged members to
cooperate in correcting these abuses." Nevertheless, the president continued to assign the FBI greater responsibility for the internal security program. Given the need for the cooperation of the program's congressional
backers and the costs of reducing FBI control over it, Truman believed the
price of correcting this "outrageous condition" was too high.

In spite of misgivings in the White House, the internal security program expanded rapidly after 1950 under the control of the FBI and smaller
bureaucracies in the Department of Defense. Its scope widened, and
although the members of the NSC received reports on it, they rarely discussed them, apparently content to leave the program alone. Patrick
Coyne's semiannual progress reports to the NSC on the internal security
program rarely elicited comment, in spite of the remarkable information
they contained. A typical discussion of these reports by the council, from
April 18, 1951, was summarized as follows:

> MR. LAY explained briefly the Progress Report on NSC 17/4 and
> NSC 17/6, and informed the Council that Mr. Coyne was on hand to
> answer any questions the Council might have.
>
> There were no questions, but MR. FORD [the deputy attorney gen-
> eral] remarked that the report was excellent.[50]

Despite NSC apathy, this particular report mentioned several striking
new developments in the program not discussed before. Earlier reports

gave no information on the activities of any particular agency, only on the general coordinating actions of the IIC and ICIS. This report was much more specific, noting that the FBI had

> identified approximately 14,500 individuals as dangerous or poten-tially dangerous to the national defense and the public safety of the United States. These individuals are being considered for apprehen-sion and detention should circumstances require such action. The number of individuals in this category is increasing as additional derogatory information is received and as investigations are con-ducted.

It also commented that the FBI had expanded its internal security efforts in plants on the key facilities list developed by the secretary of defense.

> As of November 25, 1950, there were 5,300 plants designated by the Secretary of Defense as vital facilities, and as of December 20, 1950, over 13,000 informants had been developed by the FBI with respect thereto. This program is continuing and the number of informants is steadily increasing.[51]

The FBI had long been involved in some of these activities, but NSC acknowledgment gave Hoover additional political and legal cover. Hoover probably would not have disclosed this information if he had believed that it would create opposition from the members of the NSC. His willingness to include these details is indicative of the change in the atmosphere within the administration between mid-1950 and early 1951. A political equilib-rium had been reached in which the administration no longer seriously questioned the prerogatives of the FBI in the area of internal security, and the Nationalist Republicans in Congress no longer sought to block the rearmament program. Hoover, an alert veteran of 33 years in the federal bureaucracy, took full advantage of the situation.

Had any serious attention been paid to the report, it would have been apparent that the FBI was moving beyond even the broad scope of the internal security program originally authorized by the NSC. There is some evidence that the recruitment of plant informants mentioned in the April 1951 report, perhaps the most directly antilabor aspect of the internal security program, was particularly important to the FBI. At the Septem-ber 8, 1950, NSC meeting, when the previous progress report had been dis-cussed, Deputy Attorney General Peyton Ford stated that "he had men-tioned to Mr. Coyne the desirability of emphasizing our industrial security program." This was the only substantive comment recorded on internal security at the meeting.[52] The FBI also appears to have been somewhat overeager in extending its informant program to industrial facilities around the country. The April 1951 report incorrectly states that there were 5,300 plants designated as "vital facilities." In fact, there were only 3,282 plants on the key facilities list as late as 1953, although the number was reported to be slowly growing. Furthermore, not all of these plants were designated as "vital," the highest security category.[53] Apparently, the FBI was at work in a broader range of plants than those included on the key facilities list. Some indication of the energy with which the FBI pursued this aspect of the program can be found in the rapid increase in the number of informants reported to the NSC. By the end of 1951, it had risen from about 13,000 to 52,791. The report also noted that some 62,000 members of the American Legion had agreed to furnish information to the FBI on suspected subversive activities.[54]

While the FBI's industrial security program gained momentum in 1951, the Department of Defense was not left far behind. Defense Department bureaucrats anxious to prevent any interruption of defense production brought pressure to bear on organized labor. In early 1951, a strike by the United Automobile Workers at the Fairchild Aircraft Plant in Hagerstown, Maryland, raised fears in the Pentagon that the production of C-119 troop carrier aircraft would be slowed. The Air Force urged both the UAW and Fairchild to settle the dispute as quickly as possible. At the same time, the Defense Department leaked information about this and other expected strikes to Drew Pearson, who noted ominously in his "Washington Merry-Go-Round" column that the Defense Department feared communists were behind it.[55]

In general, views of the labor movement among Defense Department officials ranged from distrust to outright hostility. John Fanning, the director of labor relations in the Office of the Assistant Secretary of Defense for Manpower, Personnel and Reserve, alerted Defense Department officials to the dangers of dealing with union officers, especially those "accused of following the Communistic party line." His deputy, F. A. O'Connell, was openly hostile to "union people," arguing in a memo to the assistant secretary of defense that they should not be permitted to fill government labor relations positions, since they would inevitably side with labor and were unlikely to accept government policy. O'Connell also had a close working relationship with Fred Haught, an officer in the National Association of Manufacturers, soliciting his suggestions on strengthening an "Anti-Communist Union amendment" to a 1953 labor relations bill.[56] As if their own proclivities in this direction were not enough, bureaucrats in the Defense Department concerned with labor matters received anti-union newsletters produced by defense industries such as General Electric, whose "Employee Relations News Letter" darkly hinted at the subversive intentions of even such conservative labor leaders as James Carey of the International Union of Electrical Workers (IUE).[57]

Those in the Department of Defense who did not share this antilabor attitude were in a weak position. John Ohly appears to have been concerned about the direction of the military's internal security program prior to his departure from the department in 1949. He argued that those accused of disloyalty should be given the right to examine their FBI files, something the FBI consistently refused to allow. Given Ohly's distaste for the direction of the internal security program, it is not surprising that he pleaded with Louis Johnson to allow him to leave the department for a post in the administration of the Mutual Defense Assistance Program.[58] Anna Rosenberg, the Assistant Secretary of Defense for Manpower, Personnel and Reserve, also appears to have been somewhat sympathetic to concerns expressed by labor. She was the subject of sexist and anti-Semitic prejudice both inside and outside the department, however, so her position was quite tenuous.[59] Beginning in February 1950, the Office of the Secretary of Defense had its own loyalty review board to investigate the "loyalty, character, [and] associations" of those working there. Under such scrutiny themselves, Defense Department administrators were unlikely to show much sympathy for those accused of being loyalty or security risks in industry.[60]

The Department of Defense emulated the FBI's methods as well as its policy goals. The Physical Security Equipment Agency (PSEA) was established in 1951 to furnish surveillance equipment and expertise for covert investigations by "all agencies of the Department of Defense."[61] At least initially, the agency appears to have been an amateurish operation, purchasing and testing equipment from magazine advertisements.[62] Consultation with the FBI, which had considerable expertise in this area, was difficult because of Hoover's preoccupation with protecting the bureau's bureaucratic turf and sources of information. By the end of 1952, the PSEA was drawing criticism from other investigative agencies within the Department of Defense. In particular, they complained that the PSEA was not coordinating its operation with the FBI and CIA, and that it was freely distributing its equipment and expertise to civilians not affiliated with the Department of Defense.[63]

The aggregate impact of the internal security program administered by the FBI and the Department of Defense is difficult to assess, even though examples of its excesses abound.[64] Brown (1958, 181) conservatively estimates that one person out of every five, in a labor force of about 65 million, was subjected to some sort of loyalty test, oath, or investigation by 1958 and that about 11,500 persons were denied employment as a result. Caute (1978, 364) found that about four million people were investigated and 5,312 persons were denied clearance under the Industrial Personnel Security Program, the Port Security Program, and the Atomic Energy Commission Program through 1956. Both Brown and Caute note, however, that it is difficult to estimate the number of people who actually lost their jobs because of the program, since many chose to resign rather than be fired and were thus not included in the statistics of those denied clearance. In addition to the difficulty of estimating the number of people who resigned in connection with the program, it is also likely that the number of people actually dismissed has simply been underreported. It is worth noting that entry 253 of the finding aid for the records of the Office of the Secretary of Defense (RG 330) in the National Archives contains "dossiers on suspended or discharged employees suspected of being disloyal or engaging in subversive activities while employed in government-owned, -operated, or -controlled industries, 1950–51." This still-classified entry is unusually large, consisting of 104 linear feet of records, raising the possibility that more people than previously thought may have been affected by the program.[65]

A 1953 draft report by the PSEA on the use of polygraph examinations provides additional evidence that internal security measures were sometimes applied very broadly and that the proportion of people directly affected in a given organization could be quite large. According to the report, between November 1951 and December 1952, polygraph examinations were administered to all 5,056 employees and job applicants at an unnamed federal agency. These examinations focused on such broad areas as "Sympathy toward Communism," "Past or present participation in any type of Communist activity," and "Close friends or relatives having Communist sympathy," as well as "homosexual activity." Of the 1,147 employees tested, 641 (56 percent) exhibited some form of deception, according to the report. Of these 641 individuals, 111 were either fired or allowed to resign, mostly for "sex deviations." An additional 70 investigations were still pending at the time the report was written. In all, during 1952, nearly 10 percent of the agency's employees were forced out of their jobs as a result of the lie detector tests. This number is especially staggering in light of the fact that all federal employees had already been investigated and cleared under the 1947 Federal Employee Loyalty Program. Those applying for employment fared even worse. Of the 3,865 job applicants tested, 1,352 (35 percent) were dismissed after the polygraph examination indicated some deception. All 1,703 who passed the test were hired. The investigators were enthusiastic about the results of the study, noting that although current polygraph technology was difficult to deceive, technical improvements were still desirable. The chilling effect of these examinations on the employees not fired as a result of them can only be imagined.[66]

In addition to its effects on left-liberals and radicals in the federal bureaucracy, the program had a disproportionate impact on the left wing of the labor movement. Even without state intervention, left-led unions would have faced a serious challenge from anticommunist elements of the union movement in the postwar era. The added problem of state action made the task facing these unions much more difficult. For example, as noted earlier, the United Electrical Workers Union (UE), the largest of the 11 unions expelled from the CIO in 1949 and 1950, was singled out by members of the Industrial Advisory Committee during the planning of the industrial personnel security program. UE suffered a precipitous decline in membership—from over 500,000 in 1945 to about 100,000 by 1955—but remained active. Most of the expelled unions were not so fortunate; only four of the eleven survived. Waterfront and maritime unions had especially radical reputations and faced the most serious repression. Under the Port Security Program initiated by the Coast Guard in July 1950, all maritime employees were investigated, and 3,783—0.6 percent of all those in these occupations—were denied clearance. Many others left maritime work rather than face the investigation, and some were reportedly still living and working under false identities as late as 1964. The National Union of Marine Cooks and Stewards (NUMCS) ultimately voted itself out of existence in 1954 rather than merge with a more conservative union, but the larger International Longshoremen's and Warehousemen's Union (ILWU) managed to survive.[67]

An incident chronicled in the papers of Averell Harriman illustrates both the attitude toward union activity of those administering the internal security program and the lengths to which they were able to go by 1951. The reach of the program extended to family members of suspected labor radicals as well as to the radicals themselves. Harriman was asked to intervene on behalf of David Lasser, an officer in the conservative International Union of Electrical, Radio and Machine Workers. Lasser's son, an officer candidate in the Air Force, had been questioned extensively about his father's radical activities in the 1930s and was about to be denied his commission based on this information. While Lasser successfully handled the problem with Harriman's help, few could boast this sort of political connection.[68] Without any defenders in either major political party, those targeted by the internal security program had no political recourse. Conversely, with few influential critics, those running the program faced little oversight.

**"A full understanding of the problems that we face
ahead of us"**

Why did the administration accept the linkage between the internal security program and rearmament? Although acceding to Republican domestic priorities helped secure approval for the rearmament program, one could argue that the administration might have forced its political opponents to accept rearmament without making any such concessions simply by playing on the political imperative of supporting American troops in Korea. While plausible, such a strategy would have been difficult and risky for at least two reasons. First, although it made congressional rejection of the program costly, the Korean War did not guarantee support for rearmament. Throughout much of the time Congress considered the rearmament program, the Korean War appeared likely to end in the near future, endangering the future of the program. Even if the war continued, administration efforts to prevent its opponents from deriving some benefits from the crisis would have increased the chance that they would turn against the war altogether and reject the rearmament program. Second, blocking the issue linkage between the internal security program and rearmament would have required a reversal in the administration's prior ideological rhetoric and a dismantling of the institutional apparatus that supported it, an especially difficult task during an election year. While Cold War ideology—the factor most often used to explain the link between McCarthyism and the Cold War—may have played a role in getting the administration to accept the issue linkage, its importance should not be overstated. This ideology was more a product of contemporary politics than a causal factor shaping them.

Because of the centrality of the Korean War to the administration's strategy for getting the rearmament program through Congress, the prospect of a quick end to the war was viewed with some concern. Frank Pace, then serving as secretary of the army, recalled a conversation with Secretary of Defense George Marshall that illustrates this concern. Having just returned from the October 1950 conference between Truman and MacArthur at Wake Island, Pace informed Marshall that MacArthur believed the war would end by Thanksgiving. At the time, preparations for the submission of a second supplemental defense appropriations bill were in progress but not yet complete.

> Well, [Marshall] said, "Pace, that's troublesome."
> Well, I said, "Sir, you must not have heard me, I said, the war would be over by Thanksgiving and the troops home by Christmas."

He said, "I heard you, but," he said, "too precipitate an end to the war would not permit us to have a full understanding of the problems that we face ahead of us."

And I said, "But General Marshall, do you mean by that that the American People would not have fully had an opportunity to grasp the implications of the cold war?"

He said, "I certainly do."

But I said, "General Marshall this has been a very, very difficult and expensive war from the American People's point of view."

"Yes," he said, "I know, Pace, but you didn't live through the end of World War II the way I did, and watch people rush back to their civilian jobs and leave the tanks to rot in the Pacific and the military strength that was built up to fade away."

I said, "I know General Marshall, but a great deal of water has passed under the bridge since then." I said, "Would you say I was naive if I said that the American people had learned their lesson?"

And he looked at me with those cold blue eyes and he said, "No, Pace, I wouldn't say you were naive, I'd say you were incredibly naive."[69]

As the course of the Korean War shifted in favor of the United States, there are indications that other administration decision makers shared Marshall's concern about the consequences of peace. George Kennan (1967, 492–95) recalled State Department objections to the admission of the People's Republic of China to the United Nations as a way to facilitate a negotiated settlement in Korea. John Foster Dulles argued that such a move would "confuse American public opinion and weaken support for the president's program looking toward the strengthening of our defenses." Just before the Chinese intervention, the president told the NSC that, without the Chinese threat, passage of a $45 billion military budget was unlikely. "Our main objective must be to convince an almost hostile Congress of the need for the program."[70]

These concerns make sense in light of the incomplete state of the rearmament program at the time. While the first supplemental appropriation had been signed by the president on September 27, the second supplemental appropriation, not submitted to Congress until November 27, was still in the preparation stages. As early as August, prominent Republicans and conservative Democrats began to question publicly the wisdom of such high levels of military spending.[71] An early end to the war would have reduced the chance for congressional approval of the additional $19.9 billion requested. The use of the Korean War as a mechanism to impose costs on congressional opponents of rearmament placed a premium on the prompt submission of defense spending proposals. Throughout the late summer of 1950, the administration rushed to produce program estimates that could be turned into appropriations requests as quickly as possible. Truman ordered the preparation of estimates speeded up after submission of the first supplemental appropriations request on July 19, setting a September 1 deadline.[72] The Pentagon, where Louis Johnson was still secretary of defense, was slow to produce acceptable budget figures. In late August, the Ad Hoc Committee on NSC 68 had to request an additional extension of the deadline after deciding that the military estimates submitted to the group were inadequate.[73]

Concerns about getting the rearmament program through Congress also encouraged acceptance of plans to continue the war after the North Korean forces had retreated beyond the thirty-eighth parallel. As was noted earlier, plans for a "rollback" of communist influence in North Korea were put forward as early as July 1. Among others in the State Department, John Allison, director of the Office of Northeast Asian Affairs, argued in favor of such a course of action. On the other hand, the Policy Planning Staff expressed concerns that Soviet or Chinese intervention might result from the rollback. The issue was referred to the NSC staff for discussion on July 17.[74] Although the resulting policy statement, NSC 81, authorized the move across the thirty-eighth parallel, it was not utterly reckless, cautioning that a Soviet or Chinese move into North Korea would be a sufficient cause to cancel the move into North Korea. Given widespread support for rollback in the State Department and the Pentagon, the decision to proceed with it may have been a foregone conclusion, but the policy was not finalized until September 11, when Truman approved NSC 81/1.[75] Operational orders were issued to MacArthur later that month, and on September 30, South Korean forces crossed into North Korea.

Despite the concerns about Chinese intervention, the administration was peculiarly reckless in both the authorization and the execution of rollback in Korea. In deciding to cross the parallel, the concerns raised by both Paul Nitze's Policy Planning Staff and George Kennan that the Soviets or Chinese might intervene were disregarded. The Policy Planning Staff wrote that the risks of such intervention exceeded the benefits of controlling the entire Korean peninsula.[76] Kennan similarly suggested that "[i]t is not essential to us to see an anti-Soviet Korean regime extended to *all* of Korea for all time." He went on to argue that "we should make it an objective of our policy to terminate our involvements on the mainland of Asia as quickly as possible and on the best terms we can get."[77]

Once the rollback had begun, U.S. decision makers consistently, even willfully, misjudged Chinese and Soviet intentions, continuing the march to the Yalu River in spite of clear indications that the Chinese were planning to intervene. They ignored the mildly cautious advice contained in NSC 81/1 about Soviet or Chinese intervention. While U.S. allies expressed great concern about the likelihood of such intervention, American decision makers were apparently unconcerned, even discouraging the British from investigating a settlement acceptable to the Chinese.[78] They refused to believe further Chinese warnings not to continue moving north, despite the enormous buildup of Chinese troops along the border and even a limited Chinese intervention in late October. These signals were coupled with a direct threat of intervention made by the Chinese to the Indian ambassador in Beijing.[79] In his memoirs, Acheson (1969, 452) comments simply that this threat was not considered "an official statement of policy."

The administration's insensitivity to Chinese warnings and its indifference to opportunities for a negotiated settlement make sense in light of the role the war played in the effort to gain congressional approval for rearmament. Those most closely involved in the rearmament program were concerned that a premature end to the war—even an early victory—might not produce the political support required to insure implementation of the rearmament program. Not only would halting MacArthur's northward advance have removed the war as a basis for political support, it would have had far-reaching political consequences in view of the broad coalition supporting the rollback and the readiness of administration opponents to interpret any hint of a diplomatic concession as an act of treason. It may be true, as Leffler (1992, 379) argues, that the administration could have found some domestic support for a negotiated settlement, but such an effort would not have served its larger policy goals. The potentially disastrous consequences of rollback in Korea are not merely obvious in retrospect—they were clear to Kennan, Nitze, and most U.S. allies at the time. Indeed, the domestic political arena is virtually the only one in which the advantages of this policy were clear.

While the administration recklessly disregarded warnings of Chinese intervention, Acheson and Truman were far more cautious and attentive when it came to their domestic opponents. At the time the crossing of the thirty-eighth parallel was authorized, they took steps to insure that the proponents of preventive war, or a military move into China, would not subsequently dominate administration policy. On September 11, the same day he approved NSC 81/1, Truman asked Louis Johnson for his resignation. Johnson's ties to the Nationalist Republicans as well as the China lobby raised the possibility that these groups might make it difficult for the president and the secretary of state to control the rollback effort once they had initiated it. The inevitable pressure from these groups for a move into China would be easier to manage with the help of a secretary of defense who was loyal to the administration's overall policy goals.[80] While Acheson and Truman probably wanted to signal their intention to maintain the U.S. position in the Third World, they also wanted to retain control over the implementation of this commitment.

Even if administration decision makers had been sure the war would continue until the rearmament program was in place, they still would have had good reasons to make concessions to the Republicans and seek a cooperative outcome. While the Korean War made opposition to the rearmament program difficult, opposition to rearmament—or even the war itself—was not impossible. As noted earlier, the Nationalist Republican leadership harbored serious doubts about the real wisdom of intervention even though they publicly supported it. Administration officials were justifiably worried that the war might not provide the base of political support they believed was necessary to preserve the new national security policy in "the long pull," a crucial element of the NSC 68 program.[81] Acceptance of the issue linkage in 1950, including the set of policies and political actors accompanying it, gave Nationalist Republicans a stake in the Cold War. To the extent that they made use of the crisis brought on by the Korean War to serve their own political ends, they were unlikely to reject the underlying premise that the United States had to respond to the global threat posed by international communism. While some in the administration worried about the implications of the internal security program—just as some Nationalist Republicans worried about the impact of the administration's national security policy—neither side was willing to forgo the gains it made from the issue linkage in order to address these concerns.

Nationalist Republican behavior can only have increased administration concerns that the war in Korea might not be sufficient to insure their support for rearmament. Especially after the Chinese intervention, Nationalist Republican leaders indicated that they might turn against the war. The fact that the crisis brought on by the Korean War affected both domestic and foreign policy issues sheds light on the curious positions some Nationalist Republicans took on the war. After Chinese intervention, some Nationalists who had expressed public support for the war vacillated between arguing for a withdrawal from Korea and demanding an all-out war against China. This sort of position-taking makes sense in light of the political situation facing the Republicans. While demanding the strongest possible military action in Korea helped reduce the political advantage that normally accrued to the administration under these circumstances—an important consideration immediately before an election—Republicans also needed to keep alive the possibility that they might turn against the war. This gave the administration an incentive to continue making concessions to them.

Combined with the rapid military reversals that characterized the first six months of the fighting in Korea, these contradictory incentives gave rise to some peculiar rhetoric from Republican leaders. Patterson (1972, 454–55) notes that Robert Taft argued publicly on July 6 that it was necessary "to march right on over the thirty-eighth parallel and occupy at least the southern part of North Korea," while worrying privately that the United States was "in real danger of becoming an imperialistic nation." After the Chinese intervention, Taft argued alternatively for withdrawal and for expansion of the war into China.[82] He also maintained contact with figures on the pacifist left, including Norman Thomas and A. J. Muste, keeping alive the possibility of working with them in opposition to the war, which became much less popular after the Chinese became involved.[83] Kenneth Wherry was equally inconsistent, privately admitting his uncertainty. Responding to a letter from a political ally in Nebraska in December of 1950, Wherry refused to endorse any policy, confining himself to the presentation of three possible options: "appeasement," an all-out effort to roll back Chinese forces in Korea using the atomic bomb and Nationalist Chinese forces, and "to pick up and come home and establish a new perimeter in the West."[84]

Other Republicans echoed this uncertainty about the war. Like Taft and Wherry, many vacillated between calls for preventive war and demands that the United States abandon its commitments in Europe and withdraw from Korea. In January, General Bonner Fellers, serving as a military consultant to the Republican National Committee, wrote to Robert Taft that the Republican party should seek a withdrawal from both Korea and Europe and urge instead a reliance on air power to defeat any Soviet attack on the United States. Fellers later revised his opinion on withdrawal, opposing any movement toward a cease-fire. While Fellers consistently supported the use of air power, the political and military purposes for which he wanted to use it varied.[85] Herbert Hoover was more consistent than many, asserting in December that the United States was the "Western Hemisphere Gibraltar of Western Civilization" and that it should rely on air and sea power to defend itself against the Soviet threat.[86]

The welter of apparently contradictory positions taken by the Nationalist Republicans has led some observers to comment on their apparent lack of understanding of the reality in Korea. Cumings (1990, 31) comments that

> [t]he utter unrealism of rollback policies (proved in the frozen wilderness of North Korea) and the predilection for losing gloriously instead of winning shrewdly (MacArthur) expresses the typical lack

of interest in or knowledge of the world at large for these quintessential American nationalists.

Another understanding of this apparent confusion, as with the administration's ambivalent attitude toward the internal security program, can be found in the linkage between domestic and foreign policy priorities. Just as many in the administration sincerely worried about the course of the internal security program, many Nationalists were genuinely concerned about the implications of extensive American commitments all over the world. As events altered their assessment of the implicit trade-off they were making, their positions shifted. The trade-off was attractive, but enthusiasm for it varied with the expected costs of the administration's national security policy, including the war in Korea. Indeed, the real possibility that Republicans might turn against the war made the trade-off possible, since it forced the administration to consider other ways to secure their support.

In addition to the tactical reasons for accepting the linkage between rearmament and the internal security program, the administration was constrained, to some extent, by its prior rhetoric on the two issues. As Theoharis (1971), Freeland (1972), and Griffith (1970) have pointed out, the Truman administration discovered soon after the end of World War II that broad rhetoric against the communist threat was a useful way to generate public support for its foreign policy. The linkage between the Soviet threat and domestic communism had been part of administration rhetoric long before NSC 68, playing a particularly prominent role in its campaign against the Progressive party in 1948. Truman's establishment of the Federal Employee Loyalty Program and other actions designed to counter the threat of domestic communism did nothing to end discussion of the issue, as Truman and his staff appear to have hoped. By the time Joseph McCarthy launched his campaign against communists in the government with his famous speech at Wheeling, West Virginia, in February of 1950, the Truman administration had already invested heavily in the rhetoric of domestic anticommunism. Backing away from this rhetoric would have been costly, especially in an election year.

While the costs of questioning the rhetorical connection between domestic and international anticommunism were real, the ideological linkage alone does not adequately explain the development of the internal security program. Genuine concerns about domestic communism do not explain the particular policies chosen to address these fears. Why was so much power given to the FBI when the White House was clearly very suspicious of the organization? If an appeal to mass anticommunism was a goal of these programs, why were many of them carried on in secret or with very limited public knowledge? These programs can be better understood as a response to political imperatives rather than products of the ideology of Truman and key figures in his administration.

The ideological linkage between domestic and international anticommunism reflected an emerging political and institutional structure more than a consistent set of beliefs on the part of individual political leaders. Events and decisions made during the 1949–51 period set up enduring institutional structures that perpetuated the policies associated with them. By 1950, the conceptual linkage between the two areas of policy would have been difficult to sever, not only because of the burden of the administration's own previous rhetoric, but also because each step forward in the internal security program helped strengthen the institutional position of those favoring even more drastic action. The concessions granted the FBI in response to congressional pressure would have been difficult to reverse even if the administration had attempted to do so. Once the industrial personnel security program was developed, it quickly fell under the control of elements of the Defense Department that had strong incentives to cooperate with the industry representatives who had helped develop the program. In general, the FBI and the Defense Department had neither the motive nor the inclination to consider the position of the labor movement or radicals within it. Similarly, having set up the Federal Employee Loyalty Program as a temporary expedient, the administration found it difficult to refuse demands to tighten loyalty standards. The internal security program was also self-reinforcing because criticism of it, from inside or outside the government, could be hazardous to one's career.

A similar dynamic helped sustain the rearmament program. The struggle over the policy within the administration had resulted in the removal of most of those favoring alternative policies based on lower levels of military spending. Edwin Nourse, Louis Johnson, and Frank Pace, all of whom had advocated defense cuts in late 1949, were no longer in a position to do so again after losing the battle over NSC 68. Once the policy was selected, personnel changes reinforced it. Similarly, George Kennan, who did not believe the buildup was necessary, left the State Department in August 1950. Furthermore, the rearmament program represented an enormous financial windfall to U.S. defense industries and created new supporters for itself. When the Eisenhower administration sought to cut the military budget a few years later, it met significant resistance, and not only from those who had originally worked to establish large defense budgets in the first place. As Fred Block (1980) has pointed out, the rearmament program established the military-industrial complex as a lasting feature of U.S. politics.

There is nothing particularly impressive about the arguments that joined the issue of the Soviet threat with a campaign against domestic radicals. The issue linkage is not a necessary one, and it was not chosen because it made more sense than the available alternatives. An equally cogent argument could have been made for the implementation of greater domestic social reforms in order to demonstrate the superiority of democratic capitalism as a way of life for the working class. Indeed, most of the principal actors involved in the political process that established the issue linkage were not especially comfortable with it. Truman worried about the consequences of the internal security program even as he facilitated its implementation. Taft and other Nationalist Republicans worried about the eventual consequences of growing U.S. imperialism even as they voted to support the programs that made it possible. After the fact, the policies of the early Cold War period may appear to be a coherent whole rooted in the ideology of anticommunist internationalism. When they were developed, however, they were more the product of political bargaining and conflict than a response to any single ideological appeal. The ideology of the Cold War, which linked domestic and international anticommunism, is best understood as a result of the politics of the 1949–51 period, rather than as a driving force behind them. Ultimately, the prevailing ideas of the Cold War came to reflect the prevailing political arrangements.

CHAPTER 8

Conclusion: Domestic Politics and Theories of National Security Policy

It is technically impossible to isolate foreign policy from all other aspects of life and consider it purely a matter of government concern, although such a view has been encouraged by the documentary publications of the Foreign Office. Such a view may be valid for the detailed course of a single negotiation and the methods used during it, which are revealed in the documents, but it fails to do justice to the fundamental factors in the foreign policy of a whole era.

—Eckart Kehr

Things don't break down into neat little compartments. You don't draw a distinction between domestic and foreign.
—George Elsey, Assistant to the President, 1946–51

In addition to explaining the linkages between domestic and foreign policy choices during the early Cold War era, this book has compared two theoretical approaches to the policy-making process. In chapter 1, I outlined a domestic political economy theory of foreign policy, contrasting it with the more familiar realist and statist approaches. The domestic political economy theory emphasizes political conflict among divergent foreign policy interests rooted in differently situated sectors of the domestic economy. It treats policy outcomes as the result of policymakers' efforts to build and maintain coalitions of these interests in order to retain power and implement their chosen policies. Domestic and foreign policies are linked because the political leaders of coalitions with opposing interests also bargain across the full range of domestic and foreign policy issues in order to secure their most important policy priorities. Statist and realist approaches to the policy-making process treat central state decision makers as if they were relatively autonomous from societal pressure. In these accounts, a set of consensual core values or objective constraints and incentives from the international system shape policy. The evidence presented here indicates that the domestic political economy model explains this particular historical policy-making process better than do realist and statist approaches.

The Domestic Political Economy and National Security Policy

The domestic political economy account presented here focused on two aspects of the policy-making process: (1) the sources of policymakers' preferences on national security policy, and (2) the nature of the coalition-building and bargaining processes on national security policy issues. I found a systematic relationship between senators' preferences and the economic structure of their home state. Senators from states where a high proportion of the largest firms had foreign direct investments, where banks lent relatively heavily to Europe, or where the import-competing sector was relatively small tended to support the administration's internationalist foreign policy. Senators from states where relatively few large corporations invested outside the Western Hemisphere, where banks tended to lend to Asia, or where the import-competing sector was relatively large tended to oppose this foreign policy. In short, there was a statistically discernible relationship between conflicting economic interests and political actors' preferences on U.S. foreign policy during the 1949–51 period.

The requirements of coalition building and maintenance and the need to obtain the acquiescence of political opponents in order to secure high-priority policy items provide a good way to understand the behavior of major political actors in this case. Major personnel changes in his administration, as well as the need to maintain the support of internationalist elites, help explain President Truman's decision to discard his plans to reduce military spending and instead accept NSC 68's call for rearmament. The need to secure the acquiescence of the administration's opponents in Congress helps explain the reversal of the decision to avoid military involvement in Korea, as well as the administration's abandonment of its domestic social welfare agenda and its acceptance of a campaign against domestic radicals. The imperatives of political bargaining also help explain the behavior of the Nationalist Republicans. Their attacks on the loyalty of many State Department employees, as well as their vacillation on the war in Korea, make sense in light of their need to keep political pressure on the administration and link the international crisis in Korea to their domestic policy priorities.

This case suggests three general conclusions about U.S. national security policy: (1) it is influenced by many of the same factors that affect policy in other areas; (2) it is the product of a whole political system, not just a discrete portion of it; and (3) an effort to incorporate both the interests of major political actors and their institutional position in the concrete, historical political system is required to explain it.

National security policy is not fundamentally different from other policy issues. The distributional politics that occur over other issues may occur over national security policy as well. Not everyone has the same stake in the values the policy protects. Cases where the interests of the entire nation are equally threatened are quite rare. The United States did not face a threat of this sort during the early Cold War period and does not face one now. In the absence of such a threat, national security policy, like policy in other areas, is likely to reflect the interests of the coalition controlling the state and the political bargaining required to enact the policy. The principal goal of the rearmament program associated with NSC 68 was to preserve an international system in which Europe and other economically important parts of the world were open to U.S. trade and investment. The program was directed against both military and economic threats to the establishment of such a system. The varying interests of different sectors of the economy in the success of the national security program, and their corresponding willingness to help bear its considerable costs, shaped support and opposition to the program. National security policy is often presented in terms of idealistic goals and patriotic symbols. This rhetoric does not insulate it from the same sort of political conflict found in other areas of policy.

Not only do the politics of national security policy not stop at the water's edge, they continue up to the highest levels of the state. The executive branch is also an arena of political conflict over the distributional consequences of this policy. During the early Cold War period, conflicting interests over national security policy existed in the executive branch as well as the Congress. Internationalists drawn primarily from eastern financial and legal circles dominated the State Department. They were able to draw on the political support of others with ties to this segment of the political economy. Louis Johnson, who was building a constituency with very different interests, opposed the commitment of greater resources to the national security program. While the internationalists in the State Department eventually became the dominant faction, their triumph was not unproblematic. Unless the executive branch is dominated by a party with completely homogenous interests and insulated from society, the divisions over national security policy evident in the domestic political economy are likely to be found there as well. Even if no political divisions existed within the executive branch, one would still have to consider the president's need for political support from diverse interests outside the government.

A second set of theoretical conclusions concerns the advantages of considering national security policy as the output of a complete political system instead of some discrete subsystem. At the highest levels of the state, substantially the same political actors face each other on a wide range of issues, including national security policy. As long as this is the case, political trade-offs across those issues are likely when their relative importance differs to the actors involved. Because of the possibility of such bargaining, outcomes on substantively unrelated issues may affect each other. While the administration used the Korean War to get congressional acceptance for its rearmament program, Nationalist Republicans and their allies in the executive branch used the war and the need to secure congressional approval of rearmament to persuade the administration to make concessions on domestic issues. If the administration had viewed the Fair Deal or a balanced federal budget as equally important policy goals, it is quite possible that rearmament would not have been successfully implemented. Indeed, the administration might never have proposed it.

Because of strategic interaction among actors in the political system and the connections between outcomes on substantively unrelated issues, it is difficult to assess the behavior of political actors in one area without knowing what is taking place on other issues and in other parts of the political system. The connections between issues are often discussed in terms of the political climate. Examining the specific connections between the preferences of the actors and the resolution of the issues offers a less nebulous way of understanding how issues are linked. The vacillation of many Nationalist Republicans between calls for a withdrawal from Korea and demands that the war be expanded into China is puzzling at first glance. However, it makes sense when one considers the bargaining process linking the expansion of the Cold War with domestic policies they favored. Truman's grant of greater authority to the FBI, an organization he generally mistrusted, is also more comprehensible when this connection is considered. Acheson's and Truman's willingness to support MacArthur's march toward the Chinese border despite signs of impending Chinese intervention makes little sense unless one examines the effects of the war on other U.S. political actors. Of course, all of these actions could be explained in terms of mistakes and individual idiosyncrasies, but such an explanation offers no help in developing theory of any sort. It does not contribute to a broader understanding of the political system or the policies it produces.

A final set of conclusions concerns the need for theories linking the political actors' interests with important aspects of the historical context that are not directly reducible to these interests. The approach taken here primarily uses interests to explain the linkages between official policymakers and societal actors. It suggests that the positions taken by policymakers reflect the interests that back them. It also characterizes the policymaking process in terms of bargaining between the representatives of policy perspectives rooted in the domestic political economy. However, some consideration of the influence of factors not related to interests is necessary in order to explain how the final outcome was reached. Two categories of variables not reducible to the interests of the actors helped shape the outcome in this case: the institutions of the particular historical political system and the legacy of past actions by the major actors.

Knowledge of the institutional features of a particular case is necessary in order to apply what would otherwise be an ahistorical model to a historical case. If some of these institutional factors had been different, even the same distribution of interests in the political economy might have produced a different outcome. By institutions, I mean the rules granting the actors special prerogatives or restricting their behavior in a way not directly related to their interests. The position of political actors in the institutional context of the time can enable them to influence other actors' choices. Although some idiosyncratic features of this historical case, such as the political skills of J. Edgar Hoover and Dean Acheson, are of limited interest beyond it, the institutional features found here may help explain other outcomes in the U.S. context.

Above all, because of the institutional advantages afforded by the office, foreign policy interests favored by the president have important advantages over their opponents. Not only does the president have a significant claim on the loyalty of members of his party in Congress, but he can also manipulate external events in ways his opponents cannot. Truman's decision to intervene in Korea made it very difficult to oppose rearmament openly. While Nationalist Republican leaders like Robert Taft protested the intervention, they had no politically viable choice but to support it. Similarly, Truman was able to take action on internal security policy without first gaining the approval of all elements of his party, some of which would probably have opposed him. No such option was open to any group in Congress. The ability of the president to take actions of this sort, particularly intervening in Korea, was very important in securing his most important policy priorities in this case.

Although the president has important institutional advantages, they are not unlimited. While presidents can initiate international commitments, as Truman did in Korea, they cannot always control the consequences of those commitments. Other states may create situations not anticipated when the commitment was made. In the case of Korea, the need to keep the war going until, as George Marshall told Frank Pace, there was "a full understanding of the problems that we face ahead of us" prompted the administration to support an expansion of the war that eventually provoked Chinese intervention.

A related consideration in applying this approach to actual historical cases is the role of ideology, understood as a persistent commitment to a particular set of policy ideas. In the sense I am using the term here, ideology refers to constraints on policy choices caused by similar choices in the past. Like institutions, this notion is not directly reducible to the interests of the actors involved. While institutions are relevant because of the persistence of the political system's rules, ideology is relevant because of the persistence of certain ideas even after the interests they originally served have changed. While ideas must appeal to a coalition of supporting interests sufficient to secure their initial acceptance, they are likely to change more slowly than the interests of those who originally put them in place.

The reasons for the persistence of ideology have less to do with the intellectual appeal of the ideas themselves than with the costs of changing them. There are at least two reasons why ideas about policy change more slowly than do interests. First, it is difficult for individual policymakers to abandon long-held ideas, even if there is political pressure on them to do so. Both acquiring expertise and developing a reputation as an advocate of a certain line of thinking are costly for individuals. Of course, individuals also develop a genuine personal belief in particular policies and may refuse to change. In the case I examined here, it was more common for individual policymakers to be replaced than for them to change their minds. Frank Pace, Louis Johnson, and Edwin Nourse, each of whom opposed high levels of defense spending, all eventually resigned or were replaced rather than reversing their positions on this issue.

A second reason ideas are likely to change more slowly than interests is that policy currents are costly to develop and do not exist for every imaginable set of policies. Building a political coalition behind a particular set of policies, including a committed set of experts to implement them, is costly and fraught with risk. This consideration presumably played a role in Truman's decision to accept NSC 68, even though he was probably uncomfortable with its fiscal implications. Had he rejected it, he would probably have had to rebuild much of his foreign policy apparatus and the supporting coalition behind it, since they were strongly committed to the program.

In this sense, ideology amounts to a bias in favor of declining interests and the status quo. For example, Robert Griffith (1979) notes that William Langer (R-ND) was an "old progressive," representing interests in the political economy that had virtually disappeared by 1950. In the regression models presented in chapter 4, Langer was an unusual case, one of only two senators to both favor the Fair Deal and oppose the national security program. Similarly, the bloated size of the FBI and the large number of former agents that J. Edgar Hoover used to promote his influence and the interests of his organization were products of World War II. After the war, Hoover was able to shift quickly from wartime internal security tasks to the search for domestic communists, a mission for which there was a ready set of supporting interests in society. The size of his organization gave him an added advantage that would not have been available if he had had to build the organization from its prewar size starting in 1945. In general, institutions and ideologies make it easier to maintain an existing policy than to establish a new one.

While ideology may play a role in explaining policy outcomes if it is understood in this way, evidence in this case suggests there are good reasons to be suspicious of explanations treating ideology as a system of beliefs divorced from any material source of support. First, accounts of this sort, which focus on the consciousness of decision makers, must address the evidence that there is no necessary relationship between personal beliefs and actual policy choices. Truman was suspicious of J. Edgar Hoover and his organization, but he nevertheless increased the authority of the FBI and accepted the political intelligence Hoover offered him. Robert Taft's concerns about the validity of McCarthy's charges against the State Department did not prevent him from facilitating McCarthy's efforts. Much of the apparent hypocrisy that fills the early Cold War period can be understood as politicians taking actions to which they saw no politically attractive alternative. The disjunction between beliefs and actions extends to collective outcomes as well. Very few political actors appear to have wanted all of the policies associated with rearmament by 1951. As realists have long argued, politics has its own logic, and it may encourage the acceptance of alternatives that run counter to the real preferences of decision makers. In any event, this appears to have been the case during the 1949–51 period.

Realist and Statist Approaches to Rearmament

The 1950 rearmament decision should be a strong case for realist and statist approaches. The new policy was planned at the highest levels of the state in great secrecy, and it involved central questions of national security. Furthermore, realists have often cited U.S. and Soviet behavior during the Cold War as a supporting example. Many historical accounts of Cold War U.S. national security policy, such as the work of Melvyn

Leffler, take a statist perspective, arguing that U.S. decision makers acted to defend a set of core values stemming from the historical development of American society.

Despite the apparently favorable conditions for the application of realist and statist approaches in this case, the evidence presented here raises some serious questions about these analytical frameworks. Realist and statist accounts of this case face problems both in explaining the origins of conflicting views on national security policy and in accounting for the policy-making process. These weaknesses of realist and statist theories do not mean that they should be discarded entirely. However, the scope of the questions to which they are applied should be restricted.

Realist and statist theories cannot explain the origins of divergent views on national security policy. Indeed, the very existence of divergent views in this area is problematic because policy choices are supposed to stem either from the constraints and incentives of the international system or from consensual core values rather than from the views of the group that happens to control the state. Strictly speaking, realist and statist theories offer no basis for understanding competing views of "the national interest." If the international environment does not imply some identifiable set of policy responses, then these theories cannot be used to explain policy outcomes. A more generous reading of these approaches might be that they predict a central tendency across a range of policy views. Since most, although perhaps not all, policymakers will be able to discern the demands placed on the state by its position in the international system, this view is most likely to become policy over time. Alternative beliefs about the national interest, then, can be understood as error in the statistical sense. They are always present but are randomly distributed and cancel each other out over time.

While this account of divergent views of the national interest seems plausible, it does not explain the case at hand. In chapter 4, I presented statistical evidence that opposition to the Truman administration's national security program should not be understood as random error. Indeed, opposition to the administration's national security program varied systematically with the economic structure of the senators' home states, their political party, and their region of origin. These statistical results strongly suggest that senators associated with segments of the domestic political economy that would benefit most from the administration's internationalist policies were more likely to support them. While this finding should not be surprising, it cannot be accommodated in realist or statist theory except by limiting its scope to cases where there is no variation in the costs and benefits of a policy across different segments of the nation. The development of Cold War national security policy would have to be excluded from this restricted range of cases.

Another plausible variant of the realist-statist approach that might account for the existence of multiple policy views would be to argue that the understanding of core values or the imperatives of the international system applies only to central government decision makers, rather than to the society as a whole. In such an account, Congress might be understood as reflecting the uninformed views of those not directly concerned with the imperatives of the international system on an everyday basis. Persons not involved in making foreign policy may become preoccupied with other issues, such as the condition of the economy or the size of their tax bill. Since few people apart from government decision makers are likely to be well informed about the general substance of international relations, let alone the secret information on which policy may be based at any given time, only these decision makers can be expected to have a genuine understanding of the national interest. Realist or statist theory, it might be argued, predicts only the dominant tendency among those who are directly concerned with making these decisions. As Hans Morgenthau (1956, 5) expressed it, this version of the theory "allows us to retrace and anticipate, as it were, the steps a statesman—past, present or future—has taken or will take on the political scene."

While this "statesmen only" version of realist or statist theory is also plausible, it faces at least two serious problems in this case. First, there was no consensus about the national interest within the state, and those holding the eventually triumphant "correct" view had no assurance that it would be adopted as national policy. Archival evidence about how the administration decided to proceed with rearmament, presented in chapters 2 and 3, indicates that differences existed among decision makers at the highest level. Furthermore, there was also no certainty that those favoring rearmament would prevail. Even after the Soviet acquisition of the atomic bomb and the victory of the Chinese Communists—the events generally credited in realist and statist accounts with providing the final push toward rearmament—the military budget was cut. Concern about the consequences of a large federal budget deficit, considered by the chairman of the Council of Economic Advisers to be "no less a risk than our diplomatic and military risks," was sufficient to override the impact of these events. While it is true that Acheson and Nitze were eventually able to get their view accepted, the reasons for their victory in the executive branch had nothing to do with the structure of the international system. Without the use of arbitrary lags on the influence of international events, a realist or statist approach cannot explain the administration's decision to rearm.

A second problem with the "statesmen only" version of these approaches is that even consensual understandings of the national interest on particular matters among top policymakers were not consistent across time, even when circumstances in the international system did not change. As noted in chapter 3, the National Security Council maintained throughout 1948 and 1949 that "the U.S. should not become so irrevocably involved in the Korean situation that any action taken by any faction in Korea or by any other power in Korea could be considered a *casus belli* for the U.S." Indeed, even Douglas MacArthur, when consulted on the matter, argued that an effort to maintain stability in South Korea was likely to fail. In keeping with this policy, U.S. troops were withdrawn in 1949. Nevertheless, without ever discussing any change in its official policy, the United States quickly moved to commit troops to Korea when the North Koreans invaded the South—an event specifically anticipated when the discarded policy was developed.

Realist and statist concepts about the making of national security policy offer no easy explanation for this sudden change. One could probably construct a realist-statist account of why Korea was not strategically important, given the international position of the United States or the core values decision makers sought to defend, in order to explain U.S. policy in 1948 and 1949. NSC 8/2 would provide a good first draft in developing such an account. Alternatively, one might develop an account of why Korea was strategically important in order to explain the decision to intervene. Explaining the sudden shift in policy when decision makers were confronted with a previously anticipated event, however, would require identifying some change in the international system or American core values between the last reassessment of U.S. policy toward East Asia and the beginning of the Korean War. Since NSC 48 reaffirmed the policy toward Korea contained in NSC 8/2 in December 1949, the first half of 1950 would be the relevant period for such a search. Although it is difficult to discern any major changes in the international environment during this period, it is not hard to identify political changes in Washington that made the use of force in Korea a much more congenial option for central state decision makers. These domestic political changes can provide a good explanation for the shift in policy, but this explanation is not compatible with a realist or statist approach.

In addition to their failure to account for the existence of multiple views on national security policy during the 1949–51 period, realist and statist approaches offer a weak and misleading account of the policy-making process. This is an important flaw in a theory even when its predictions are correct, because the failure to provide a sense of process raises the possibility that the cause-and-effect relationships it posits may be spurious. It also limits its usefulness as a guide to historical research. The range of possible realist and statist accounts of the policy-making process is rather narrow. In order for neorealist theory to explain policy choices, events and circumstances in the international system must evoke an identifiable policy response or set of responses from decision makers. Historical accounts rooted in realist or statist assumptions about the policy-making process, such as those offered by Wells (1979) and Leffler (1992) for NSC 68, generally use external events as explanatory devices. These external events make the demands of the state's position in the international system clear to the decision makers.

In this case, however, the external events generally offered to explain rearmament fail to do so. The collapse of the Nationalist regime in China and the detonation of an atomic bomb by the Soviet Union were met with a decision to reduce military spending. Furthermore, those who wrote NSC 68, especially Paul Nitze, had believed a large increase in spending on the national security program was necessary since at least the summer of 1949—before any of these events took place. The Korean War is similarly problematic as an explanation for the acceptance of NSC 68 in the administration, since the bulk of the archival evidence suggests that the president made this decision before the North Korean attack.

One might still argue that the Korean War effectively produced rearmament by mobilizing support for the program. While the domestic political impact of the Korean War explains much of this case rather well, it only superficially supports a realist or statist account of rearmament. The North Korean attack itself did little to change policymakers' minds about the size of the military budget. The decision to commit U.S. ground troops to the fighting was the crucial event, since it left the opponents of rearmament with few politically viable alternatives to supporting the administration's proposals for increased defense spending. This decision was not an external event emanating from the international system, however, but a use of the institutional powers of the presidency to produce a particular domestic political result. It cannot be treated as an unproblematic response to the international environment because it contradicted prior U.S. policy as well as the judgments of policymakers close to the event such as John Foster Dulles and Douglas MacArthur. The North Korean attack might have been met with less drastic measures that would not have forced the acceptance of rearmament. Indeed, one probably would have expected such a response given prior U.S. policy. The argument that the Korean War produced rearmament simply begs the question of what prompted the decision to become involved in the Korean War.

Furthermore, even if intervention in Korea were interpreted as a necessary response to the international system, evidence about the role of the international system in producing the changes necessary to secure support for rearmament is not encouraging. There is no evidence that the Korean War produced any change in the preferences of the major opponents of rearmament. Of course, events in Korea did change some minds about the wisdom of Truman's foreign policy. However, the major opponents of large military budgets in Congress continued to harbor doubts about both rearmament and the decision to intervene in Korea. The private comments of Robert Taft and other Nationalist Republican leaders indicate they felt compelled to support the administration's requests for more spending on the national security program because of the engagement of U.S. troops in Korea. The changes produced by intervention in Korea depended on the domestic political consequences for U.S. politicians of failure to support U.S. troops once they were committed. Though their doubts about the policy persisted, they were inhibited from acting on them.

Realist and statist approaches also miss some potentially important aspects of the policy-making process entirely. Because they begin by assuming a consensus on core values or the imperatives of the international system, they pay little attention to the political process by which other policy options are ruled out. This process had important consequences in this case. The administration achieved rearmament only through the sacrifice of its domestic labor and social welfare agenda. One might argue that this price was worth paying in order to secure political support for the new world role of the United States. Indeed, NSC 68 makes just such a case. Clearly, though, a theory that misses this aspect of the policy-making process will produce an incomplete account of the policy's costs and its implications for American society.

A more extreme modification of realist and statist theories to correct the problems in their account of the policy-making process would be to include domestic political factors. One could argue that policymakers are beset with pressures both from within their own society and from the position of their state in the international system. The task facing them is to find a way to balance these potentially conflicting sets of demands. Indeed, Putnam (1988) and others suggest just such a theoretical approach. As Snyder (1991, 14–17) does, one could argue that domestic political forces may sometimes become strong enough to "hijack the state" in pursuit of policies that fail to consider the defense of core values or the demands of the state's position in the international system. The apparent virtue of this approach is that it combines a realist-statist notion of the national interest with an acknowledgment of the importance of domestic politics.

While many of those who share realist or statist convictions about the national interest have adopted this strategy, theorists of neorealism usually try to avoid it. Waltz (1979) is quite explicit about the irrelevance of "unit-level variables." The introduction of domestic factors into neorealist theory erodes its usefulness and intellectual appeal in several important ways. First, variation in the motives of the units undermines its conclusions about the character of the international system. Waltz derives the characteristics of the international system by considering the cumulative consequences of a large number of undifferentiated units pursuing the same goals in competition with one another. By asserting that states seek to maximize their chances of survival in the international system—an assumption placing security issues at the center of the foreign policy agenda—Waltz is able to derive a system structure in a manner similar to the way microeconomic assumptions can be used to examine the structure of a market. The power of his theory is generated by the assumptions he makes. If the policy goals of states are allowed to vary and are not assumed to center around security issues, then the elegant system structure developed by Waltz becomes much more difficult to derive.

Furthermore, many of the interesting counterintuitive predictions made by realist models are rooted in their argument that domestic political factors do not have a significant impact on the international behavior of states. John Mearsheimer's argument (1990) that there will be increasing conflict in Europe after the Cold War is provocative because he contends that the structure of the international system is a more important influence on foreign policy than the ideological affinities and institutional ties between European states. His argument would have been much less distinctive had he argued that domestic political factors might be just as important as the structure of the international system. Similarly, the introduction of conflict and bargaining over basic policy goals into a statist account robs it of its parsimony and intellectual appeal. If there is no consensus on core values, then the concept is of little use for explaining outcomes.

Even if one believes that the costs of introducing domestic variables into realist or statist approaches is worth paying, doing so does not resolve the problems with other realist and statist concepts. Adding other variables into the mix does not produce a satisfactory way to identify the "national interest." Assuming that the interests of those who control the state are inherently more "national" than others carries an obvious political bias with which most analysts would not be comfortable, if they recognized it. Treating the interests of those with a greater stake in the international system—and therefore more reason to be concerned about the position of the state in it—as the national interest poses the same problem. One may argue that the interests of the state as a set of institutions correspond to the greatest good for the greatest number of people in society, but the truth of this proposition is far from obvious. Any account of foreign policy that treats certain policy goals as "core values" or "the national interest" will inevitably serve as an ideological weapon against those who do not share those goals.

In terms of this case, there is no basis, other than ideological affinity of the analyst, for arguing that Dean Acheson's version of U.S. core values or the national interest was any more valid than Robert Taft's. Each was rooted in a different segment of the domestic political economy, and neither represented the interests of the whole nation. Indeed, the "whole nation" had no single set of interests. Accounts of the early Cold War period that use statist or realist notions about core values or the national interest tend to ignore or downplay political conflict over foreign policy, because they do not take seriously the possibility that alternative views might also have become policy. In short, the problems of realist and statist concepts are rooted in the unit of analysis they use, the unitary state, and cannot be solved simply by adding auxiliary considerations. Analyses of the policy-making process can only avoid these problems if they focus on the interests of subnational actors actually involved in this process rather than on some presumed set of core values or the supposed interests of an abstraction like the unitary state.

National Security Policy after the Cold War

In many respects, the circumstances surrounding U.S. national security policy today resemble those of the early Cold War period. The collapse of the Soviet Union has made many of the assumptions that have organized policy since 1950 obsolete, and some basic questions about the proper world role of the United States that have been closed since 1950 are once again open for broad discussion. Given the subject matter of this work, these parallels deserve comment. The purpose of developing theory is to understand not only the past, but the present as well. The approach presented here identifies some areas about which questions should be asked in order to help understand the national security policy likely to be pursued by the United States after the Cold War. My research also suggests that several common lines of inquiry are not likely to improve our understanding of how national security policy is made.

The best place to begin an inquiry into the future of U.S. national security policy is with the structure of the domestic political economy. What are the interests of the major political investors in the United States today? Along what lines are they divided, and which of the two political parties do they tend to support? The debates over the General Agreement on Tariffs and Trade (GATT) and the North American Free Trade Agreement (NAFTA) indicate that a broad spectrum of political interests in both parties support internationalist foreign policy initiatives. At the same time, they show that labor may no longer be willing to back an internationalist foreign policy, as it did during the immediate postwar era, and that some elements of the political right may be returning to their nationalist roots. Trubowitz and Roberts (1992) point out that defense industries are politically important in many parts of the country, especially the Sunbelt states, and these industries will certainly have a stake in an internationalist foreign policy. Beyond generalizations about regional differences, a closer look at the interests and political orientations of particular industries is likely to be fruitful in understanding the policy positions taken by the major political parties.

If both major parties are essentially internationalist, as seems to be the case, then the differences on national security policy may center around less general issues. As in the 1949–51 period, the relative importance of different world regions may be an issue. In the case examined here, Republicans from the Midwest and the West were generally more concerned about U.S. policy toward Asia than were Democrats from the East, who were usually preoccupied with Europe. While these regional orientations are obsolete now, new ones may have emerged. An examination of policy toward a region of the world over which segments of the two parties disagree sharply, as they did over Latin America during the 1980s, might shed some light on this issue. Cox (1994) presents a very interesting analysis along these lines.

In addition to differences in the relative priority of various regions of the world, major political investors and the corresponding policy currents in the major parties are likely to differ over the policies they believe are necessary to sustain their interests. For example, the statistical evidence in chapter 4 supports Frieden's argument (1989; 1994) that direct investors in Third World extractive industries have distinctive foreign policy views. While this particular tendency may no longer be very important, since host countries have since expropriated many of these industries, international investors are still likely to have different policy preferences based on what they consider necessary to protect their interests. These differences may lead to divergent views about particular policy instruments or about the general diplomatic and military posture of the United States. The probable preference of defense industries for a more militant national security policy is an obvious example, but others are possible.

Another set of considerations likely to be relevant to the future of U.S. national security policy are the effects of policy outcomes on other issues. What other major policy outcomes are currently at stake? How do coalitions constructed on these issues overlap with positions taken on national security policy? How salient are outcomes in the area of national security policy compared to outcomes in other issue areas to the most important political actors? The 1993–94 debate over the reform of the health care system provides another echo of the politics of the 1949–51 period. Those who opposed Truman's social welfare agenda during that period were generally less internationalist in their orientation than those who supported it. Concessions to its opponents on labor and social welfare issues helped facilitate the administration's efforts to build support for rearmament. It may turn out that coalitions formed in debates over domestic issues such as health care have distinctive views about national security policy as well. If so, the outcome of substantively unrelated debates over domestic policy might well influence the future of national security policy, just as it did during the early Cold War period.

Much of the current commentary on the post–Cold War future of U.S. national security policy focuses on the content of the national interest. Does it include humanitarian efforts to end the war in Bosnia or restore the elected government of Haiti, or is it strictly limited to security issues such as the possible possession of nuclear weapons by North Korea? These questions are complicated, it is often said, by the fact that the position of the United States as the only remaining superpower in the international system offers no clear set of threats and interests on which policy must be based. Unlike the early Cold War era, the argument goes, there is now no unifying threat to the national interest around which policy can be constructed.

The research presented here suggests not only that this view of the early Cold War era is inaccurate, but also that the national interest and related concepts such as the idea of core values are not a useful way of understanding the making of national security policy. External threats make a difference for national security policy, but one must specify precisely whose interests are threatened. A genuine threat to the nation as a whole is very unlikely. Realist and statist approaches and the conceptual apparatus associated with them, especially the notion of the national interest and the practice of interpreting international threats in terms of this supposed interest, seemed plausible during much of the postwar era partly because of the events of the late 1940s and early 1950s. After the Korean War, the wide acceptance of an ambitious global foreign policy justified in terms of anticommunism and the Soviet threat made "the national interest" seem real. During this period, arguments in favor of alternative foreign policies were forced to the margins of American political life. I have tried here to demonstrate the problems with this conception of the policymaking process even where it should have been most useful. At present, when the "threats" are even more difficult to agree upon, the concept of the national interest is even less likely to be useful.

As it always has been, foreign policy is a political matter. It is bound up with many other issues at stake in the domestic political arena. Whatever national security policy the United States ultimately adopts, there will be winners and losers. Foreign policy is not simply a question of how we will deal with the outside world, but above all a matter of who "we" actually are. Are we people who will gain from continuing the vast military expenditures initiated in 1950, or are we people who would rather use most of those resources for other purposes? The answer, of course, is that the "we" in this question has no real meaning. Both alternatives have interested advocates, and even the middle ground between them will produce winners and losers in much the same fashion. Appeals to a mythical national interest only cloud the issue.

Data Collection

Collecting the quantitative data used in chapter 4 was a formidable task. The data were generally unavailable in machine-readable form and transforming it into the variables I used raised some important problems. Data were collected in four general categories, each of which merits some comment here: (1) Congressional voting; (2) direct foreign investment; (3) international lending; and (4) international trade. In all cases, while the problems must be noted, they do not invalidate the results I presented in chapter 4, since the data are the best available and are not biased toward finding the relationships I was seeking.

Data on Congressional Voting

The data used to calculate the voting scores, the dependent variable used in the models presented in chapter 4, were by far the easiest to gather. These were available in machine-readable form from the Inter-University Consortium for Political and Social Research (ICPSR), as are data on all recorded congressional votes. The ICPSR database also includes information on the party and home state of each member of Congress, further simplifying data collection. A useful discussion of the subject and context of each vote is presented in the *Congressional Quarterly Almanac,* which was published annually during the 1949–51 period.

Data on Direct Foreign Investment

To develop an indicator of the level of foreign direct investment by corporations headquartered in each state, I relied mostly on the data provided by the annual *Moody's Industrial Manual* and the comparable volumes on utilities, merchandising, and railroads. I examined the 200 firms with the greatest assets according to the earliest *Fortune* listing, for 1954, categorizing them based on their ownership of subsidiaries outside the Western Hemisphere and their ownership of subsidiaries in extractive industries in Third World areas. The best source for general information on foreign investment by U.S. corporations is Wilkins (1974).

Data on International Lending

Data on international lending were difficult to gather for legal and bureaucratic reasons. Each year, the Federal Reserve publishes a single national aggregate figure on international activity by member banks. In addition, a few Federal Reserve banks publish their own statistics on international lending, but these are incomplete and may not be comparable across Federal Reserve districts. When I contacted the Department of the Treasury, which controls the financial data that banks are required to submit to the Federal Reserve, officials there initially refused to release any unpublished figures on international lending, citing the confidentiality agreements under which these data were originally collected. When confronted with a Freedom of Information Act request, however, they agreed to release some annual figures for each Federal Reserve district.

　　　Each month, U.S. banks are required to submit information on their "claims on foreigners" on Foreign Exchange Form B-2. These B-2 forms contain figures on both "short-term claims," with a maturity of less than one year, and "long-term claims," with a maturity of more than one year, for each applicable country and region. The B-2 forms are then aggregated in each Federal Reserve city and sent to the Treasury Department. The Treasury Department released to me the year-end figures for each Federal Reserve district.

　　　In order to approximate each state's share of the total claims on foreigners in its Federal Reserve district, I multiplied the district figure by each state's share of total banking activity in the Federal Reserve district. I also assumed that the noncoastal states included in the San Francisco Federal Reserve district did not participate in international lending activity.[1] In order to control for the total volume of lending activity in each state, I divided total short- and long-term claims on foreigners listed in the B-2 form by the figure for total loans and discounts for the states in the Federal Reserve district given in the *Statistical Abstract of the United States.* The variables I used are estimated figures for claims on foreigners, on Asians, or on Europeans by banks in the state as a proportion of their total lending activity.

Data on International Trade

By far the most time-consuming data to collect and use were those on international trade. Reliable figures on exports and imports by each state are not available. In order to estimate the relative size of the export and import-competing sectors in each state, I first converted the figures for exports and imports into the sectors given in the Standard Industrial

Classification (SIC) system. I then calculated the value of the goods exported by each three-digit SIC sector as a proportion of the total value added in that sector in the United States. Similarly, I calculated the value of imported goods from each industrial sector as a proportion of the total value added in that sector. Assuming that the export orientation and import-sensitivity of a sector were constant across states, I then estimated the export orientation and import sensitivity of the state based on the size of each sector as a proportion of total value added in the state. The indicator of the size of the export sector, then, is the sum, over all sectors in each state's economy, of the proportion of the sector's products exported multiplied by the size of the sector as a proportion of all value added in the state. Similarly, the size of the import-competing sector is indicated by the sum, over all sectors in a state's economy, of imports as a proportion of total value added in the sector multiplied by the size of the sector as a proportion of all value added in the state.

Aside from the potential for error inherent in the assumption that the export orientation and import sensitivity of industrial and agricultural sectors do not vary across states, the greatest problems in developing these variables occurred in the process of translating the data on exports and imports into a useful form. During the 1940s, imports were recorded under a classification system known as Schedule A. Exports were recorded under a different system known as Schedule B. These systems organize exports and imports by commodity, rather than by the type of industry that produced them. By contrast, the industrial censuses use the SIC system, which hierarchically organizes the economy into major industry groups (assigned a two-digit identification number), industry groups (assigned a three-digit identification number), and industries (assigned four-digit identification numbers).[2]

The differences between a classification system based on commodities and a system based on industrial sectors make some error unavoidable in converting trade data from Schedule A and Schedule B into the SIC system. Not all of the commodities in the Schedule A and Schedule B classification systems are specified in ways that facilitate their conversion. In many cases, a single classification in these two systems includes commodities from more than one SIC sector. This problem exists even when converting trade data into the very general two-digit SIC sectors, and it becomes more serious as one moves to the more specific industrial classifications at the three- and four-digit levels. These incomparabilities are an inevitable result of the fact that the export- and import-classification systems were designed to classify commodities, while the SIC system was designed to classify industries. In the 1960s, some of these difficulties were resolved by the adoption of a new system for recording data on trade that is more closely related to the SIC system. Unfortunately, data in this form are not available for earlier historical periods.

A less serious problem that is also worth mentioning is that data from the industrial censuses are not recorded in such a way that one can move from the three- or four-digit level to the two-digit level simply by adding figures for all of the industries contained in each two-digit major industry group. Below the two-digit level, sectors that either are very small or contain an insufficient number of firms to allow the presentation of data without violating confidentiality rules are omitted from the census figures. As a result, the aggregate figures for major industry groups in each state are usually greater than the sum of their three-digit industry groups and almost always greater than the sum of the figures for their subsidiary four-digit industries. As a result, greater disaggregation can only be purchased at the price of greater incompleteness in the data.

Notes

Chapter 1

1. The set of positions I refer to here as "nationalism" is also commonly referred to as "isolationism." Given the stigma attached to the latter term, however, I have chosen to use the former in this work. (An alternative method of placing the two perspectives on linguistically equal footing would be to refer to internationalism as "imperialism.") Doenecke (1979) provides an interesting overview of nationalist-isolationist politics after World War II. The linkage between the economic and military proposals of nationalists and internationalists is widely acknowledged. Some historians, such as Leffler (1992), Gaddis (1982; 1983), and Jones and Woods (1993), stress security concerns, while others, such as Kolko and Kolko (1972), Block (1977; 1980), Eden (1984; 1985), Hogan (1987), Cumings (1990; 1993), Pollard (1985), McGlothlen (1993), and Trubowitz (1992), treat economic concerns as more fundamental. Few recent writers argue that the two concerns were unrelated.

2. The prominence of this eastern foreign policy elite is often observed by historians and others writing on the period. Burch (1980) presents an encyclopedic account of the interest group affiliations of major officials in the Truman administration. Isaacson and Thomas (1986) examine the backgrounds of some senior administration officials drawn from the eastern establishment. Shoup and Minter (1977) and Schulzinger (1984) examine the role of the Council on Foreign Relations. Ferguson (1984) and Frieden (1988) both stress the role of eastern, internationally oriented investment banks in the elite coalition that backed the Democratic party and the New Deal after 1932.

3. Yergin (1977), for example, treats the history of U.S. foreign policy during the early Cold War era in terms of an ideological conflict between advocates of the accommodationist "Yalta axioms" and those committed to the more confrontational "Riga axioms."

4. Ikenberry (1992, 321) stresses the ability of successful ideas to attract political support and assemble interest-based coalitions. Similarly, Goldstein (1989, 71) argues that ideas influence policy only when they are backed by power, and that their inherent logic is secondary to this requirement. These insights are not new. Kehr (1977a, 174–88), reacting to the prevalence of "the history of ideas" in interwar German academia, strongly disparaged the historical importance of ideas, arguing that material interests were more fundamental. Indeed, Kehr attributed even the tendency to study the history of ideas during this period to material forces.

5. Other works that examine the foreign policy implications of conflict between industry groups include Gourevitch (1977; 1986), Kurth (1979), Ferguson (1984), Davis and Huttenback (1986), Frieden (1988), Maxfield and Nolt (1990), Gibbs (1990), Nowell (1994), and Cox (1994). These works follow in a longer tradition of research established in earlier work including that of Hobson ([1902] 1965), Beard and Smith (1934), Schattschneider (1935), and others.

6. For a review of the way this question is handled in the endogenous trade literature, see Nelson (1988). Factor-based accounts generally follow the Stolper and Samuelson argument (1941) that the scarce factor will oppose trade liberalization because exposure to the world market will drive down its wage. Particularly interesting results using this approach include those presented by Rogowski (1989) and Magee, Brock, and Young (1989). Both acknowledge the shortcomings of a factor-based approach, however. Rogowski notes that U.S. labor should have opposed free trade in the postwar era and states that its support for "U.S. policies toward taxation and investment that virtually guaranteed the export of jobs" is hard to explain (1989, 120).

7. See, for example, Agnew (1987, 89–129) and Bensel (1984, 6).

8. See, for example, biographical accounts of major internationalists, such as Isaacson and Thomas (1986), Bird (1992), and Hershberg (1993). A similar argument could be made about the nationalists, as Griffith (1979) does.

9. Frieden (1988) argues that the Democratic and Republican parties represented distinctive blocs of societal interests between 1914 and 1940. Trubowitz (1992) found linkages between regionally defined blocs of interests and political parties. Hogan (1987) cites Ferguson's theory in his argument that the character of internationally oriented U.S. business interests influenced the development of the Marshall Plan. Gibbs (1990) presents evidence of the influence of mineral interests and the different policies pursued by the Eisenhower and Kennedy administrations during the Congo crisis. Cox (1994) shows that business interests associated with the two parties have supported different policies toward Latin America since the end of World War II.

10. Concerning the advantageous position of business interests in the political process, see Schattschneider (1935), Key (1965), Lindblom (1977), and Salamon and Siegfried (1977).

11. Although Joseph echoes Schurmann's discussion (1974, 33–39) of "politically significant currents" in mass politics, his account of these currents differs significantly because it focuses instead on elite politics.

12. Trubowitz and Roberts (1992) argue that military spending policies during the Cold War altered the balance of societal interests in some regions of the country, but this process appears to have taken decades.

13. Schurmann (1974) makes the parallel observation that the executive inhabits a "realm of ideology" and can afford to take a more expansive view of policy than can bureaucrats and others who inhabit the "realm of interests." In Schurmann's account, ideological visions encompass a broader range of interests than those represented by a single bureaucracy. Political actors who are tied to such a narrow range of interests cannot articulate an "ideology" in this sense.

14. There are a few noteworthy exceptions to this rule, including Krasner (1978).

15. For a concise summary of the problems of finding a rational "social welfare function" for a society with preferences on more than one issue, see Mueller (1989) and Hinich and Munger (1994, 23–37).

16. Gilpin (1981, 25) also uses the Cold War confrontation between the United States and the Soviet Union to illustrate his notion of "vital interests."

17. Jones and Woods (1993) review this recent historiographical trend toward interpreting American Cold War foreign policy in terms of a "national security imperative" quite similar to Leffler's argument about core values.

18. Leffler's shorter 1994 work pays more attention to various influences on the development of core values.

19. My purpose here is not to present a complete review of the vast historiography of the early Cold War era, but only to point out some similarities in the assumptions and concepts used by these historians with the theoretical arguments made by realists and statists. Useful reviews of the literature include Gaddis (1983), Crapol (1987), and Leffler (1994). The end of the Cold War, as well as the publication of Melvyn Leffler's well-received book (1992) on the subject, prompted several other very good literature reviews, including Eden (1993) and Cumings (1993), which argues persuasively that efforts to place historians into gross categories such as "revisionist" or "postrevisionist" are politically loaded and analytically dubious. Hogan (1992) contains several interesting interpretative essays touching on the origins as well as the end of the Cold War.

20. Halle's account (1967, xiii) holds most closely to the neorealist stress on international structure. "But the historical circumstances, themselves, had an ineluctable quality that left the Russians little choice but to move as they did. Moving as they did, they compelled the United States and its allies to move in response."

21. In view of my argument here, it is perhaps ironic that Gaddis (1992/93) has been quite critical of Waltz. His announced position on neorealism does not release him from the underlying thrust of his other work, however.

22. Fischer and Kamlet (1984) treat budgets in precisely this way: as the outcome of the "competing aspiration levels" of executive agencies and the programmatic concerns of the chief executive. Kamlet and Mowery (1987) incorporate congressional action into this competing aspiration levels model. Su, Kamlet, and Mowery (1993) expand this model to include additional variables and consider possible interdependence between budgetary categories.

23. McNeil Oral History Interview, September 19, 1972, p. 160. Gaddis (1982, 354–55) argues that budgetary considerations were critical to policy planning throughout the Cold War.

24. There are many outstanding accounts of German foreign policy before World War I that consider the requirements of domestic coalition building. These include the work of Eckart Kehr (1977b), Hans-Ulrich Wehler (1970), and Geoff Eley (1976, 1980), among others. Although they do not examine the political bargaining that established it in much detail, some examinations of the early Cold War era in the United States treat foreign policy as part of a larger political and economic order that included not only an expanded world role, but also a labor-management accord that traded labor peace for increasing wages and government man-

agement of the economy through Keynesian macroeconomic policies. Maier (1977) refers to this arrangement as the "politics of productivity." Bowles, Gordon, and Weisskopf (1983, 62–79) include institutional arrangements providing for the protection of U.S. foreign investments, the preservation of labor peace, and government intervention to moderate the effects of the business cycles as part of an overarching "postwar corporate system." Griffith (1989, 60–62) singles out the development of a postwar political and economic order as one of the most important legacies of the Truman years. Other works linking the domestic and foreign policy trends initiated after World War II include Harris (1982), Kemp (1990), Galambos and Pratt (1988), and Vatter (1985).

Chapter 2

Notes to epigraphs: Nourse to Truman, 8/26/49, Keyserling Papers, Box 3; Off-the-record comments by Johnson to the American Society of Newspaper Editors, 4/26/49, Johnson Papers, Box 140; Nitze (1980, 171).

1. *FRUS 1950,* 1:262, 283–84. The entire text of NSC 68 is on pp. 235–92. NSC 68 is also reprinted in May (1993) and Etzold and Gaddis (1978).

2. Many examinations of the history of the German officer corps before World War I, for example, stress its ties to the interests of the upper class in German society. See, for example, Craig (1964, 233–53) and Herwig (1973, 31–36). Kehr (1977b, 7–12) argues that the German navy was able to maintain a strategically irrelevant battleship construction program because of support from the emerging industrial elite, which benefited from both increased purchases of steel and the search for external markets the fleet was supposed to support. In the U.S. context, the linkages between societal and bureaucratic interests in the area of military procurement provide some useful insights. For example, Kurth (1971), Lieberson (1971), Magdoff (1970), Pilisuk and Hayden (1965), and Trubowitz and Roberts (1992) offer evidence of linkages between defense industries and the military in a number of areas. Cumings (1990), Eden (1984; 1985), Joseph (1987), and Schurmann (1974) describe other linkages between bureaucratic interests within the state and societal interests outside it.

3. Concerning process-tracing, see George and McKeown (1985).

4. May (1993, 14–15) presents a different, but equally incorrect, set of reasons for the president's approval of NSC 68. He argues that Truman accepted the necessity for more defense spending before the Korean War, but only because of the potential reaction of "hostile members of Congress and newspaper editors" to a rejection. In fact, hostile members of Congress were pressing for cuts in defense spending, not rearmament.

5. Examining the origins of the policy of containment between 1944 and 1947, Deborah Larson (1985, 255–57) found that such conversion experiences rarely occurred. Events are usually interpreted in accordance with prior beliefs.

6. The National Military Establishment did not become the Department of Defense until the passage of amendments to the National Security Act in the fall of 1949. The decision to reduce the ceiling for the defense budget is discussed in detail by Rearden (1984, 369–72), Leffler (1992, 304–5), and Hammond (1962, 280–82).

7. Budget Bureau—Staff Meetings, Lawton Papers, Box 3.

8. Note attached to Pace's resume, undated, Johnson Papers, Box 139. The article, awkwardly entitled "Director Pace's Young Ideas Will Show Up in New Style Budget: His Aim Is to Help Ordinary Citizens Understand Federal Spending," appeared in the December 16, 1949, edition of *U.S. News and World Report,* pp. 38–39. See also "Budget in Brief," *Washington Post,* January 25, 1950.

9. Undated draft entitled "Should the Federal Budget Be Balanced?" with handwritten comments by Bell; Bell to Pace, 11/22/49, Pace Papers, Box 3.

10. Pace to Dawes, 2/1/49; Dawes to Pace, 3/49, Pace Papers, Box 3. According to Pace's February 1 letter, Dawes had apparently also been in touch with Webb on matters such as "budgeting military expenditures." Pace wrote that "[a]ll of us hope that the reports of the Hoover Commission will help us to strengthen the Bureau of the Budget, especially increase its ability, under the President, to control military expenditures and coordinate business management of the departments and agencies."

11. The letter requesting this assessment by the Council of Economic Advisers is reprinted in Nourse (1953, 250–51).

12. Johnson to Frank Pace, Sr., 7/29/49, Johnson Papers, Box 108.

13. Pace to Early, 4/14/49; Early to Pace, 4/16/49, Pace Papers, Box 3.

14. Marx Leva Oral History Interview, June 12, 1970, p. 76.

15. Rearden (1984, 47) discusses Johnson's appointment of Matthews. Matthews's activities in the United States Chamber of Commerce are discussed in some detail in Irons (1974).

16. Johnson speech to the 37th Annual Meeting of the Chamber of Commerce, May 5–June 9, 1949, Johnson Papers, Box 130.

17. *Time,* February 27, 1950, p. 20.

18. Page wrote Johnson on December 16, 1949, about the most recent such encounter. "I think the meeting did a considerable amount of good and I feel that it can be built up for the benefit of the Defense Department by mail and occasional contact with these people." Johnson responded on December 20, noting that "I am sure it was worthwhile even if only a few people contributed to the cause." It is not clear whether "the cause" was Johnson's eventual plan to run for president or the plan proposed by Page that these corporations pass along to the Defense Department useful information acquired in the course of their overseas business (Page to Johnson, 12/16/49; Johnson to Page, 12/20/49, Johnson Papers, Box 126).

19. Johnson's meetings with the Washington press corps appear to have taken place mostly during April of 1949, shortly after his installation as secretary of defense (Invitation lists, 4/49, Johnson Papers, Box 126). Despite his best efforts, Johnson was much less successful in cultivating the media than were officials in the State Department and others sympathetic to them—especially Averell Harriman, whose papers are full of evidence of his media ties.

20. Osborne to Johnson, 1/25/50, Johnson Papers, Box 126.

21. Johnson to Wherry, 5/20/49, Johnson Papers, Box 130. The letter was written to "My dear Ken" and signed "Louis." Wherry wrote Johnson to express his regret that he never got a chance to defend his record before Congress after he was forced to resign (Wherry to Johnson, 4/27/51, Wherry Papers, Box 12).

22. Concerning the defense budget, the commission report concluded: "The costs of the National Military Establishment, currently about $15,000,000,000 a year, appears to be unduly high, in terms of both the ability of the Nation's economy to sustain them and of the actual return in military strength and effective national security." The Republican National Committee prepared a special report summarizing the commission's findings and planned to make extensive use of it in the 1950 campaign ("The Hoover Commission Reports," 7/49, Bridges Papers, File 81, Folder 13).

23. This practice did not escape notice at the time. Joseph and Stewart Alsop, "Truman Must Choose," *Washington Post,* March 31, 1950, notes this tendency and alleges that Republican leaders had endorsed a "Get Acheson" campaign. See also Stewart Alsop, "Get Acheson, Lay Off Johnson," *Washington Post,* August 21, 1950. Marquis Childs, "'Get Acheson' GOP Drive," *Washington Post,* August 25, 1950, charges that Johnson was furnishing Acheson's opponents with derogatory information about the secretary of state.

24. The efforts of the Air Force to secure a larger budget by contacting sympathetic Republicans during the 1948 session of Congress are discussed extensively by Eden (1985). The "revolt of the admirals" over funding for the so-called super carrier is discussed in Schilling (1962). Both are mentioned in Rearden (1984, 309–30, 335–57).

25. According to Marx Leva, "[t]he chief difference between Forrestal and Johnson I would say, is that Johnson, having seen Forrestal's battle [with Truman to increase the budget], having heard of it or read of it, never fought for more funds. If Truman said it was twelve billion or eleven billion, 'Well, that's it'" (Marx Leva Oral History Interview, June 12, 1970, p. 61).

26. Johnson's regulation of contacts between the State and Defense Departments is mentioned by Rearden (1984, 127–28) and began with directives issued in April 1949, shortly after Johnson became secretary of defense. The responsibilities of Defense Department officials in managing politico-military affairs are laid out in an August 3, 1949, memo found in *FRUS 1949,* 1:365–68.

27. Leffler (1992, 309) mentions State Department objections to the new limits on foreign aid. NSC 52/1 requested the study of the impact of the budget cuts and is reproduced in *FRUS 1949,* 1:352–57. The final report, NSC 52/3, which included comments on the State Department's additions by the Department of the Treasury, the Council of Economic Advisers, and the Department of Defense, are in the same *FRUS* volume, pp. 385–98. Concerning State Department work on MDAP, see Pach (1991). Joseph and Stewart Alsop, who generally echoed State Department concerns, also began calling for a greater military aid budget at about this time ("Defense of Europe," *Washington Post,* September 21, 1949).

28. Nourse (1953, 275–80) recounts his own view of the events. In his oral history interview, Nourse asked John Steelman, a senior assistant to the president, if Keyserling could be replaced. Steelman declined, stating that Keyserling's outside supporters would "raise merry hell" if he were removed (Nourse Oral History Interview, March 7, 1972, p. 61). Keyserling demanded to see the loyalty file of Bertram Gross after Gross was cleared by the Loyalty Review Board and wrote an

angry memo to Nourse protesting the Loyalty Review Board's refusal of his request. Apparently, Keyserling had his own ideas about what constituted a sufficient standard of loyalty for his employees (Keyserling to Nourse, 11/5/48, Keyserling Papers, Box 7).

29. Nourse to Truman, 8/26/49, Keyserling Papers, Box 3. Keyserling has written "wrong" in the margins next to Nourse's argument that domestic programs were more desirable in themselves than were military programs.

30. Keyserling and Clark to Truman, 8/26/49, Keyserling Papers, Box 3.

31. Keyserling and Clark to Truman, 8/26/49, Keyserling Papers, Box 3.

32. Nourse (1953, 249) notes that he suspects it was Pace who secured an invitation for him to the National Security Council meeting.

33. Memorandum by the Chairman of the Council of Economic Advisers (Nourse) to the National Security Council, September 30, 1949, *FRUS 1949,* 1:394–96.

34. The invocation of these events, a practice maintained by Leffler and Wells, began with accounts written when little archival evidence was available and before the report itself was even declassified. See, for example, Huntington (1963, 47). Hammond (1962, 285) stresses the role of the Soviet A-bomb. In their own accounts of the development of NSC 68, Acheson (1969, 345) and Nitze (1980, 173) downplay the motivational importance of these events, arguing that they had believed that the defense budget was too small since at least the summer of 1949.

35. CIA Special Evaluation Number 32, "Possible Collapse of Chinese National Government Control," 7/21/48, DDRS 1990 Collection, Document 1259.

36. Summary for the President of the discussion at the 33rd meeting of the National Security Council, 2/4/49, PSF, NSC Meeting Summaries; also included in the DDRS 1983 Collection, Document 1284.

37. Quoted in Acheson (1969, 303).

38. Kennan to Acheson, 2/17/50, *FRUS 1950,* 1:161.

39. Most contemporary press accounts support this interpretation. See, for example, Arthur Krock, "Capital Views Soberly Russia's Atomic Bomb," *New York Times,* September 25, 1949; Richard H. Parke, "Atomic Leaders Are Reassuring," *New York Times,* September 24, 1949; and Marshall Andrews, "Soviet A-Blast Fails to Jolt Pentagon," *Washington Post,* September 24, 1949. The Alsop brothers, who saw the Soviet atomic bomb as further evidence that greater military and foreign aid spending was necessary, lamented the "trancelike reception of the news that the Soviets have exploded an atomic bomb" ("Matter of Fact," *Washington Post,* September 28, 1949).

40. "Gabrielson Accuses Truman," *New York Times,* September 25, 1949.

41. The underlined quote reads "There has been as yet no indication that the general lines of Soviet foreign policy have been altered by the possession of atomic secrets" (State Department Weekly Review, 10/49, White House Confidential File, Box 59).

42. ORE 74–49, "Governmental Programs on National Security and International Affairs for FY 1951," 9/22/49, DDRS 1991 Collection, Document 170.

Chapter 3

Notes to epigraphs: Acheson (1969, 374); Murphy Oral History Interview, May 25, 1970, p. 524.

1. Nourse (1953, 283) quotes his own diary entries concerning the August 26 meeting.

2. "Nourse Calls Rift in Capital Typical," *New York Times,* October 22, 1949.

3. *FRUS 1949,* 1:412. For the budget message itself, see *PPP: HST, 1950,* 44–106.

4. Hammond (1962, 310); Nitze (1980, 171).

5. Dean Acheson to the President, 2/16/50, White House Confidential File, Box 41. This document is also reproduced in *FRUS 1950,* 1:834–41.

6. Snyder to Acheson, 7/9/49, 7/10/49; Acheson to Harriman, 6/23/49, 6/25/49, Harriman Papers, Box 272.

7. Pace to Truman, 3/10/50, White House Confidential File, Box 41.

8. See, for example, Schulzinger (1984) and Isaacson and Thomas (1986). Ferguson (1984) and Frieden (1988) discuss the origins of the linkages between this elite and the Democratic party.

9. Wells (1979, 141–48) includes an interesting discussion of the origins of the Committee on the Present Danger. Hershberg (1993, 491–514) makes clear the close connections between the committee and the State Department. Sanders (1983, esp. 51–114) offers the most detailed account.

10. Truman to Acheson, 1/31/50, *FRUS 1950,* 1:143–44; Wells (1979, 125); Rearden (1984, 524).

11. Most of the reports of disagreement over actual spending figures in the interagency group come from Hammond's interviews (1962, 306, 318–19). Nitze (1989, 96) says that Acheson instructed him to leave out any cost estimates.

12. Pace's correspondence, calendars, and phone records contain evidence of only one contact with Keyserling, a phone call on March 1, 1950 (March 1950 Appointment Calendar, Pace Papers, Box 13). In his account of his resignation, though, Pace cites his disagreement with Keyserling (Pace Oral History Interview, January 22, 1972, p. 64).

13. Pace to Charles P. Stokes, 2/15/50, Pace Papers, Box 5.

14. Robert Oppenheimer met with the group on February 27, 1950; James Conant, president of Harvard University, on March 2; Chester I. Barnard, president of the Rockefeller Foundation, and Henry Smyth, a member of the Atomic Energy Commission, on March 10; Robert Lovett on March 16; and Ernest O. Lawrence, director of the Radiation Laboratory at the University of California, on March 20 (Nitze to Acheson, *FRUS 1950,* 1:202–3).

15. Record of the Meeting of the State-Defense Policy Review Group, 3/16/50, *FRUS 1950,* 1:196–200. Lovett, a partner in the investment banking firm of Brown Brothers Harriman, brought up the need to increase American imports from Europe to reduce the balance-of-payments surplus.

16. "Defense Chief Will Hew to Line in Armed Forces 'Fat' Trim," *Washington Post,* March 20, 1950.

17. Firsthand accounts of the meeting agree on the major details, although

Acheson's and Nitze's versions add some dubious dramatic flourishes not included in other versions. A State Department Memorandum of Conversation (*FRUS 1950,* 1:203–6) provides the most detail. Sidney Souers, who had been serving as a part-time consultant to the group drafting the report, also wrote a memo on the meeting (Souers Papers, Box 1). Acheson (1969, 373–74) reports that General Burns "wept in shame" after the meeting and comments that the incident convinced him Johnson was mentally ill. Contradicting Acheson's tale of crashing chair legs, Nitze (1989, 95) states that "Johnson entered the room in a towering rage and announced that he had no intention even of sitting down."

18. The completion of NSC 68 was also noted by Stewart Alsop on March 26 ("Matter of Fact," *Washington Post,* March 26, 1950). See also his "Truman Must Choose," *Washington Post,* March 31, 1950.

19. Johnson's statement is quoted at length in Hammond (1962, 338–40).

20. Statement before the Senate Appropriations Committee, July 25, 1950, Johnson Papers, Box 145.

21. Elsey Oral History Interview, March 9, 1964, p. 241.

22. Connelly Oral History Interview, November 30, 1967, pp. 162–63, 168, 205, 380–83.

23. The details of the president's vacation, including with whom he met, were recorded in a log by Lieutenant Commander William Rigdon, the president's naval aide. According to oral history accounts, the staff spent the bulk of the trip playing cards with the president, having contests to see who could find the most outrageous flowered shirt (Truman won), and taking side trips to Havana.

24. Joint Oral History Interview with Charles Murphy, Richard Neustadt, David Stowe, and James Webb conducted by Anna Nelson and Hugh Heclo, February 20, 1980, pp. 63–67. The presence of the other three White House staffers, especially Charles Murphy, adds to the credibility of Webb's version of events. None of them questioned his story, even though they disagreed with one another concerning other events during the interview.

25. Joint Oral History Interview with Charles Murphy, Richard Neustadt, David Stowe, and James Webb conducted by Anna Nelson and Hugh Heclo, February 20, 1980, p. 66.

26. Since Pace did not accompany the president to Key West, this meeting may have taken place before Webb's trip there to ask for his removal. Pace's calendars indicate that he met with NSC staffers James Lay and S. Everett Gleason on March 17. There is no record of any meeting with Nitze, but the date of the meeting with Lay and Gleason indicates that it is possible they presented him with NSC 68 (1950 Calendars, Pace Papers, Box 13).

27. Pace Calendars, 1950, Pace Papers, Box 13. There was also a program for his speech to the Detroit Economic Club entitled "A Federal Budget Deficit, Why?" 3/13/50, Pace Papers, Box 3. "Truman Picks Lawton to Head Budget, Pace for Army," *Washington Post,* March 30, 1950. Pace's own version of events is contained in the Pace Oral History Interview, February 25, 1972, pp. 154–55.

28. The meetings and phone calls between Pace and Murphy are indicated on Murphy's daily calendar, Murphy Papers, Box 16. Since they are not listed on Pace's calendar, they appear to have been planned by Murphy.

29. Lawton to the Citizen's Committee for the Hoover Report, 8/11/49, Lawton Papers, Box 7.

30. *FRUS 1950,* 1:298–306.

31. Murphy Daily Record of Telephone Calls and Appointments, March and April 1950, Murphy Papers, Box 16; Murphy Oral History Interview, May 25, 1970, pp. 521–22.

32. Clifford and Elsey had written a memo in 1946 detailing hostile Soviet intentions and calling on the United States to upgrade its military capabilities in response. Leffler (1992, 130–38) offers an extensive discussion of the Clifford-Elsey Report.

33. "A Report to the President Pursuant to the President's Directive of January 31, 1950," 4/7/50, Elsey Papers, Box 89. The text of this document is identical to the one reprinted in *FRUS 1950,* 1:235–92.

34. Murphy Daily Record of Telephone Calls and Appointments, April 1950, Murphy Papers, Box 16; Murphy Oral History Interview, May 25, 1970, pp. 523–24.

35. Memo to the President on the 55th Meeting of the National Security Council, 4/21/50, PSF, NSC Meeting Summaries.

36. For example, based on his interviews with participants, Hammond (1962, 331) states that after the NSC discussed the report, policy development proceeded on two tracks—one favoring a buildup and the other opposing it—but also comments that NSC 68 "was under consideration with Presidential blessing." Huntington (1963, 52–53) argues that the administration was probably planning "small adjustments upward" in the military budget. Rearden (1984, 535) states that "what Truman had in mind is by no means clear." Nitze (1989, 98) avoids the issue of when Truman accepted the report, stating only that he was unsure what the president would do at the time NSC 68 was presented to him.

37. "If his decision is affirmative, it is assumed that the various agencies of the Government will be instructed, under the coordination of the NSC, to develop programs in connection therewith; and that at that time the full machinery of the Department will be called into action" (Webb to Rusk, Jessup, and other State Department officials, RG 59 [Records of the Policy Planning Staff, 1947–53], Box 54).

38. "Johnson Says Reds Aiming at Our Economy," *Washington Post,* May 12, 1950.

39. Elsey memo for the files, 9/16/50, Elsey Papers, Box 72. As was noted earlier, Webb also recalled talking Truman out of firing Johnson when he visited the president in Key West in March (Joint Oral History Interview with Charles Murphy, Richard Neustadt, David Stowe, and James Webb conducted by Anna Nelson and Hugh Heclo, February 20, 1980, pp. 63–67).

40. Richard Bissell to Averell Harriman, 5/12/50, Harriman Papers, Box 272.

41. Murphy Oral History Interview, May 19, 1970, p. 524. Paul Nitze (1980, 173; 1989, 96–97) has also commented on the support he received from Keyserling.

42. Nourse continued to speak out against a large military budget after his resignation. "We must have the imperturbability of a General McAuliffe to say 'nuts' when an industrially primitive and illiterate country tries to bluff us as to our

respective abilities to wage industrialized warfare" (Charles Egan, "Hoffman Predicts Red Collapse," *New York Times,* May 3, 1950).

43. Hamilton Q. Dearborn to James Lay, 5/8/50, *FRUS 1950,* 1:306–11.

44. *FRUS 1950,* 1:323–24.

45. Bohlen to Nitze, 4/5/50, *FRUS 1950,* 1:221–25.

46. Murphy Oral History Interview, May 19, 1970, p. 522.

47. In the press, Acheson's call for a closer examination of the actual military strength of the United States was contrasted with Johnson's statement that U.S. defenses were "in grand shape." *Time* (February 20, 1950, p. 13) favorably compared Acheson's argument that the United States should "recognize the military situation for what it is and speedily redress it" with Johnson's "complacency." Joseph and Stewart Alsop had privileged access to Acheson's thinking and attacked Johnson's economy program regularly throughout the winter and spring of 1950. See also Arthur Krock, "Mr. Johnson's Record: The Pros and the Cons," *New York Times,* February 26, 1950.

48. Richard Bissell to Averell Harriman, 5/12/50, Harriman Papers, Box 12; *FRUS 1950,* 1:297–98.

49. Truman to James Lay, 4/12/50; Minutes of the 55th Meeting of the National Security Council, 4/20/50, PSF, Box 207.

50. *PPP: HST, 1950,* 441. Given the broad range of arguments from NSC 68 appearing in the press in spite of the president's secrecy order, Truman probably had to dissemble in order to keep his intentions hidden from his congressional opponents.

51. Souers memorandum for the file, 6/8/50, Souers Papers, Box 1.

52. Ferdinand Kuhn, "U.S. Policies to Be Unified by Harriman for Truman," *Washington Post,* June 17, 1950. Curiously, Donovan (1982, 261) cites an interview with Harriman commenting that he was brought in after the beginning of the Korean War with instructions from Truman to "Help Dean—He's in trouble." The timing is incorrect, but Truman's sentiment is appropriate given the vigorous attacks then being made on Acheson by congressional Republicans.

53. Memorandum to the President summarizing the discussion at the 55th meeting of the NSC, 4/21/50, PSF, NSC Meeting Summaries.

54. Bonesteel to Harriman, 3/13/50; Harriman to Bonesteel, 3/17/50, Harriman Papers, Box 271. Bonesteel and Harriman had been working together to argue for the importance of military aid to Europe since at least late 1948. Harriman assembled some of their correspondence on this issue and kept it with the materials he was sent concerning NSC 68 (Harriman to Secretary of State, 11/2/48; Bonesteel Memorandum, 11/11/48; Harriman to Paul Hoffman, 12/26/48, Harriman Papers, Box 272).

55. Concerning State Department thinking on offshore procurement, see Kofsky (1995, 16–18).

56. Bissell to Harriman, 5/12/50, Harriman Papers, Box 272.

57. *FRUS 1950,* 1:297–98; Wallace Carroll to Barrett and Nitze, 6/13/50, RG 59 (Records of the Policy Planning Staff, 1947–53), Box 54; Barrett to Spingarn, undated, Spingarn Papers, Box 24.

58. Bissell to Harriman, 5/26/50, Harriman Papers, Box 271. The preliminary

estimates included in the National Security Resources Board's comments on NSC 68 have no figure for the Department of Defense, indicating that all of the other relevant executive agencies had these preliminary figures ready by the time Bissell wrote to Harriman (Memorandum by the National Security Resources Board, 5/29/50, *FRUS 1950*, 1:316–21).

59. Memorandum by James Lay summarizing the first meeting of the Ad Hoc Committee on NSC 68, 5/2/50, *FRUS 1950*, 1:298.

60. *PPP: HST, 1950*, 445–49. The fact that the president requested the amount that Bissell had suggested to Harriman supports the argument that this request was linked to progress on NSC 68.

61. Dulles to Acheson, 2/9/50, Dulles Papers, Box 47. This telegram praising a statement by Acheson urging bipartisan cooperation was one of several. Hoopes (1973, 85–88) notes that Dulles's efforts to secure a position in the State Department began within a few weeks of the special election, sending out feelers to State Department officials through Carl McCardle, a sympathetic journalist. Dulles believed he and Vandenberg were the chief architects of bipartisanship and expressed his concern that it would break down because of his electoral loss and Vandenberg's enforced absence (Dulles to Lawrence Fuchs, 12/5/49, Dulles Papers, Box 40). Webb's account of his trip to Key West, referred to earlier with respect to the transfer of Frank Pace from the Bureau of the Budget, is found in the Joint Oral History Interview with Charles Murphy, Richard Neustadt, David Stowe, and James Webb, February 20, 1980, p. 65.

62. Dulles memorandum of conversation with Arthur Vandenberg, 3/30/50; Vandenberg to Acheson, 3/31/50, Dulles Papers, Box 47; Acheson memorandum of conversation with Truman, 4/4/50; Acheson memorandum of conversation with Herbert Lehman, 4/5/50; Acheson memorandum of conversation with Dulles, 4/6/50, Acheson Papers, Box 65.

63. Kepley (1988, 82) discusses this arrangement in the context of efforts to renew bipartisanship but does not link it to the development of NSC 68. Bridges had suggested this sort of arrangement to Jack McFall, who handled congressional relations for the State Department, in February 1950, arguing that Republicans on the Foreign Relations Committee did not represent the dominant perspective held by Senate Republicans (McFall memorandum of conversation with Styles Bridges, 2/21/50, RG 59 [McFall], Box 1). Vandenberg encouraged acceptance of the idea, informing Acheson that Bridges was "coming around" to the idea of cooperating with the administration. Vandenberg urged Acheson to ignore Bridges's antiadministration rhetoric (Acheson to Truman, 4/5/50, Acheson Papers, Box 65).

64. James Webb to Robert Taft, 4/27/50, Taft Papers, Box 750.

65. Statement attached to invitation to 5/10/50 smoker, Taft Papers, Box 750.

66. Taft to St. Clair Archer, 4/8/50, Taft Papers, Box 920.

67. "Review of Bipartisan Foreign Policy Consultations since World War II," 10/1/51, Elsey Papers, Box 59. This study, conducted by Kenneth Hechler, lists all presidential appointments with Republicans between 1945 and 1951. It was presented to the Senate and was intended to show that Republicans were frequently consulted. Nevertheless, it probably does not contain off-the-record meetings.

There is no mention of any meetings of the Republican senators named at the April 18 meeting in the papers of Styles Bridges, Robert Taft, or Dean Acheson.

68. Styles Bridges, for one, was advised by his staff to stay away from these meetings since they could damage his reputation (Dick Auerbach to Styles Bridges, 6/11/50, Bridges Papers, File 27, Folder 111). Jack McFall was disappointed at the Republican turnout for these events, although he attributed it to a scheduling conflict with a dinner given by Styles Bridges (McFall to William Hall, 4/27/50, RG 59 [McFall], Box 1).

69. Souers memorandum for the file, 6/8/50, Souers Papers, Box 1.

70. James Lanigan to Harriman, 11/30/50, Harriman Papers, Box 282.

71. Harriman's papers also contain correspondence with media figures such as Al Friendly of NBC, Edward R. Murrow of CBS, and many others in business and government.

72. Robert Albright, "Truman's 'New Technique' Still Faces Acid Test," *Washington Post,* May 21, 1950.

73. Handwritten list of "Top Musts" attached to the printed Summary of the Status of Legislation Relating to the Recommendations of the President, 11/2/49, Spingarn Papers, Box 26; Urgent Legislation [a printed list], 5/31/50, Spingarn Papers, Box 26. Similar printed lists appear in the papers of other White House staff members and apparently served as the basis for discussion at meetings on legislative strategy.

74. *FRUS 1950,* 1:285.

75. Memorandum of Conversation between the Secretary and Representative Herter, 3/24/50, Acheson Papers, Box 65. This document can also be found in *FRUS 1950,* 1:206–9.

76. Carlton Savage to Nitze, 5/2/50, RG 59 (Records of the Policy Planning Staff, 1947–53), Box 54.

77. Memorandum for the President on the 50th Meeting of the National Security Council, 12/30/49, PSF, NSC Meeting Summaries. This memo can also be found in the DDRS 1982 Collection, Document 2100.

78. Robert Cutler to the President, 2/23/53, DDRS 1987 Collection, Document 534. NSC 8 is reproduced in *FRUS 1948,* 6:1164–69. During the 1952 election campaign, the *Boston Herald* ran two editorials arguing that the decision to remove American troops from Korea was based on a misinterpretation of a message sent to Washington by Douglas MacArthur in January 1949. After the election, the newspaper asked the Eisenhower administration to make public the facts concerning the American withdrawal. Cutler assembled the relevant documents and summarized them for Eisenhower. In fact, MacArthur had supported the withdrawal in spite of the expectation that the South Korean regime would not survive. Cutler wanted to release the information, but Eisenhower decided to keep the entire matter secret.

79. Robert Cutler's Extracts from General MacArthur's January 19, 1949, Message (CX 67198, CM IN 17171), 2/23/53, DDRS 1987 Collection, Document 535.

80. *FRUS 1949,* 7:969–78.

81. NSC Progress Report on NSC 8/2, 8/3/50, RG 59 (Records of the Policy Planning Staff, 1947–53), Box 20.

82. Cumings (1990, 568–621) offers some evidence that the attack did not come as a surprise to everyone. Nitze (1980, 173–74) says that in February 1950, Alexander Sachs brought him a paper predicting a North Korean attack in the summer.

83. NSC 67, approved on April 12, 1950, states that "[i]n the event that the communists gain participation in the Italian Government by legal means and threaten to achieve control of the Italian Government, or in the event that the Italian Government ceases to evidence a determination to resist communist internal or external threats, the United States should be prepared to initiate measures designed to prevent communist domination and to revive Italian determination to oppose communism" (DDRS 1978 Collection, Document 247B).

84. For example, May (1993, 135) reprints excerpts from Wells's article on NSC 68 in his textbook on the subject and introduces it as an example of "neorealism." Similarly, Stephanson (1993, 288) regards both Leffler and John Lewis Gaddis as neorealists.

Chapter 4

Notes to epigraphs: Wherry to Henry Doorly [publisher, *Omaha World Herald*], 1/25/50, Wherry Papers, Box 11; *FRUS 1950*, 1:290.

1. Graham and Kefauver visited the White House with this group to plan strategy against the Internal Security Act in September 1950 (Spingarn memo for the files, 9/6/50, Spingarn Papers, Box 13).

2. Fried (1974) recounts some of the details of the 1950 campaign and argues that race was a bigger issue in Pepper's reelection campaign in Florida and Graham's in North Carolina than was communism.

3. "Alabama 'Loyalist' Democrats Expect to Oust States' Righters," *New York Times,* May 6, 1950.

4. The Republican Party Steering Committee in late 1949 divided the Senate into "reliable conservatives," "short-term conservatives," "confused Senators," "short-term New Dealers," and "incorrigible New Dealers" based on their votes on labor legislation in the Eightieth and Eighty-first Congresses. Those not in the Senate during the passage of the Taft-Hartley Act in 1947 were listed as "short-term," since their position on the issue could not be known. Frear, who took office in 1949, was listed as a "short-term conservative." The selection of labor votes as the sole criterion by which senators were evaluated also demonstrates the importance of this issue to the Nationalist Republicans who controlled the Steering Committee, as well as their belief that it would become an issue again during the second session of the Eighty-first Congress in 1950.

5. DuPont's efforts to secure trade protection during the 1930s are discussed by Ferguson (1984, 72–79).

6. This report was based on votes from the first half of the 1950 session of the Eighty-first Congress. Taylor and Hayden received a perfect +30, O'Mahoney a +25, McFarland a +15, Johnson a +10, and Chavez and Gillette a +5. Interestingly, three of the six issues used to determine the rating concerned foreign policy, two concerned housing, and one concerned natural resources (the Columbia River

Basin projects amendment to the Rivers and Harbors bill). This gives some indication of the priority the administration accorded its foreign policy agenda, even before the Korean War (Report on the United States Senate, undated [probably May 1950], Elsey Papers, Box 80).

7. Kenneth Wherry (R-NE) was minority leader, and Eugene Millikin (R-CO) chaired the Republican Party Conference. Robert Taft (R-OH) chaired the powerful Policy Committee. Leverett Saltonstall (R-MA), the minority whip, was the only internationalist in a leadership position.

8. George H. E. Smith to Taft, 1/17/51, Taft Papers, Box 626.

9. Nitze's remarks in "Clinton's Foreign Policy Affairs Similar to Truman's," National Public Radio, *Morning Edition,* February 17, 1994, Transcript No. 1284–5.

10. Marshall to Nitze, 11/15/50, RG 59 (Records of the Policy Planning Staff, 1947–53), Box 8. The memo estimated that roughly one quarter of the Senate would fully support the administration's policy in the Eighty-second Congress, one quarter would be "irreconcilable," and half would be critical of some aspects of it.

11. Of course, this argument about regional orientation could be made for trade as well as investment. Unfortunately, appropriate data for testing this hypothesis were not available.

12. Bensel (1984) and Agnew (1987) are among those who treat the differences among regions as differences in economic structure. As was noted in chapter 2, Eden (1985, 176–85) also uses region as a proxy for economic structure, arguing that the "business nationalists" who opposed the internationalism of the Truman administration came mostly from Midwest and mountain states with few ties to the international economy. Trubowitz (1992) treats region in the same way, examining changes in sectional conflict over foreign policy during the postwar era. Conflicting interpretations of regional differences exist, however. For example, Daniel Elazar (1970) has argued that regional variations in political behavior are based on cultural differences rooted in the historical development of the area.

13. The persistence of class "remnants" based on previously dominant forms of economic activity has often been noted in other contexts. For example, Kehr (1977b), Wehler (1970), and others have examined the effects of the persistence in Wilhelmine Germany of institutions and political forces rooted in precapitalist economic activity after German industrialization.

14. Baldwin derived his measures of import and export sensitivity from the *Congressional District Data Book,* 93rd Congress, published by the Bureau of the Census. These figures represent the relative number of workers employed in the export and import-competing sectors rather than the value of goods produced by each sector. There is a close relationship between the number of employees in a sector and the value of the goods produced by it, and the same results are produced regardless of which specification is used for the size of the sector.

15. Rieselbach (1966); Eden (1985, 178–85).

16. Stanley Botner to Fred Hobart, 10/2/50; Everett Bellows to Stanley Botner, 10/11/50, Harriman Papers, Box 309.

Chapter 5

Notes to epigraphs: FRUS 1950, 1:285; Charles Murphy Oral History Interview, June 24, 1969, p. 262.

1. For accounts of the Turnip Day Special Session—so named because its opening day, July 26, was the traditional day for planting turnips in Missouri—see Donovan (1977, 406–16) and Hamby (1973, 244–47). Fair Deal programs were a frequent theme in Truman's rhetoric during the first half of 1950. See, for example, Robert C. Albright, "Truman's 'New Technique' Still Faces Acid Test," *Washington Post,* May 21, 1950.

2. The Truman administration's domestic program has its defenders. See, for example, Hamby (1973) and Smith (1976).

3. Oral History Interview with Charles Murphy, June 24, 1969, p. 276.

4. George Elsey's handwritten notes on a draft of the Legislative Program for the Second Session of the 81st Congress, Elsey Papers, Box 38.

5. McAuliffe (1978) discusses this split within the American left in some detail. Concerning the Progressive party and the Wallace campaign, see Markowitz (1973), Walton (1976), and Yarnell (1974).

6. Memo by Douglas McGregor, David Edelstein, and Joseph Duggan, 7/24/47, Vanech Papers, Box 1. Concerning the role of the attorney general's list, see Caute (1978, 169–72) and Goldstein (1978, 309–11).

7. On the fate of the expelled unions, see O'Brien (1968). Other historical accounts of the expelled unions and the role communists played in them include Rosswurm (1992), Levenstein (1981), and Cochran (1977).

8. J. Edgar Hoover sent frequent reports on the meetings and strategy planned by the Progressive party to Harry Vaughan, the president's military aide, including a several-hundred-page report on the Wallace campaign and its leadership ("Communists and Pro-communists for Wallace," undated [probably mid-1948], PSF, Box 168). On the provision of FBI information to employers, see Caute (1978, 116) as well as the discussion in the Minutes of the Industrial Labor Relations Committee, 7/12/50, RG 330, Office of the Secretary of Defense, Munitions Board, Office of Administrative Management, Box 1. Major radical figures who left the labor movement for political reasons found it very difficult to find work, because their record followed them wherever they went. See De Caux (1970, 522–45) and Nelson, Barrett, and Ruck (1981, 399–424) for personal accounts.

9. Connelly Oral History Interview, August 21, 1968, p. 440. Connelly also noted that in 1948, "[a]ll the so-called liberals were backing Eisenhower. Whatever liberals are, I don't know" (November 30, 1967, p. 276). Truman's suspicion of the liberal wing of the Democratic party apparently ran very deep. The White House received regular reports on the efforts of political figures associated with the New Deal to undermine Truman's political position. The White House received reports based on FBI wiretaps on Thomas Corcoran, a well-known former official in the Roosevelt administration, and secret investigations of New Dealers such as Harold Ickes in search of political intelligence or useful scandal. Connelly, military aide Harry Vaughan, and NSC Executive Secretary Sidney Souers were the usual con-

duits for this information. These activities are discussed by Donovan (1977, 29–30) and Theoharis (1978, 160–63).

10. Donovan (1977, 417–19) discusses the poor financial condition of the Truman campaign. Connelly commented that "[p]eople didn't think he was going to win so why back a losing horse. So that's what happened. That's why he didn't get any money" (Connelly Oral History Interview, November 30, 1967, p. 285).

11. Donovan (1977, 26–29); Hamby (1973, 54–59).

12. Elsey Oral History Interview, July 10, 1969, p. 319.

13. Connelly Oral History Interview, August 21, 1968, p. 331.

14. *U.S. News and World Report,* December 16, 1949, p. 1; *Time,* January 9, 1950, p. 10; April 3, 1950, pp. 21–22. Demands for cuts in military spending came from many sources. See, for example, "State Chamber Group Asks 5 Billion Cut in Budget and Spending Kept within Income," *New York Times,* January 31, 1950.

15. Memorandum of conversation between the Secretary and Representative Herter, 3/21/50, Acheson Papers, Box 65. This document is also included in *FRUS 1950,* 1:206–9. The Alsop brothers consistently reflected Acheson's view that more spending was necessary. More typical is Hanson Baldwin's argument that military spending cuts were a necessary calculated risk ("Armed Strength Cuts," *New York Times,* January 16, 1950).

16. Wherry to Henry Doorly, 1/25/50, Wherry Papers, Box 11.

17. Handwritten note by Robert Taft, undated, Taft Papers, Box 750.

18. "General Program of Republican Congress," undated [1948], Bridges Papers, File 26, Folder 10. This document was probably prepared for Bridges's 1948 reelection campaign following the Eightieth Congress.

19. Wherry speech notes, undated [1950], Wherry Papers, Box 9.

20. Patterson (1972, 146–59, 315–34) summarizes Taft's views on domestic and foreign policy.

21. Eden (1985, 172–76), Patterson (1972, 339–41), and Kepley (1988, 11–12) all mention this arrangement. The main source for this "tacit and informal understanding" is Vandenberg (1952, 318–19).

22. Minority Party Policy Committee report, undated [late 1949], Taft Papers, Box 813. Foreign policy issues did not influence their assessment of senators' reliability.

23. Carr to Paul Walter, 9/12/50, Taft Papers, Box 279; Taft to Herbert Hoover, 11/21/50, Taft Papers, Box 920.

24. Staff memo summarizing the RNC report, 9/22/49, Bridges Papers, File 25; S. E. Dennis to Wherry, 2/27/50, Wherry Papers, Box 11.

25. Kofsky (1993) presents evidence that the administration had previously exaggerated the threat of war after the Czech coup in 1948 in order to facilitate the passage of the Marshall Plan and additional funding for aircraft procurement.

26. These meetings are summarized in detail in *FRUS 1950,* 7:157–65, 178–83, 200–202. The summary of the June 28 meeting is not included in the *FRUS* collection but can be found in the Acheson Papers, Box 65.

27. Memorandum of Conversation on the Meeting of the NSC in the Cabinet Room at the White House, 6/28/50, Acheson Papers, Box 65. The memorandum states that "the usual members of the NSC" were present, as well as the vice presi-

dent, Treasury Secretary John Snyder, National Security Resources Board Director Stuart Symington, Averell Harriman, Dean Rusk, H. Freeman Matthews, and Philip Jessup. While the "usual members" of the NSC might include the Joint Chiefs of Staff Chairman Omar Bradley, there is no indication that he attended the meeting. The only military officer whose remarks are recorded was Air Force Chief of Staff Hoyt S. Vandenberg. By contrast, all four members of the JCS were present at the June 26 meeting.

28. Memorandum of Conversation by the Ambassador at Large (Jessup), 6/25/50, *FRUS 1950,* 7:157–61.

29. "Korean Prospect," *Washington Post,* May 25, 1950. This prompted a letter from Earnest Fisher, a former official with the U.S. Military Government in Korea. He noted that the United States did not contemplate holding the peninsula in the event of war. "There is, therefore, no question of our being militarily involved in Korea" (*Washington Post,* May 31, 1950).

30. Cumings (1990, 430–31). Connally remained ambivalent immediately after the North Korean attack, stressing that the issue had been referred to the United Nations ("North Korea's Attack Catches 'Hill' by Surprise," *Washington Post,* June 26, 1950).

31. See, for example, James Reston, "War in Korea Overwhelms Atlantic Arms Opposition," *New York Times,* June 27, 1950; Arthur Krock, "Two Great Postwar Questions Are Intensified," *New York Times,* June 27, 1950; and Ferdinand Kuhn, "Policy Now Bars Sending Troops," *Washington Post,* June 26, 1950.

32. "South Korea Should Win, Johnson Says," *Washington Post,* June 26, 1950.

33. Memorandum of conversation with Secretary Acheson, Secretary Pace, and others of the State Department, 7/1/50, Dulles Papers, Box 47.

34. Dulles to Lippmann, 7/13/50; Lippmann to Dulles, 7/18/50, Dulles Papers, Box 48.

35. Murphy Oral History Interview, May 25, 1970, pp. 523–24.

36. Kolodziej (1966) notes that the first supplemental appropriations bill included $11.7 billion for the military services and an additional $4 billion in MDAP funds. The second supplemental contained $16.85 billion for defense, and the third had $6.39 billion.

37. Fellers to Taft, 7/19/50, Taft Papers, Box 670.

38. Memorandum of Conversation by Philip Jessup, 7/3/50, Acheson Papers, Box 65. This document is also reproduced in *FRUS 1950,* 7:286–91.

39. Acheson Memorandum of Conversation with the President, 7/10/50, Acheson Papers, Box 65. Acheson's memo betrays some aggravation at Truman's failure to give him additional details. He notes that "I will see Mr. Harriman later today about this matter and try to be clearer as to exactly what was discussed by the Big Four and what the present thinking is on the subject."

40. Truman did not share his political strategies with his staff, allowing only Matthew Connelly to attend Big Four meetings. Charles Murphy recalled that "the President, I think, quite purposefully decided that he wanted to conduct these meetings by himself, and did not want staff there" (Murphy Oral History Interview, June 24, 1969, p. 237).

41. Murphy Oral History Interview, May 25, 1970, pp. 525–26.

42. Budget memoranda with handwritten notes, 7/12/50 and 7/15/50, Elsey Papers, Box 71.

43. Symington to the members of the National Security Council, 7/6/50, *FRUS 1950,* 1:338–41. David Stowe, a member of the White House staff, recalled that "Stu Symington in those days was really one of the biggest hawks we had" (Joint Oral History Interview, February 20, 1980, pp. 76–77).

44. Notes on Acheson's Comments at the cabinet meeting, 7/14/50, Acheson Papers, Box 65.

45. Acheson memorandum of telephone conversation, 7/13/50, Acheson Papers, Box 65.

46. Notes on discussion of Defense paper, 7/14/50, Acheson Papers, Box 65.

47. The president's message to Congress can be found in *PPP: HST, 1950,* 527–37. The radio and television address made the same day can be found on pp. 537–42.

48. *CR,* 81st Congress, 2nd Session, June 28, 1950, pp. 9319–23.

49. *CR,* 81st Congress, 2nd Session, June 30, 1950, pp. 9537–39.

50. Press Release from the Office of Senator George W. Malone, 7/26/50, Bridges Papers, File 80, Folder 80.

51. Patterson (1972, 453) notes that this quote appeared in *Newsweek.*

52. Taft to McCormick, undated [1950], Taft Papers, Box 924.

53. Wherry to Mrs. R. L. Huston, 7/18/50, Wherry Papers, Box 11. Wherry's papers appear to contain only favorable comments from his constituents on most issues, so those on Korea stand out as an exception.

54. Ickes to Taft, 7/28/50; Taft to Ickes, 8/1/50; Ickes to Taft, 8/9/50, Taft Papers, Box 924. Although their political views were far apart, Ickes considered Taft "the Babe Ruth of the Republican Party," commenting after the 1948 election that, with the nomination of Dewey, the Republicans "sent in a batboy with the bases full and only one run needed" (Ickes, "Taft Minus Hartley," *New Republic* 121 [July 18, 1949], p. 16, quoted in Patterson 1972, 425).

55. Long to Bridges, 8/17/50, Bridges Papers, File 27, Folder 16A.

56. *Congressional Quarterly Almanac* 6:121–25.

57. Spingarn Oral History Interview, March 20, 1967, p. 70.

58. "Fair Deal a Dim Memory as 'War Congress' Wanes," *Washington Post,* September 3, 1950.

59. Donovan (1982, 365) comments that Truman's domestic agenda was destroyed by "the political crosswinds of war and rising military expenditures" and confines his account to domestic scandals and foreign policy after the beginning of the Korean War. Gosnell (1980, 449–50) argues that after the Korean War, "the legislative situation changed radically," scuttling the Fair Deal while giving the president wider authority in foreign policy. McCoy (1984, 221) observes that "less concern for attacking domestic social problems and greater partisanship in all matters" followed the beginning of the Korean War, but he does not explain why this occurred and focuses primarily on foreign policy.

60. *Congressional Quarterly Almanac* 6 (1950) provides a brief discussion of each item handled by Congress during the second session of the Eighty-first Congress.

61. Some of the activities of the Truman White House bear a disturbing resem-

blance to those that would cost another president his job two decades later. Truman's staff met to set up a "dirty tricks department" to embarrass the China lobby, and the president asked the attorney general to investigate their tax records (Elsey to Truman, 3/28/51; Lloyd to Murphy, 11/1/51, Murphy Papers, Box 10; Truman to the Attorney General [Howard McGrath], 6/11/51, Elsey Papers, Box 59).

Chapter 6

Notes to epigraphs: Emerson Schmidt to Francis Matthews, 9/4/46, Matthews Papers, Box 10; ILRC Minutes, 11/27/48.

1. Charles Wilson, the chief executive officer of General Electric named to head the Defense Production Administration in 1951, commented in 1946 that "the problems of the United States can be captiously summed up in two words: Russia abroad and labor at home" (quoted in Irons 1974, 77–78).

2. McQuaid (1982, 135). According to the Bureau of Labor Statistics, 10.5 percent of American workers were involved in work stoppages. The largest annual figure since 1881, the first year for which records exist, is 20.8 percent in 1919. Interestingly, both 1946 and 1919 were reconversion years, and both marked the beginnings of major red scares.

3. Rupert (1990) argues that the way the neoliberal assumptions of the politics of productivity were articulated within the labor movement was critical to the success of the arrangement. While Rupert stresses the bureaucratization of the union movement during World War II, he makes little mention of the elimination of elements of the labor movement that refused to adhere to the neoliberal consensus after the war ended.

4. McAuliffe (1978, 29–30) and Oshinsky (1974, 132–33) note that the noncommunist CIO leadership supported the Marshall Plan but opposed—or at least refrained from endorsing—the Truman Doctrine.

5. More extensive discussion of anticommunism in the labor movement during the immediate postwar era can be found in Cochran (1977), Levenstein (1981), Lichtenstein (1989), and Rosswurm (1992). De Caux (1970) and Nelson, Barrett, and Ruck (1981) offer personal accounts of this conflict in the labor movement. Griffith (1988) treats the issue in the context of the CIO's effort to expand its membership in the South, and McAuliffe (1978) examines its role in the broader ideological currents of the American left.

6. Confidential Appendix to "Communists within the Labor Movement," January 1946, Matthews Papers, Box 13. Most of the information contained in this document appears to have been based on a 1945 report sent to Matthews by Father John F. Cronin, who assisted Matthews and Schmidt in assembling the three USCC reports ("The Problem of American Communism in 1945," undated [1945], Matthews Papers, Box 10). Theoharis (1978, 133) notes that Cronin's information, in turn, came from the FBI. The information was to be kept confidential to avoid both the exposure of FBI informants and potential libel suits from those listed as Communist party members. Concerning other aspects of the business campaign to promote free enterprise, see Fones-Wolf (1994).

7. Quoted in Irons (1974, 86).

8. Quoted in McQuaid (1982, 152–53).

9. John S. Sinclair to Harriman, 12/29/50; Harriman to Sinclair, 1/4/51, Harriman Papers, Box 310.

10. Quoted in Stein (1963, 99).

11. Griffith (1988) attributes the failure of Operation Dixie in part to the strength of the social control mechanisms wielded by Southern industrialists and the widening ideological schism within the CIO, which led it to withdraw support for some of the organizing campaigns it had previously supported.

12. Hoover to Vaughan, 3/18/46, PSF, Box 168. Bridges's papers do not indicate how he obtained Magdoff's lie detector test results (Magdoff polygraph results, undated, Bridges Papers, File 27).

13. Remarks of Major T. W. Heffernan, Department of the Air Force, ILRC Minutes, 7/14/48.

14. Remarks of Alexander Corey, Department of the Army, ILRC Minutes, 9/8/48.

15. Remarks of Captain William J. Marshall, Department of the Army, and Rear Admiral Charles W. Fox, Department of the Navy, ILRC Minutes, 9/16/48.

16. Remarks of Major Hartley Dame, Department of the Army, ILRC Minutes, 11/7/48.

17. John Fanning to the Chairman of the Munitions Board, 1/6/49, RG 330, Munitions Board, Office of Administrative Management. The complaint actually represented a minority view on the committee since none of the uniformed military officers on the committee believed procedures should be changed (ILRC Minutes, 1/4/49).

18. Remarks of John Fanning, Chairperson of the Industrial Labor Relations Committee, ILRC Minutes, 10/27/49. UE was expelled from the CIO less than one month later as a communist-dominated union.

19. In addition to Munitions Board officials, the IAC included representatives of the Atlantic Refining Company, Western Electric, AT&T, General Electric, United Aircraft Corporation, American Smelting and Refining Company, the American Cyanamid Company, Thompson Products, Standard Oil Company of New Jersey, the Glenn L. Martin Company, Bausch & Lomb Optical, and Pennsalt International Corporation (IAC Minutes, 4/20/49). Representatives of a few other defense contractors attended other meetings.

20. IAC Minutes, 11/9/49.

21. Plants on the key facilities list were classified as "vital," "critical," or "very important." The list itself is still classified.

22. IAC Minutes, 4/20/49 and 3/11/53.

23. IAC Minutes, 4/20/49. Concerning the Schenectady plant, see Schatz (1983).

24. Remarks of Leland W. Miller of Consolidated Vultee Aircraft, IAC Minutes, 7/12/50.

25. IAC Minutes, 11/9/49 and 7/12/50. Concern about the loyalty oaths was expressed at the November 11, 1949, meeting. Union work rules governing the dismissal of employees came up at every meeting. The exchange between Howard and Miller occurred at the July 12, 1950, meeting.

26. Remarks of Robert Applegate of the Munitions Board, IAC Minutes, 7/12/50.

27. IAC Minutes, 4/20/49.

28. IAC Minutes, 11/9/49.

29. Notes on the St. Louis Conference, 4/43, Ohly Papers, Box 32; Ohly to the File, 9/8/42, Ohly Papers, Box 34.

30. Harry Truman, quoted in Ferrell (1983, 513).

31. Theoharis and Cox (1988, 45–48, 62–63); Summers (1993, 29–31, 35–38); Gentry (1991, 85–88, 103–4).

32. Theoharis and Cox (1988, 157, 203); Gentry (1991, 197).

33. Hoover to Vaughan, 10/31/45, PSF, Box 167; Hoover to Vaughan, 12/7/45, PSF, Box 168. There are many other memoranda of this sort in the President's Secretary's File, especially from the 1945–46 period.

34. Summers (1993, 84) and Gentry (1991, 218) note that Winchell was a personal friend of Hoover and that the director frequently sent him useful information for his newspaper column and radio program. Pearson also had a close relationship with Hoover, although the two eventually came into conflict, according to Gentry (1991, 380–82). Summers (1993, 101) reports that Hoover referred to Lippmann as a "coyote of the press" and collected information on Alsop's homosexuality.

35. National Security Council Progress Report by the NSC Representative on Internal Security on the implementation of Internal Security (NSC 17/4; 17/6), 12/20/51, PSF, Records of the NSC; see also DDRS 1988 Collection, Document 1691. Theoharis (1985) and Theoharis and Cox (1988, 193–98) discuss the American Legion Contact Program in detail.

36. "Over the years you have been a real bulwark of strength to the FBI and I can never begin to thank you for all the fine things which you have done" (Hoover to Bridges, 12/23/50, Bridges Papers, File 28).

37. Hillman to Bridges, 9/21/49, Bridges Papers, File 25; Report on Alex L. Hillman, 4/3/53, Bridges Papers, File 28; Report on Eugene Daniell, undated [1954], Bridges Papers, File 42, Folder 52.

38. List of 26 Communist party members and 46 suspected sympathizers living in New Hampshire, undated [probably 1946 or later], Bridges Papers, File 26, 1941–54: Assorted files on Communism, Mutual Security, Canadian Spy Report, and State Department Personnel; Hoover to Bridges, 7/8/48, Bridges Papers, File 42, Folder 52.

39. George H. E. Smith to Robert Taft, 12/19/50, Taft Papers, Box 750.

40. Sidney Souers to James Forrestal, 1/5/49, Files of the NSC, Box 10. Coyne helped bring information developed by the FBI to the attention of the NSC staff (Coyne to the Executive Secretary of the NSC, 3/1/49, Files of the NSC, Box 10).

41. James Lay to the Chief of Personnel of the CIA, 5/16/49, Files of the NSC, Box 10.

42. NSC 7, "The Position of the United States with Respect to Soviet-Directed World Communism," 3/30/48, *FRUS 1948,* 1:545–50. This document is also reproduced in the DDRS 1975 Collection, Document 278B. NSC 7 was canceled by the NSC on November 23, 1948, after its contents were superseded by NSC 20/4,

which was approved on that date. An earlier draft of this report, NSC 20/2, had not mentioned internal security issues at all (*FRUS 1948*, 1:615–24). The subject was added by the time NSC 20/4 was approved, however, and that report included a statement that it was necessary to "assure the internal security of the United States against the dangers of sabotage, subversion, and espionage" (*FRUS 1948*, 1:668).

43. The FBI is the only agency mentioned by name in the directive authorizing the study. At the April 2, 1948, meeting of the NSC, Souers informed the NSC that he planned to hire a consultant to conduct the study (Memorandum for the President summarizing the discussion at the 9th meeting of the NSC, 4/2/48, PSF, NSC Meeting Summaries. This document is also reproduced in the DDRS 1982 Collection, Document 1226).

44. Coyne to the Executive Secretary of the NSC, 4/18/48, PSF, Box 9. Theoharis and Cox (1988, 178–84) note that the FBI was not entirely satisfied with the delimitation agreement and that Hoover continued to worry that other intelligence services would encroach on what he considered his own bureaucratic turf.

45. NSC 17, "The Internal Security of the United States," 6/28/48, DDRS 1979 Collection, Document 52A. Theoharis and Cox (1988) and Gentry (1991) both frequently note that Hoover often sought broad approval for various activities from the attorney general or the president without revealing that the actions for which permission was requested had already been taken.

46. NSC 17, "The Internal Security of the United States," 6/28/48, DDRS 1979 Collection, Document 52A.

47. Memorandum for the President summarizing the discussion at the 18th meeting of the NSC, 8/20/48, PSF, NSC Meeting Summaries. This document is also included in the DDRS 1982 Collection, Document 2110.

48. Souers to the NSC, 8/26/48; Souers to Russell J. Hopley, 9/13/48, Records of the NSC, Box 9.

49. Spingarn Oral History Interview, March 24, 1967, p. 781.

50. Souers to SANACC, 9/16/48, NSC Records, Box 9; Coyne to Souers, 11/1/48, NSC Records, Box 9. Theoharis (1978, 77–78) notes that the issuance of such a statement had been a priority for Hoover for several years.

51. Forrestal to the President [included in NSC 17/3], 10/7/48, DDRS 1979 Collection, Document 53A.

52. Spingarn to the President, 10/15/48, Spingarn Papers, Box 31.

53. Dissent of the Department of Justice Representative to SANACC 401 [included in NSC 17/3], 11/4/48, DDRS 1979 Collection, Document 53A.

54. Tom Clark to the President [included in NSC 17/3], 10/23/48, DDRS 1979 Collection, Document 53A.

55. Memorandum from the Department of Justice to the Ad Hoc Committee of SANACC on Internal Security [included in NSC 17/3], 11/4/48, DDRS 1979 Collection, Document 53A.

56. Souers distributed the document to the NSC immediately prior to the November 26, 1948, meeting, but the summaries of that and three subsequent meetings contain no indication that NSC 17/3 was discussed (Souers to the NSC, 11/26/48, NSC Records, Box 9; Memoranda for the President summarizing the meetings of the NSC, 11/26/48, 12/3/48, and 12/17/48, DDRS 1982 Collection,

Documents 1227, 1228, and 1229; 12/10/49, DDRS 1983 Collection, Document 1283).

57. Coyne to Souers, 12/8/48, 12/30/48, NSC Records, Box 9.

58. Souers to the NSC, 2/8/49, DDRS 1980 Collection, Document 376A. This version was evidently an early draft of the memorandum. The final draft, mentioned in the NSC minutes, was dated March 3, 1949 (Minutes of the 36th Meeting of the National Security Council, 3/22/49, PSF, Box 205. This document is also reproduced in the DDRS 1978 Collection, Document 58B).

59. Souers to Forrestal, 1/5/49, NSC Records, Box 10. Souers passed along a memorandum written by Hoover to the attorney general discussing his January 4 meeting with Forrestal.

60. Memorandum for the President summarizing the discussion at the 36th meeting of the NSC, 3/23/49, PSF, NSC Meeting Summaries. This document is also reproduced in the DDRS 1982 Collection, Document 1230.

61. Policies Developed through the NSC—Chronological List, undated, PSF, Box 194.

62. Coyne to Souers, 4/26/49, NSC Records, Box 10. Hoover was initially elected to serve until July 1, 1950, but was repeatedly reelected.

63. Souers to members of the IIC, 3/23/49, NSC Records, Box 10.

64. Coyne to Souers, 6/20/49, NSC Records, Box 10.

65. "Policies of the Government Relating to National Security," vol. 3, 1950, PSF, Box 195. The annex to NSC 68 pertaining to internal security policy is still classified, but a schematic summary was included in this report.

Chapter 7

Notes to epigraphs: CR, 81st Congress, 2nd Session, July 6, 1950, p. 9716; Acheson (1969, 421–22).

1. For a more detailed account of the activities of the Dies Committee, see Fried (1990, 46–58), Green (1979, 69–76), Griffith (1970, 30–34), and O'Reilly (1983, 37–74).

2. In denouncing the detention provisions offered as a substitute for the McCarran bill by Senator Harley Kilgore (D-WV), Senator Homer Ferguson (R-MI) declared: "I am sincerely interested in doing something about communism in America, but I am also sincerely interested in obeying the Constitution, even when dealing with Communists" (*CR,* 81st Congress, 2nd Session, September 12, 1950, p. 14591). McCarran agreed, stating solemnly that "[f]or two or three days we have been reciting phrase after phrase of the Kilgore bill that is obnoxious to the organic law of this country" (*CR,* September 12, 1950, p. 14593).

3. *CR,* 81st Congress, 2nd Session, September 20, 1950, p. 15201.

4. Address to the Executives Club of Milwaukee, 5/8/48, Taft Papers, Box 841.

5. William Hoover to Taft, 9/14/49; Taft to Hoover, 9/19/49, Taft Papers, Box 683. Taft monitored the Justice Department's perjury investigation of Travis's affidavit (Tom Shroyer to Taft, 12/29/49, Taft Papers, Box 673). Taft criticized the administration for failing to pursue perjury charges against some union officers who signed the affidavit ("Truman Nullifies T-H Act, Taft Charges," *Washington*

Post, April 5, 1950). The 1954 Communist Control Act, which extended many of the provisions in the Internal Security Act, was even more specifically directed against the labor movement. See McAuliffe (1978, 132–44).

6. *CR,* 81st Congress, 2nd Session, September 20, 1950, p. 15188.

7. *CR,* 81st Congress, 2nd Session, September 12, 1950, p. 14599.

8. IAC Minutes, 7/12/50.

9. Spingarn to the White House Staff, undated [June 1950], Spingarn Papers, Box 31.

10. *CR,* 81st Congress, 2nd Session, September 12, 1950, p. 14596.

11. *CR,* 81st Congress, 2nd Session, September 12, 1950, p. 14597.

12. Murphy and Spingarn to Truman, 5/16/50; Spingarn memo for the files, 5/20/50, Spingarn Papers, Box 36; Spingarn memo for the file, 8/11/50, Spingarn Papers, Box 31. This incident, as well as Justice's general support for internal security legislation, is discussed in Theoharis (1971, 140–45).

13. Richard Neustadt to Spingarn, 7/3/50, Spingarn Papers, Box 19.

14. "Anti-Red Bill Death without Vote Is Hinted," *Washington Post,* March 6, 1950.

15. Report by the RNC Research Division, October 1946, Bridges Papers, File 26.

16. Spingarn to the President, 7/14/50, PPF, Box 94.

17. George H. E. Smith to Robert Taft, 12/19/50, Taft Papers, Box 750; Alphabetical list of names from the State Department, undated [probably 1950], Bridges Papers, File 27, Folder 49.

18. Maurice Joyce to Scott McLeod, 4/20/50, Bridges Papers, File 27, Folder 86.

19. Theoharis and Cox (1988, 280–300), Summers (1993, 178–79), and Gentry (1991, 377–82) note that Hoover helped select Don Surine, a former FBI agent, to serve as McCarthy's staff investigator and that the bureau furnished McCarthy and Surine with information from FBI files. After Hoover withdrew his support for McCarthy in 1953, refusing to provide him with any additional information and discouraging former agents from joining his staff, McCarthy was increasingly unable to provide any evidence to support the charges he made. As Oshinsky (1983, 430–32) makes clear, this situation contributed to his embarrassment in the course of hearings on internal security in the Army and to his censure by the Senate in 1954.

20. Bridges received two letters alleging communist infiltration of the CIO from Lewis H. Brown, the chairperson of the board of the Johns-Manville Corporation, which he placed in a file labeled "Matters to be taken up with Lovett and Puerifoy" (Brown to Bridges, 11/1/47 and 12/12/47, Bridges Papers, File 27, Folder 21).

21. *CR,* 81st Congress, 2nd Session, August 14, 1950, p. 10153.

22. *CR,* 81st Congress, 2nd Session, September 14, 1950, p. 14796.

23. *PPP: HST, 1950,* 641–42.

24. "McCarran's 'Reds' Bill Seen Victor Today," *Washington Post,* September 12, 1950.

25. Spingarn memo for the file, 9/19/50, Spingarn Papers, Box 13. Truman publicly committed himself to prompt action on the bill immediately after meeting with congressional leaders ("'Tough' Red Curbs Set by Conferees," *New York*

Times, September 18, 1950). In fact, House and Senate leaders decided to recess rather than adjourn on September 21. At the time Truman made his decision, though, an adjournment was planned, so the threat of a pocket veto still existed ("Tax Raise Bill Ready; Recess Set Saturday," *Washington Post,* September 21, 1950).

26. Spingarn to Hopkins, 9/25/50, Spingarn Papers, Box 13.

27. Spingarn to Donald Dawson, 9/30/50, Spingarn Papers, Box 13.

28. The 18 Democrats were Lister Hill (AL), John McClellan (AR), Edwin Johnson (CO), J. Allen Frear (DE), Spessard Holland (FL), Walter George (CO), Richard Russell (LA), Paul Douglas (IL), Guy Gillette (IA), Virgil Chapman (KY), Russell Long (LA), Herbert O'Conor (MD), Patrick McCarran (NV), Robert Kerr (OK), Harry Byrd (VA), A. Willis Robertson (VA), Warren Magnuson (WA), and Lester Hunt (WY).

29. The two who supported the Wherry amendment on September 23 were the ultraconservative Harry Byrd (D-VA) and Walter George (D-GA). Guy Gillette (D-IA), Patrick McCarran (D-NV), and Lester Hunt (D-WY) were not present for the September 23 vote. The administration also picked up the support of seven Internationalist Republicans, including William Knowland (CA), Margaret Chase Smith (ME), Leverett Saltonstall (MA), Edward Thye (MN), H. Alexander Smith (NJ), Wayne Morse (OR), and Chan Gurney (SD).

30. Quoted by Hamby (1973, 413).

31. Spingarn memo for the file, 9/25/50, Spingarn Papers, Box 32.

32. Spingarn Oral History Interview, March 28, 1967, p. 1059.

33. Murphy Oral History Interview, June 24, 1969, pp. 233–35.

34. NSC Progress Report by the NSC Representative on Internal Security on the Implementation of NSC 17/4 and 17/6, 3/26/51, PSF, Box 212. This report is also reproduced in the DDRS 1988 Collection, Document 1690.

35. Spingarn had circulated to the White House staff ADA literature condemning the Internal Security Act and was personally congratulated by ADA officials after the veto (Spingarn to White House staff, 8/21/50, Spingarn Papers, Box 31; Rauh to Spingarn, 9/28/50, Spingarn Papers, Box 32).

36. Spingarn Oral History Interview, March 28, 1967, pp. 1059–63.

37. Spingarn to Murphy, 10/7/50, Murphy Papers, Box 13.

38. Max Lowenthal to Charles Murphy, "Memo re: the McCarthy Business," 5/5/50, Murphy Papers, Box 10.

39. Spingarn to Murphy, 6/19/50, Spingarn Papers, Box 13; Spingarn memo for the files, 6/23/50, Spingarn Papers, Box 31. Concerning State Department support for the idea, see the McFall Oral History Interview, June 24, 1970, pp. 37–38.

40. Spingarn memo for the file, 9/19/50; Spingarn to Dawson, 9/30/50, Spingarn Papers, Box 13.

41. Hamby (1973, 467–68); Donovan (1982, 367).

42. *PPP: HST, 1950,* 571–76.

43. *PPP: HST, 1950,* 545.

44. Spingarn to Clifford, 9/21/48, OF 10-B, Box 102. Keller (1989) suggests that liberals sought to develop "an internal security state" by placing policy in this area in the hands of professionals in the FBI. Keller's thesis is hard to square with evi-

dence that liberals in the White House, as well as the president, seriously mistrusted the FBI.

45. Theoharis (1971, 255–57) notes that the Loyalty Review Board was also criticized by liberals for violations of individual rights. These protests were generally ignored.

46. Loyalty standards continued to be ratcheted upward during the rest of the Truman administration and especially under Eisenhower, when loyalty tests were replaced with even broader "security" standards. Employees had to prove that their retention was "clearly consistent with the interests of national security." Concerning the details of the Federal Employee Loyalty Program, see Brown (1958, 21–60), Theoharis (1971, 242–68; 1978, 196–228), and Caute (1978, 267–345), among other works.

47. The quote is from a 9/27/47 letter from Harry Truman to Bess Truman, in Ferrell (1983, 513).

48. Handwritten note signed "H.S.T." on a memo from Clifford to Truman, 5/23/47, PSF, Box 155.

49. Stephen Spingarn's mistrust of the FBI was shared by others working in the White House (Max Lowenthal to Elsey and Murphy, undated [1950], Murphy Papers, Box 10).

50. Memorandum for the President summarizing the discussion at the 89th meeting of the NSC, 4/18/51, PSF, NSC Meeting Summaries. The president presided at this meeting, which was chiefly concerned with Korea and a plan for dealing with defectors from the Soviet bloc.

51. NSC Progress Report by the NSC Representative on Internal Security on the implementation of Internal Security (NSC 17/4; 17/6), 3/26/51, PSF, Box 212. This report is also reproduced in the DDRS 1988 Collection, Document 1690.

52. Memorandum for the President summarizing the discussion at the 67th meeting of the National Security Council, 9/8/50, PSF, NSC Meeting Summaries. The president and Louis Johnson both praised the report at the meeting, but only Ford, speaking on behalf of the Department of Justice, made any suggestions.

53. The 1953 figures are included in the minutes of the March 11, 1953, meeting of the Industrial Advisory Committee, Office of Industrial Security, Munitions Board, Office of the Secretary of Defense, RG 330. According to the minutes of the April 20, 1949, meeting, plants could be designated as "vital," "critical," or "very important," in descending order of importance.

54. NSC Progress Report by the NSC Representative on Internal Security on the implementation of Internal Security (NSC 17/4; 17/6), 12/20/51, PSF, Box 216. The report is also reproduced in the DDRS 1988 Collection, Document 1691. Regarding the cooperation of the American Legion, see Theoharis (1985; 1988, 193–98).

55. Small to Rosenberg, 1/22/51; Eugene Zuckert to Walter Reuther and Richard Boutelle, 1/16/51; Clipped article by Drew Pearson, "Strikes Slow Jet Engine Output," in the file, RG 330 (Office of the Secretary of Defense), Assistant Secretary of Defense (Manpower, Personnel and Reserve), Office of Domestic Programs, Subject File, 1951–July 1954, Box 1032-E.

56. Fanning to Colonel Mee, 11/14/52; O'Connell to Rosenberg, 11/9/51; O'Connell to Haught, 5/22/53, RG 330 (Office of the Secretary of Defense), Assis-

tant Secretary of Defense (Manpower, Personnel and Reserve), Office of Domestic Programs, Subject File, 1951–July 1954, Box 1032-C.

57. General Electric Employee Relations News Letter, RG 330 (Office of the Secretary of Defense), Assistant Secretary of Defense (Manpower, Personnel and Reserve), Office of Domestic Programs, Subject File, 1951–July 1954, Box 1032-B. Carey's IUE was set up by the CIO in 1949 in an effort to supplant the more radical UE, which had been expelled from the organization.

58. Ohly to Townsend Hoopes, 8/8/49, Ohly Papers, Box 79; Ohly to Johnson, 7/22/49 and 7/29/49, Johnson Papers, Box 140.

59. Comptroller Wilfred McNeil claimed that the presence of a woman made everyone uncomfortable and used her appointment as an example of the poor administrative choices sometimes made by George Marshall (McNeil Oral History Interview, September 12, 1972, pp. 188–89). Rosenberg was also a lightning rod for congressional criticism. Robert Taft received a letter from a major campaign contributor, Wallace Templeton, demanding that Taft oppose her nomination. "Certainly the appointment of a Jewish foreigner of the original Roosevelt gang does not make much sense. All this holds true when there are so many decent well-educated capable real Americans who in these desperate times would and could patriotically serve their country." Taft's response was polite but noncommittal. "It is not always easy to defeat an appointment in the absence of some clear scandal in connection with the appointee. . . . All I can say is, we will do the best we can to prevent the confirmation of those who are obviously disqualified." He later voted to confirm her appointment (Templeton to Taft, 11/10/50, and Taft to Templeton, 11/21/50, Taft Papers, Box 914). Other members of Congress were less scrupulous. Confusing her with a different Anna Rosenberg, Joseph McCarthy and a coterie of anti-Semitic House members accused her of being a member of the communist-affiliated John Reed Club in New York during the 1930s. When the accusation turned out to be untrue, McCarthy, in an uncharacteristic display of responsible behavior, voted to confirm her nomination (Oshinsky 1973, 203–5).

60. Assistant Secretary of Defense (Manpower and Personnel) to the Chairmen of Boards, Staffs and Committees, and the Directors of Offices, Office of the Secretary of Defense, 2/6/50, RG 330, Assistant Secretary of Defense (Manpower and Personnel), Budget & Finance Division, Subject File, 1947–55, Box 15.

61. Charter of the Physical Security Equipment Agency, undated, RG 330 (Office of the Secretary of Defense), Assistant Secretary of Defense (Manpower and Personnel), Ralph Stohl's File, Office of Personnel Security and Reserve, 1951–54, Box 1.

62. RG 330 (Office of the Secretary of Defense), Assistant Secretary of Defense (Manpower and Personnel), Ralph Stohl's File, Office of Personnel Security and Reserve, 1951–54, Box 1. The file contains clipped advertisements for high-speed cameras, lie detectors, and hidden recording devices.

63. Clear to Long, 3/16/53, RG 330 (Office of the Secretary of Defense), Assistant Secretary of Defense (Manpower and Personnel), Ralph Stohl's File, Office of Personnel Security and Reserve, 1951–54, Box 1.

64. Brown (1958), Warner (1954), and Yarmolinsky (1955) provide fascinating contemporary accounts of particular cases.

65. When I asked to see these records in the summer of 1993, I was told that sometime during the mid-1980s they had been deaccessioned and taken from the National Archives to Fort Holabird by the Army.

66. Draft of Final Report on Use of Polygraph for Security Clearances, 5/14/53, RG 330 (Office of the Secretary of Defense), Assistant Secretary of Defense (Manpower and Personnel), Ralph Stohl's File, Office of Personnel Security and Reserve, 1951–54, Box 1.

67. On the Port Security Program, see Caute (1978, 392–400) and Brown (1958, 71–73).

68. Lasser to Harriman, 2/6/51, Harriman Papers, Box 286. Stuart Symington remained suspicious after being contacted by a Harriman aide: "This fellow Lasser has some kind of radical background, doesn't he?" (Everett M. Kassalow to Harriman, 12/1/50, Harriman Papers, Box 286). Indeed, many of the radicals persecuted during the McCarthy era probably did have Communist party ties of some sort. See Schrecker (1994) for a recent bibliography on this and related issues. It is worth noting that, in spite of recent evidence presented by Klehr, Haynes, and Firsov (1995) that the American Communist party did have ties to the Soviet Union and that some of its members were indeed Soviet spies, evidence about individuals' political sympathies—not evidence of spying—was used to label them as security risks. Although their political views were extremely unpopular, these individuals were nevertheless as much a part of American society as Democrats and Republicans.

69. Pace Oral History Interview, February 25, 1972, pp. 115–16.

70. Memorandum for the President summarizing the 72nd meeting of the NSC, 11/24/50, PSF, NSC Meeting Summaries. See Kofsky (1995) for a good account of the relationship between the war in Korea and the military budget.

71. See, for example, "Martin Warns of War Cost," *New York Times,* August 6, 1950; "70-Billion Budget Foreseen by Byrd," *New York Times,* August 6, 1950; "General Queried on Tank Program," *New York Times,* August 8, 1950; "Taft Sees Threat of World War III in All-Out Arming," *Washington Post,* August 8, 1950; and "2,000 Ohioans Hear Taft Open Campaign," *New York Times,* August 18, 1950. The Alsop brothers responded by arguing that more military spending was necessary regardless of the good news from Korea. See Joseph Alsop, "Good News," *Washington Post,* September 1, 1950; and Stewart Alsop, "Where We Stand," *Washington Post,* September 18, 1950.

72. Executive Secretary of the NSC to the Ad Hoc Committee on NSC 68, 7/28/50, *FRUS 1950,* 1:351–52.

73. Lay Memorandum of Conversation, 8/23/50, *FRUS 1950,* 1:373–74. While it is possible that concerns about this delay contributed to Truman's decision to dismiss Louis Johnson, there is no clear reason to blame him for it, since the estimates were being prepared largely by the Joint Chiefs of Staff.

74. James Lay to the National Security Council, 7/17/50, *FRUS 1950,* 7:410.

75. Cumings (1990, 710–11) and Foot (1985, 74) argue that the decision was actually made in late August, in time for Acheson's meeting with the British prime minister. The perfunctory discussion of NSC 81 at the September 7 meeting, when no one raised any objection to the idea of rollback, supports this argument. A for-

mal decision was not very important at this point in the war in any event, since the Inchon landings, which made a move into the North an immediate possibility, did not even take place until September 15.

76. Draft Memorandum by the Policy Planning Staff, 7/22/50, *FRUS 1950,* 7:449–54.

77. Kennan to Acheson, 8/21/50, Acheson Papers, Box 65. Kennan extended his concern about U.S. military involvement in Asia to Vietnam as well. "In Indo-China we are getting ourselves into the position of guaranteeing the French in an undertaking which neither they nor we, nor both of us together, can win."

78. Memorandum of Conversation by Philip Jessup, 11/21/50, Acheson Papers, Box 65. This document is also reproduced in the DDRS 1978 Collection, Document 86A.

79. Memorandum for the President summarizing the 71st meeting of the NSC, 11/10/50, PSF, NSC Meeting Summaries. For more detailed discussions of U.S. disregard of warnings about Chinese intervention, see Bernstein (1977, 18–22; 1981, 258–60), Cumings (1990, 733–45), Foot (1985, 74–87), Gaddis (1977, 292), Leffler (1992, 374–80), and Stueck (1981, 236–50).

80. Regarding the firing of Johnson, see Acheson (1969, 441), Cumings (1990, 711), Donovan (1982, 265–67), and Nitze (1989, 105).

81. NSC 68, 4/7/50, *FRUS 1950,* 1:244.

82. Patterson (1972, 475, 485–89), Taft's principal biographer, seems genuinely confused by his subject's positions on Korea in late 1950 and early 1951. He argues in consecutive paragraphs that "Taft was usually careful to set some limits on American policy in Asia" and that he called for the use of "every means within our power" to insure the security of South Korea.

83. Thomas to Taft, 3/7/51, Taft Papers, Box 627; Taft to Thomas, 3/13/50, Taft Papers, Box 968; Patterson (1972, 475).

84. Wherry to Frank Woods [chairman of the Lincoln Telephone and Tele-graph Company], 12/11/50, Wherry Papers, Box 11.

85. Fellers to Taft, 1/12/51, Taft Papers, Box 490; Fellers to Taft, 7/2/51, Taft Papers, Box 619.

86. Kepley (1988, 104–5); Donovan (1982, 323).

Chapter 8

Notes to epigraphs: Kehr (1977b, 23); Elsey Oral History Interview, February 10, 1964.

Appendix

1. The twelfth Federal Reserve district, which is centered in San Francisco, is extremely large and includes Arizona, Idaho, Nevada, and Utah in addition to the coastal states of California, Oregon, and Washington. The volume of financial activity in the noncoastal states of this district is extremely low and probably includes very little, if any, international lending. The tenth district, centered in Kansas City and including Colorado, Nebraska, Oklahoma, and Wyoming, is

probably more like these four states than is the Pacific Coast. This district did not even have to produce a B-2 form, since the total volume of lending was less than $100,000.

2. The Census of Agriculture does not use the SIC system but instead organizes agriculture by commodities produced. For purposes of the analysis presented here, I treated each type of agricultural commodity as if it were an SIC sector. This may introduce some distortion into the model, since the same farm may produce several different "sectors" under this scheme. There is no reason to believe that this distortion is very serious, however.

References

Archives

Alderman Library, University of Virginia, Charlottesville
    Papers of Louis A. Johnson
Harry S. Truman Presidential Library, Independence, MO
    White House Central Files
        Official File (OF)
        President's Personal File (PPF)
        President's Secretary's File (PSF)
        Confidential File
        Bill File
        Records of the National Security Council
    Papers of Dean Acheson
    Papers of George M. Elsey
    Papers of S. Everett Gleason
    Papers of Leon Keyserling
    Papers of Frederick J. Lawton
    Papers of Charles S. Murphy
    Papers of John Ohly
    Papers of Frank Pace, Jr.
    Papers of Sidney Souers
    Papers of Stephen Spingarn
    Papers of Ralph Stohl
    Papers of Stuart Symington
    Papers of A. Devitt Vanech
    Papers of James Webb
Library of Congress, Washington, DC
    Papers of Tom Connally
    Papers of W. Averell Harriman
    Papers of Robert A. Taft
National Archives, Washington, DC, and College Park, MD
    Record Group 59, General Records of the Department of State
        Assistant Secretary of State for Congressional Relations, 1949–51
        Policy Planning Staff
    Record Group 330, Office of the Secretary of Defense
        Records of the Assistant Secretary of Defense (Comptroller)

Records of the Assistant Secretary of Defense (Legislative and Public Affairs)
Records of the Assistant Secretary of Defense (Manpower, Personnel and
    Reserve)
Records of the Munitions Board
    Minutes of the Industrial Labor Relations Committee (ILRC Minutes)
    Minutes of the Industrial Advisory Committee on Industrial Security
        (IAC Minutes)
Nebraska State Historical Society, Lincoln
    Papers of Kenneth S. Wherry
New Hampshire State Archive, Concord
    Papers of Styles Bridges
Mudd Library, Princeton University, Princeton, NJ
    Papers of John Foster Dulles
    Papers of H. Alexander Smith
Southern Historical Collection, Wilson Library, University of North Carolina at
    Chapel Hill
    Papers of Frank Porter Graham

Published Document Collections and Interviews

Congressional Record, 81st Congress, 2nd Session, 1950 *(CR)*
Declassified Documents Reference Service. Woodbridge, CT: Research Publica-
    tions, Inc. (1981–present); Arlington, VA: Carrollton Press (1975–81).
    (DDRS)
Foreign Relations of the United States (FRUS)
*Personal Papers of the Presidents of the United States: Harry S. Truman (PPP:
    HST)*

Oral History Interviews (Harry S. Truman Library, Independence, MO)
    Joint Interview with Charles Murphy, Richard Neustadt, David Stowe, and
        James Webb
    Matthew J. Connelly
    George M. Elsey
    Joseph G. Feeney
    Paul Griffith
    Felix Larkin
    Frederick J. Lawton
    Marx Leva
    Robert Lovett
    Max Lowenthal
    Jack K. McFall
    Wilfred J. McNeil
    Charles Murphy
    Edwin G. Nourse
    Frank Pace, Jr.
    Stephen J. Spingarn

Books and Articles

Acheson, Dean. 1969. *Present at the Creation: My Years in the State Department.* New York: W. W. Norton & Company.

Agnew, John. 1987. *The United States in the World Economy.* New York: Cambridge University Press.

Allison, Graham T. 1969. "Conceptual Models and the Cuban Missile Crisis." *American Political Science Review* 63 (3): 689–718.

———. 1971. *Essence of Decision: Explaining the Cuban Missile Crisis.* Boston: Little, Brown.

Arrow, Kenneth. 1963. *Social Choice and Individual Values.* New Haven, CT: Yale University Press.

Baldwin, Robert E. 1985. *The Political Economy of U.S. Import Policy.* Cambridge, MA: MIT Press.

Beard, Charles A., and George H. E. Smith. 1934. *The Idea of National Interest.* New York: Macmillan.

Bensel, Richard F. 1984. *Sectionalism and American Political Development.* Madison: University of Wisconsin Press.

Bernstein, Barton J. 1970. "The Ambiguous Legacy: The Truman Administration and Civil Rights." In Barton J. Bernstein, ed., *Politics and Policies of the Truman Administration.* Chicago: Quadrangle Books.

———. 1977. "The Policy of Risk: Crossing the 38th Parallel and Marching to the Yalu." *Foreign Service Journal* 54, no. 3 (March): 16–29.

———. 1981. "New Light on the Korean War." *International History Review* 3 (2): 256–77.

———. 1989. "The Truman Administration and the Korean War." In Michael J. Lacey, ed., *The Truman Presidency.* New York: Cambridge University Press and the Woodrow Wilson International Center for Scholars.

Bird, Kai. 1992. *The Chairman: John J. McCloy and the Making of the American Establishment.* New York: Simon & Schuster.

Block, Fred L. 1977. *The Origins of International Economic Disorder.* Berkeley and Los Angeles: University of California Press.

———. 1980. "Economic Instability and Military Strength: The Paradoxes of the 1950 Rearmament Decision." *Politics and Society* 10 (1): 35–58.

Bowles, Samuel, David M. Gordon, and Thomas E. Weisskopf. 1983. *Beyond the Waste Land.* Garden City, NY: Doubleday.

Brown, Ralph S. 1958. *Loyalty and Security.* New Haven, CT: Yale University Press.

Bueno de Mesquita, Bruce. 1981. *The War Trap.* New Haven, CT: Yale University Press.

Bueno de Mesquita, Bruce, and David Lalman. 1992. *War and Reason: Domestic and International Imperatives.* New Haven, CT: Yale University Press.

Burch, Philip H. 1980. *Elites in American History.* Vol. 3, *The New Deal to the Carter Administration.* New York: Holmes & Meier Publishers.

Buzan, Barry. 1983. *People, States, and Fear.* Chapel Hill: University of North Carolina Press.

Cassing, James, Timothy J. McKeown, and Jack Ochs. 1986. "The Political Economy of the Tariff Cycle." *American Political Science Review* 80 (3): 843–62.

Caute, David. 1978. *The Great Fear: The Anti-Communist Purge under Truman and Eisenhower.* New York: Simon & Schuster.

Cochran, Bert. 1977. *Labor and Communism: The Conflict That Shaped American Unions.* Princeton, NJ: Princeton University Press.

Condit, Doris M. 1988. *History of the Office of the Secretary of Defense.* Vol. 2, *The Test of War, 1950–1953.* Washington, DC: Historical Office, Office of the Secretary of Defense.

Cox, Ronald W. 1994. *Power and Profits: U.S. Policy in Central America.* Lexington: University of Kentucky Press.

Craig, Gordon A. 1964. *The Politics of the Prussian Army, 1640–1945.* New York: Oxford University Press.

Crapol, Edward. 1987. "Some Reflections on the Historiography of the Cold War." *The History Teacher* 20 (2): 251–62.

Cumings, Bruce. 1990. *The Origins of the Korean War.* Vol. 2, *The Roaring of the Cataract.* Princeton, NJ: Princeton University Press.

———. 1993. "'Revising Postrevisionism,' or, The Poverty of Theory in Diplomatic History." *Diplomatic History* 17 (3): 539–69.

Davis, Lance E., and Robert A. Huttenback. 1986. *Mammon and the Pursuit of Empire.* New York: Cambridge University Press.

De Caux, Len. 1970. *Labor Radical.* Boston: Beacon Press.

Doenecke, Justus. 1979. *Not to the Swift: The Old Isolationists in the Cold War Era.* Lewisburg, PA: Bucknell University Press.

Donovan, Robert J. 1977. *Conflict and Crisis: The Presidency of Harry S Truman, 1945–1948.* New York: W. W. Norton & Company.

———. 1982. *Tumultuous Years: The Presidency of Harry S Truman, 1949–1953.* New York: W. W. Norton & Company.

Downs, George W., and David M. Rocke. 1990. *Tacit Bargaining, Arms Races, and Arms Control.* Ann Arbor: University of Michigan Press.

Eden, Lynn. 1984. "Capitalist Conflict and the State: The Making of United States Military Policy in 1948." In Charles Bright and Susan Harding, eds., *Statemaking and Social Movements: Essays in Theory and History.* Ann Arbor: University of Michigan Press.

———. 1985. "The Diplomacy of Force: Interests, the State, and the Making of American Military Policy in 1948." Ph.D. diss., University of Michigan.

———. 1993. "The End of U.S. Cold War History." *International Security* 18, no. 1 (Summer): 174–207.

Elazar, Daniel J. 1970. *Cities of the Prairie: The Metropolitan Frontier and American Politics.* New York: Basic Books.

Eley, Geoff. 1976. "Defining Social Imperialism: Use and Abuse of an Idea." *Social History* 3:265–90.

———. 1980. *Reshaping the German Right: Radical Nationalism and Political Change after Bismarck.* New Haven, CT: Yale University Press.

Ellsberg, Daniel. 1972. *Papers on the War.* New York: Simon & Schuster.

Etzold, Thomas H., and John L. Gaddis, eds. *Containment: Documents on American Policy and Strategy, 1945–51.* New York: Columbia University Press.

Ferguson, Thomas. 1983. "Party Realignment and American Industrial Structure." In Peter Zarembka, ed., *Research in Political Economy* 6:4–120. Greenwich, CT: JAI Press.

———. 1984. "From Normalcy to New Deal: Industrial Structure, Party Competition, and American Public Policy in the Great Depression." *International Organization* 38:59–85.

———. 1995. *Golden Rule.* Chicago: University of Chicago Press.

Ferrell, Robert H., ed. 1983. *Dear Bess: The Letters from Harry Truman to Bess Truman, 1910–1959.* New York: W. W. Norton & Company.

Fischer, Gregory, and Mark Kamlet. 1984. "Explaining Presidential Priorities: The Competing Aspiration Levels Model of Macrobudgetary Decision Making." *American Political Science Review* 78 (2): 356–71.

Fones-Wolf, Elizabeth. 1994. *Selling Free Enterprise.* Urbana: University of Illinois Press.

Foot, Rosemary. 1985. *The Wrong War: American Policy and the Dimensions of the Korean Conflict, 1950–1953.* Ithaca, NY: Cornell University Press.

Freeland, Richard. 1972. *The Truman Doctrine and the Origins of McCarthyism.* New York: Alfred A. Knopf.

Fried, Richard M. 1974. "Electoral Politics and McCarthyism: The 1950 Campaign." In Robert Griffith and Athan Theoharis, eds., *The Specter: Original Essays on the Cold War and the Origins of McCarthyism.* New York: Franklin Watts.

———. 1990. *Nightmare in Red: The McCarthy Era in Perspective.* New York: Oxford University Press.

Frieden, Jeffry. 1988. "Sectoral Conflict and United States Foreign Economic Policy." *International Organization* 42 (1): 59–90.

———. 1989. "The Economics of Intervention: American Overseas Investments and Relations with Underdeveloped Areas, 1890–1950." *Comparative Studies in Society and History* 31, no. 1 (January): 55–80.

———. 1994. "International Investment and Colonial Control: A New Interpretation." *International Organization* 48 (4): 559–94.

Gaddis, John L. 1977. "Korea in American Politics, Strategy, and Diplomacy, 1945–1950." In Arika Iriye and Yonosuke Nagai, eds., *The Origins of the Cold War in Asia.* New York: Columbia University Press.

———. 1982. *Strategies of Containment.* New York: Oxford University Press.

———. 1983. "The Emerging Post-revisionist Consensus on the Origins of the Cold War." *Diplomatic History* 7 (3): 171–90.

———. 1992/93. "International Relations Theory and the End of the Cold War." *International Security* 17 (3): 5–58.

Galambos, Louis, and Joseph Pratt. 1988. *The Rise of the Corporate Commonwealth.* New York: Basic Books.

Gentry, Curt. 1991. *J. Edgar Hoover: The Man and the Secrets.* New York: Penguin Books.

George, Alexander L., and Timothy J. McKeown. 1985. "Case Studies and Theories of Organizational Decision Making." *Advances in Information Processing in Organizations* 2:21–58.

Gibbs, David N. 1990. *The Political Economy of Third World Intervention.* Chicago: University of Chicago Press.

Gilpin, Robert. 1981. *War and Change in International Politics.* New York: Cambridge University Press.

Goldstein, Judith. 1989. "The Impact of Ideas on Trade Policy: The Origins of U.S. Agricultural and Manufacturing Policies." *International Organization* 43 (1): 31–71.

Goldstein, Robert J. 1978. *Political Repression in Modern America.* Cambridge, MA: Schenkman Publishing Company.

Gosnell, Harold F. 1980. *Truman's Crises: A Political Biography of Harry S. Truman.* Westport, CT: Greenwood Press.

Gourevitch, Peter A. 1977. "International Trade, Domestic Coalitions, and Liberty: Comparative Responses to the Crisis of 1873–1896." *Journal of Interdisciplinary History* 8 (2): 281–313.

———. 1986. *Politics in Hard Times.* Ithaca, NY: Cornell University Press.

Green, George Norris. 1979. *The Establishment in Texas Politics: The Primitive Years, 1938–1957.* Westport, CT: Greenwood Press.

Greene, William H. 1997. *Econometric Analysis.* 3d ed. Upper Saddle River, NJ: Prentice-Hall.

Griffith, Barbara S. 1988. *The Crisis of American Labor: Operation Dixie and the Defeat of the CIO.* Philadelphia: Temple University Press.

Griffith, Robert. 1970. *The Politics of Fear: Joseph R. McCarthy and the Senate.* Lexington: University of Kentucky Press.

———. 1979. "The Old Progressives and the Cold War." *Journal of American History* 66 (2): 334–47.

———. 1989. "Forging America's Postwar Order: Domestic Politics and Political Economy in the Age of Truman." In Michael J. Lacey, ed., *The Truman Presidency.* New York: Cambridge University Press and the Woodrow Wilson International Center for Scholars.

Grimmett, Richard F. 1973. "Who Were the Senate Isolationists?" *Pacific Historical Review* 42 (4): 479–98.

Halle, Louis J. 1967. *The Cold War as History.* New York: Harper & Row.

Hamby, Alonzo L. 1973. *Beyond the New Deal: Harry S. Truman and American Liberalism.* New York: Columbia University Press.

———. 1993. "Hamby's Commentary." In Ernest R. May, ed., *America's Cold War Strategy: Interpreting NSC 68.* New York: St. Martin's Press.

Hammond, Paul Y. 1962. "NSC-68: Prologue to Rearmament." In Warner R. Schilling, Paul Y. Hammond, and Glenn H. Snyder, *Strategy, Politics, and Defense Budgets.* New York: Columbia University Press.

Harris, Howell J. 1982. *The Right to Manage.* Madison: University of Wisconsin Press.

Hermann, Charles F. 1972. *International Crises: Insights from Behavioral Research.* New York: The Free Press.

Hershberg, James G. 1993. *James B. Conant.* New York: Alfred A. Knopf.

Herwig, Holger H. 1973. *The German Naval Officer Corps: A Social and Political History, 1890–1918.* London: Oxford University Press.

Hinich, Melvin J., and Michael C. Munger. 1994. *Ideology and the Theory of Political Choice.* Ann Arbor: University of Michigan Press.

Hobson, J. A. [1902] 1965. *Imperialism: A Study.* Ann Arbor: University of Michigan Press.

Hogan, Michael J. 1987. *The Marshall Plan: America, Britain, and the Reconstruction of Western Europe, 1947–1952.* New York: Cambridge University Press.

———. 1992. *The End of the Cold War: Its Meaning and Implications.* New York: Cambridge University Press.

Hoopes, Townsend. 1973. *The Devil and John Foster Dulles.* Boston: Little, Brown.

Huntington, Samuel P. 1963. *The Common Defense: Strategic Programs in National Politics.* New York: Columbia University Press.

Ikenberry, G. John. 1992. "A World Economy Restored: Expert Consensus and the Anglo-American Postwar Settlement." *International Organization* 46 (1): 289–321.

Irons, Peter H. 1974. "American Business and the Origins of McCarthyism: The Cold War Crusade of the United States Chamber of Commerce." In Robert Griffith and Athan Theoharis, eds., *The Specter: Original Essays on the Cold War and the Origins of McCarthyism.* New York: Franklin Watts.

Isaacson, Walter, and Evan Thomas. 1986. *The Wise Men: Six Friends and the World They Made.* New York: Simon & Schuster.

Janowitz, Morris. 1960. *The Professional Soldier.* Glencoe, IL: The Free Press.

Jervis, Robert. 1980. "The Impact of the Korean War on the Cold War." *Journal of Conflict Resolution* 24 (4): 563–92.

Jones, Howard, and Randall B. Woods. 1993. "Origins of the Cold War in Europe and the Near East: Recent Historiography and the National Security Imperative." *Diplomatic History* 17 (2): 251–76.

Joseph, Paul. 1987. *Cracks in the Empire: State Politics in the Vietnam War.* New York: Columbia University Press.

Kamlet, Mark, and David Mowery. 1987. "Influences on Executive and Congressional Budgetary Priorities, 1955–1981." *American Political Science Review* 81 (1): 155–78.

Kampelman, Max. 1957. *The Communist Party vs. the CIO.* New York: Praeger Press.

Kehr, Eckart. 1977a. "Modern German Historiography." In Gordon Craig, ed., *Economic Interest, Militarism, and Foreign Policy: Essays on German History,* trans. Grete Heinz. Berkeley and Los Angeles: University of California Press.

———. 1977b. "Anglophobia and Weltpolitik." In Gordon Craig, ed., *Economic Interest, Militarism, and Foreign Policy: Essays on German History,* trans. Grete Heinz. Berkeley and Los Angeles: University of California Press.

Keller, William W. 1989. *The Liberals and J. Edgar Hoover.* Princeton, NJ: Princeton University Press.

Kemp, Tom. 1990. *The Climax of Capitalism.* New York: Longman.

Kennan, George F. 1967. *Memoirs: 1925–1950.* Boston: Little, Brown.

Kepley, David R. 1988. *The Collapse of the Middle Way: Senate Republicans and the Bipartisan Foreign Policy, 1948–1952.* New York: Greenwood Press.

Key, V. O. 1964. *Politics, Parties, and Pressure Groups.* New York: Crowell Press.

King, Gary. 1989. *Unifying Political Methodology.* New York: Cambridge University Press.

Klehr, Harvey, John Earl Haynes, and Fridrikh Igorevich Firsov. 1995. *The Secret World of American Communism.* New Haven, CT: Yale University Press.

Kobrin, Stephen. 1980. "Foreign Enterprise and Forced Divestment in LDCs." *International Organization* 34 (1): 65–88.

Koen, Ross Y. 1974. *The China Lobby in American Politics.* New York: Octagon Books.

Kofsky, Frank. 1993. *Harry S. Truman and the War Scare of 1948.* New York: St. Martin's Press.

———. 1995. "Did the Truman Administration Deliberately Prolong the Korean War?" Unpublished manuscript to appear in Christian G. Appy, ed., *Cold War Constructions.* Amherst: University of Massachusetts Press, forthcoming.

Kohl, Wilfrid. 1975. "The Nixon-Kissinger Foreign Policy System and U.S.-European Relations: Patterns of Policymaking." *World Politics* 28 (1): 1–43.

Kolko, Joyce, and Gabriel Kolko. 1972. *The Limits of Power.* New York: Harper & Row.

Kolodziej, Edward A. 1966. *The Uncommon Defense and Congress, 1945–1963.* Columbus: Ohio State University Press.

Krasner, Stephen. 1978. *Defending the National Interest.* Princeton, NJ: Princeton University Press.

Kurth, James. 1971. "A Widening Gyre: The Logic of American Weapons Procurement." *Public Policy* 19:373–404.

———. 1979. "The Political Consequences of the Product Cycle: Industrial History and Political Outcomes." *International Organization* 33 (1): 1–34.

Larson, Deborah Welch. 1985. *Origins of Containment: A Psychological Explanation.* Princeton, NJ: Princeton University Press.

Lave, Charles A., and James G. March. 1975. *An Introduction to Models in the Social Sciences.* New York: Harper & Row.

Leffler, Melvyn P. 1984. "The American Conception of National Security and the Beginnings of the Cold War, 1945–48." *American Historical Review* 89 (2): 346–81.

———. 1991. "National Security." In Michael J. Hogan and Thomas G. Paterson, eds., *Explaining the History of American Foreign Relations.* New York: Cambridge University Press.

———. 1992. *A Preponderance of Power: National Security, the Truman Administration, and the Cold War.* Stanford, CA: Stanford University Press.

———. 1994a. "The Interpretive Wars over the Cold War." In Gordon Martel, ed., *American Foreign Relations Reconsidered, 1890–1993.* New York: Routledge.

———. 1994b. *The Specter of Communism.* New York: Hill & Wang.

Levenstein, Harvey A. 1981. *Communism, Anticommunism, and the CIO.* Westport, CT: Greenwood Press.

Lichtenstein, Nelson. 1989. "Labor in the Truman Era: Origins of the 'Private Welfare State.'" In Michael J. Lacey, ed., *The Truman Presidency.* New York: Cambridge University Press and the Woodrow Wilson International Center for Scholars.

Lieberson, Stanley. 1971. "An Empirical Study of Military-Industrial Linkages." *American Journal of Sociology* 76 (4): 522–84.

Lindblom, Charles E. 1977. *Politics and Markets.* New York: Basic Books.

McAuliffe, Mary Sperling. 1978. *Crisis on the Left.* Amherst, MA: University of Massachusetts Press.

McCormick, Thomas. 1982. "Drift or Mastery? A Corporatist Synthesis for American Diplomatic History." *Reviews in American History* 10, no. 4 (December): 318–30.

McCoy, Donald R. 1984. *The Presidency of Harry S. Truman.* Lawrence: University of Kansas Press.

McGlothlen, Ronald L. 1993. *Controlling the Waves.* New York: W. W. Norton & Company.

McKeown, Timothy J. 1986. "The Limitations of 'Structural' Theories of Commercial Policy." *International Organization* 40 (1): 43–64.

———. 1994. "The Epidemiology of Corporate PAC Formation, 1975–1984." *Journal of Economic Behavior and Organization* 24:153–68.

McQuaid, Kim. 1982. *Big Business and Presidential Power: From F.D.R. to Reagan.* New York: Morrow.

Magdoff, Harry. 1970. "Militarism and Imperialism." *American Economic Review* 60 (2): 237–46.

Magee, Stephen P., William A. Brock, and Leslie Young. 1989. *Black Hole Tariffs and Endogenous Policy Theory.* New York: Cambridge University Press.

Maier, Charles S. 1977. "The Politics of Productivity: Foundations of American International Economic Policy after World War II." *International Organization* 31 (4): 607–33.

Markowitz, Norman D. 1973. *The Rise and Fall of the People's Century: Henry A. Wallace and American Liberalism, 1941–1948.* New York: The Free Press.

Maxfield, Sylvia, and James H. Nolt. 1990. "Protectionism and the Internationalization of Capital: U.S. Sponsorship of Import Substitution Industrialization in the Philippines, Turkey, and Argentina." *International Studies Quarterly* 34:49–81.

May, Ernest R. 1993. *American Cold War Strategy: Interpreting NSC 68.* New York: St. Martin's Press.

Mearsheimer, John J. 1990. "Back to the Future: Instability in Europe after the Cold War." *International Security* 15 (1): 5–56.

Morgenthau, Hans. 1956. *Politics among Nations.* 2d ed. New York: Alfred A. Knopf.

Mueller, Dennis C. 1989. *Public Choice II.* New York: Cambridge University Press.

Nelson, Steve, James R. Barrett, and Rob Ruck. 1981. *Steve Nelson, American Radical.* Pittsburgh, PA: University of Pittsburgh Press.

Neustadt, Richard E. 1974. "Congress and the Fair Deal: A Legislative Balance Sheet." In Alonzo Hamby, ed., *Harry S. Truman and the Fair Deal.* Lexington, MA: D. C. Heath & Company.

Niebuhr, Reinhold. 1932. *Moral Man and Immoral Society.* New York: Charles Scribner's Sons.

Nitze, Paul H. 1980. "The Development of NSC 68." *International Security* 4 (4): 170–76.

Nitze, Paul H., with Ann M. Smith and Steven L. Rearden. 1989. *From Hiroshima to Glasnost.* New York: Grove Weidenfeld.

Nourse, Edwin G. 1953. *Economics in the Public Service: Administrative Aspects of the Employment Act.* New York: Harcourt, Brace.

Nowell, Gregory P. 1994. *Mercantile States and the World Oil Cartel, 1900–1939.* Ithaca, NY: Cornell University Press.

O'Brien, F. S. 1968. "The 'Communist-Dominated' Unions in the United States since 1950." *Labor History* 9 (2): 184–209.

Olson, Mancur. 1965. *The Logic of Collective Action.* Cambridge, MA: Harvard University Press.

O'Reilly, Kenneth. 1983. *Hoover and the Un-Americans: The FBI, HUAC, and the Red Menace.* Philadelphia, PA: Temple University Press.

Oshinsky, David M. 1974. "Labor's Cold War: The CIO and the Communists." In Robert Griffith and Athan Theoharis, eds., *The Specter: Original Essays on the Cold War and the Origins of McCarthyism.* New York: Franklin Watts.

———. 1983. *A Conspiracy So Immense: The World of Joe McCarthy.* New York: The Free Press.

Pach, Chester J. 1991. *Arming the Free World: The Origins of the United States Military Assistance Program, 1945–1950.* Chapel Hill: University of North Carolina Press.

Patterson, James T. 1972. *Mr. Republican: A Biography of Robert A. Taft.* Boston: Houghton Mifflin.

Pilisuk, Marc, and Thomas Hayden. 1965. "Is There a Military-Industrial Complex Which Prevents Peace? Consensus and Countervailing Power in Pluralistic Systems." *Journal of Social Issues* 21 (3): 67–117.

Pollard, Robert A. 1985. *Economic Security and the Origins of the Cold War, 1945–1950.* New York: Columbia University Press.

Poole, Keith T., and Howard Rosenthal. 1985. "A Spatial Model for Legislative Roll-Call Analysis." *American Journal of Political Science* 29:357–84.

———. 1991. "Patterns of Congressional Voting." *American Journal of Political Science* 35:228–78.

Posen, Barry R. 1984. *The Sources of Military Doctrine.* Ithaca, NY: Cornell University Press.

Putnam, Robert D. 1988. "Diplomacy and Domestic Politics: The Logic of Two-Level Games." *International Organization* 42 (3): 427–60.

Rearden, Steven L. 1984. *History of the Office of the Secretary of Defense.* Vol. 1,

The Formative Years, 1947–1950. Washington, DC: Historical Office, Office of the Secretary of Defense.

Rieselbach, Leroy N. 1966. *The Roots of Isolationism.* Indianapolis, IN: Bobbs-Merrill.

Rogowski, Ronald. 1989. *Commerce and Coalitions.* Princeton, NJ: Princeton University Press.

Rosecrance, Richard, and Arthur A. Stein, eds. 1993. *The Domestic Bases of Grand Strategy.* Ithaca, NY: Cornell University Press.

Rosenau, James. 1968. "National Interest." In David L. Sills, ed., *International Encyclopedia of the Social Sciences.* New York: Crowell Collier and Macmillan.

Rosswurm, Steve, ed. 1992. *The CIO's Left-Led Unions.* New Brunswick, NJ: Rutgers University Press.

Rupert, Mark E. 1990. "Producing Hegemony: State/Society Relations and the Politics of Productivity in the United States." *International Studies Quarterly* 34 (4): 427–56.

Salamon, Lester M., and John J. Siegfried. 1977. "Economic Power and Political Influence: The Impact of Industry Structure on Public Policy." *American Political Science Review* 71 (3): 1026–43.

Sanders, Jerry W. 1983. *Peddlars of Crisis: The Committee on the Present Danger and the Politics of Containment.* Boston: South End Press.

Schattschneider, Elmer Eric. 1935. *Politics, Pressures, and the Tariff.* New York: Prentice-Hall.

Schatz, Ronald W. 1983. *The Electrical Workers.* Urbana: University of Illinois Press.

Schilling, Warner R. 1962. "The Politics of National Defense: Fiscal 1950." In Warner R. Schilling, Paul Y. Hammond, and Glenn H. Snyder, *Strategy, Politics, and Defense Budgets.* New York: Columbia University Press.

Schrecker, Ellen. 1994. *The Age of McCarthyism: A Brief History with Documents.* Boston: Bedford Books.

Schulzinger, Robert D. 1984. *The Wise Men of Foreign Affairs: The History of the Council on Foreign Relations.* New York: Columbia University Press.

Schurmann, Franz. 1974. *The Logic of World Power.* New York: Pantheon Books.

Shoup, Laurence H., and William Minter. 1977. *Imperial Brain Trust: The Council on Foreign Relations and United States Foreign Policy.* New York: Monthly Review Press.

Sitkoff, Harvard. 1974. "Years of the Locust: Interpretations of Truman's Presidency since 1965." In Richard S. Kirkendall, ed., *The Truman Period as a Research Field: A Reappraisal, 1972.* Columbia: University of Missouri Press.

Smith, Geoffrey S. 1976. "'Harry We Hardly Know You': Revisionism, Politics, and Diplomacy, 1945–1954." *American Political Science Review* 70 (2): 560–82.

Snyder, Jack. 1991. *Myths of Empire.* Ithaca, NY: Cornell University Press.

Snyder, Richard, H. W. Bruck, and Burton Sapin. 1954. *Decisionmaking as an Approach to the Study of International Politics.* Foreign Policy Analysis Project Series, Monograph No. 3. Princeton, NJ: Foreign Policy Analysis Project.

Stein, Arthur A. 1993. "Domestic Constraints, Extended Deterrence, and the Incoherence of Grand Strategy: The United States, 1938–1950." In Richard Rosecrance and Arthur A. Stein, eds., *The Domestic Bases of Grand Strategy.* Ithaca, NY: Cornell University Press.

Stein, Bruno. 1963. "Loyalty and Security Cases in Arbitration." *Industrial and Labor Relations Review* 17 (1): 96–113.

Stephanson, Anders. 1993. "Commentary: Ideology and Neorealist Mirrors." *Diplomatic History* 17 (2): 285–95.

Stolper, Wolfgang Friedrich, and Paul A. Samuelson. 1941. "Protection and Real Wages." *Review of Economic Studies* 9:58–73.

Stueck, William W. 1981. *The Road to Confrontation: American Policy toward China and Korea, 1947–1950.* Chapel Hill: University of North Carolina Press.

Su, Tsai-Tsu, Mark S. Kamlet, and David C. Mowery. 1993. "Modeling U.S. Budgetary and Fiscal Policy Outcomes: A Disaggregated, Systemwide Perspective." *American Journal of Political Science* 37 (1): 213–45.

Summers, Anthony. 1993. *Official and Confidential: The Secret Life of J. Edgar Hoover.* New York: G. P. Putnam's Sons.

Theoharis, Athan G. 1971. *Seeds of Repression: Harry S. Truman and the Origins of McCarthyism.* Chicago: Quadrangle Books.

———. 1978. *Spying on Americans.* Philadelphia, PA: Temple University Press.

———. 1985. "The FBI and the American Legion Contact Program, 1940–1966." *Political Science Quarterly* 100 (2): 271–86.

Theoharis, Athan G., and John Stuart Cox. 1988. *The Boss: J. Edgar Hoover and the Great American Inquisition.* Philadelphia, PA: Temple University Press.

Tobin, James. 1958. "Estimation of Relationships for Limited Dependent Variables." *Econometrica* 26:24–36.

Trubowitz, Peter. 1992. "Sectionalism and American Foreign Policy: The Political Geography of Consensus and Conflict." *International Studies Quarterly* 36 (1): 173–90.

Trubowitz, Peter, and Brian Roberts. 1992. "Regional Interests and the Reagan Military Buildup." *Regional Studies* 26 (6): 555–67.

Tucker, Nancy Bernkopf. 1983. *Patterns in the Dust.* New York: Columbia University Press.

Vandenberg, Arthur H., Jr., and Joe Alex Morris, eds. 1952. *The Private Papers of Senator Vandenberg.* Boston: Houghton Mifflin.

Vatter, Harold G. 1985. *The U.S. Economy in World War II.* New York: Columbia University Press.

Walton, Richard J. 1976. *Henry Wallace, Harry Truman, and the Cold War.* New York: Viking Press.

Waltz, Kenneth. 1979. *A Theory of International Relations.* Reading, MA: Addison-Wesley.

Warner, John. 1954. "Labor Unions and 'Security Risks.'" *The Reporter* 11, no. 1 (July 6): 14–18.

Wehler, Hans-Ulrich. 1970. "Bismarck's Imperialism, 1862–1890." *Past and Present* 48:119–55.

Weir, Margaret, and Theda Skocpol. 1985. "State Structure and the Possibilities for 'Keynesian' Responses to the Great Depression in Sweden, Britain, and the United States." In Peter B. Evans, Dietrich Rueschemeyer, and Theda Skocpol, eds., *Bringing the State Back In.* New York: Cambridge University Press.

Wells, Samuel F. 1979. "Sounding the Tocsin: NSC 68 and the Soviet Threat." *International Security* 4, no. 2 (Fall): 116–58.

Wilkins, Mira. 1974. *The Maturing of Multinational Enterprise.* Cambridge, MA: Harvard University Press.

Yarmolinsky, Adam. 1955. *Case Studies in Personnel Security.* Washington, DC: Bureau of National Affairs.

Yarnell, Allen. 1974. *Democrats and Progressives.* Berkeley and Los Angeles: University of California Press.

Yergin, Daniel. 1977. *Shattered Peace: The Origins of the Cold War and the National Security State.* Boston: Houghton Mifflin.

Zakaria, Fareed. 1992. "Realism and Domestic Politics." *International Security* 17 (1): 177–98.

Zimmerman, William. "Issue Area and Foreign Policy Process: A Research Note in Search of a General Theory." *American Political Science Review* 67 (4): 1204–12.

Name Index

Acheson, Dean, 1, 95, 110, 111, 112, 189, 193 198; 212–18nn, 223n, 224n, 235n; China policy and, 38, 178–79; dollar gap and, 43–44, 56; Korean War and, 69–70, 115–18, 178–79, 188; 1949 budget cuts and, 40–42; and NSC 68, 45–49, 51–52, 56–63; relations with Congress, 33, 66–68, 76, 119–21, 124, 151
Agnew, John, 89, 208n, 221n
Albright, Robert C., 126, 219n, 222n
Allison, Graham T., 27
Allison, John, 177
Alsop, Joseph, 32, 111, 142, 212n, 213n, 215n, 217n, 223n, 228n, 235n
Alsop, Stewart, 32, 111, 212n, 213n, 215n, 217n, 223n, 235n
Applegate, Robert, 228n
Arrow, Kenneth, 13

Baldwin, Robert E., 92, 221n
Barkley, Alben, 37
Barnard, Chester, 45, 48, 214n
Barrett, Edward, 61, 217n
Beard, Charles A., 13, 208n
Bell, David, 30, 50, 51, 211n
Bernstein, Barton, 70, 107, 236n
Bissell, Richard, 61, 62, 216n, 217n, 218n
Bohlen, Charles, 58, 217n
Bonesteel, Charles, 60, 217n
Bradley, Omar, 117, 224n
Brewster, Owen, 81, 85
Bridges, Harry, 137
Bridges, Styles, 81, 225n; anticommunism of, 135, 154, 159, 227n, 228n, 231n; consultation with Truman administration, 66–67, 218n, 219n; efforts to cut budget, 33, 112, 126, 160, 212n, 223n; member of China bloc, 85, 111, 122, 124; relations with FBI, 8, 142–43, 228n
Brock, William A., 5, 208n
Brown, Ralph, 172, 173, 233n, 234n, 235n
Bruck, H. W., 19
Bueno de Mesquita, Bruce, 2
Bundy, McGeorge, 69
Burch, Philip H., 33, 207n
Burns, James, 34, 47, 48, 215n
Buzan, Barry, 3
Byrd, Harry, 80, 82, 84, 110, 126, 232n, 235n

Cain, Harry, 81, 85
Capehart, Homer, 81, 161
Carey, James, 172, 234n
Carr, Eugene, 113, 223n
Cassing, James, 6
Caute, David, 137, 155, 173, 222n, 233n, 235n
Chapman, Virgil, 80, 232n
Chavez, Dennis, 80, 83, 220n
Clark, John D., 35, 36, 42, 213n
Clark, Tom, 147, 148, 229n
Clifford, Clark, 35, 50, 54, 107, 168, 169, 216n, 232n, 233n
Conant, James B., 45, 117, 214n
Condit, Doris M., 119
Connally, Tom, 67, 80, 117, 224n
Connelly, Matthew, 50, 63, 109, 110, 144, 169, 215n, 222n, 223n, 224n

Subject Index

Agricultural subsidies, 126, 128
Agriculture, data on, 87, 205, 237
Air Force, United States, 9, 33, 34, 122, 137, 171, 212n, 224n, 227n
Air power: Louis Johnson's support for, 33, 47; Nationalist support for strategies relying upon, 79, 84, 122, 180
Amerasia case, 159
American Cyanamid, 227n
American Federation of Labor (AFL), 134, 159. *See also* Labor movement
American Legion, 33; FBI contact program with, 142, 171, 228n, 233n
Americans for Democratic Action (ADA), 109, 165, 232. *See also* Liberals
American Smelting and Refining, 227n
American Telephone and Telegraph, 227n
Appropriations, Senate Committee on, 49, 66, 110, 142–43, 160, 215n
Armed Services, Senate Committee on, 66
Army, United States, 136, 137, 140, 146, 160, 227n, 231n, 235n
Asia, U.S. policy toward, 69–70, 84–85, 87, 125, 177, 194, 199, 236n. *See also specific countries*
Atlantic Refining, 227n
Atomic bomb, 84, 180; Soviet acquisition of, 28, 37–38, 39, 43, 45, 74, 127, 193, 195, 213n
Atomic Energy Commission, 173, 214n
Attorney General, 28, 136, 147, 148, 149, 166, 167; Internal Security Act

and, 153, 155, 157–58; list of subversive organizations of, 108, 222n; relationship with FBI, 147, 160, 168, 229n, 230n. *See also* Justice, Department of

Bausch & Lomb Optical, 227n
Big Four (Democratic congressional leaders), 50, 119–20, 163–65, 224n
Brown Brothers Harriman, 96, 214n
Balanced budget: Bureau of the Budget's concern over, 29–31, 53, 215n; Council of Economic Advisers' attitude toward, 25, 31, 35–36, 37, 193; Louis Johnson's support for, 30, 32–33; Truman's support for, 30, 62
Budget deficit. *See* balanced budget
Bureau of the Budget, 36, 44, 51, 126, 163; Frank Pace as Director of, 31, 44, 51–53, 60, 218n; Frederick Lawton as Director of, 56; James Webb as Director of, 51; NSC 68 and, 46, 52, 53, 55, 56, 59, 61, 63; seeks cuts in international programs, 29–30, 34, 39, 42, 53, 211n
Bureaucratic politics used to explain foreign policy, 27–28
Business Roundtable, 132

CBS, 67, 219n
Central Intelligence Agency (CIA), 38, 39, 147, 149, 172, 213n, 228n
Chase National Bank, 32
China, 70, 115, 124, 127, 161; intervenes in Korea, 176–80, 188, 190, 236n; possibility of attack on

259